AF252040

FIGHTER ACES
OF THE
LUFTWAFFE
IN WORLD WAR II

FIGHTER ACES OF THE LUFTWAFFE

IN WORLD WAR II

PHILIP KAPLAN

Pen & Sword
AVIATION

First published in Great Britain in 2007 by
Pen & Sword Aviation
an imprint of
Pen & Sword Books Ltd

Copyright © Philip Kaplan, 2007

ISBN 978-1-84415-460-9

The right of Philip Kaplan to be identified as Author of this Work has been
asserted by him in accordance with the Copyright,
Designs and Patents Act 1988.

A CIP catalogue record for this book is
available from the British Library

All rights reserved. No part of this book may be reproduced or transmitted in
any form or by any means, electronic or mechanical including photocopying,
recording or by any information storage and retrieval system, without
permission from the Publisher in writing.

Typeset in Times New Roman by
Phoenix Typesetting, Auldgirth, Dumfriesshire

Printed and bound in England by
Biddles Ltd, King's Lynn

Pen & Sword Books Ltd incorporates the Imprints of Pen & Sword Aviation, Pen
& Sword Maritime, Pen & Sword Military, Wharncliffe Local History,
Pen & Sword Select, Pen & Sword Military Classics and Leo Cooper.

For a complete list of Pen & Sword titles please contact
PEN & SWORD BOOKS LIMITED
47 Church Street, Barnsley, South Yorkshire, S70 2AS, England
E-mail: enquiries@pen-and-sword.co.uk
Website: www.pen-and-sword.co.uk

Contents

Acknowledgements

The author is grateful to the following people for their generous assistance and contributions made in the development of this book: Malcolm Bates, Tony Bianchi, Peter Coles, James H. Doolittle, Adolf Galland, Gerd Gloystein, Stephen Grey, Mark Hanna, Ray Hanna, Margaret Kaplan, Neal Kaplan, Wade Meyers, Michael O'Leary, Geoffrey Page, Horst Petzschler, Gunther Rall, Christine Seidel, Klaus Seidel, Peter Vogler, Duke Warren.

Introduction

Following Germany's defeat in World War One, the victorious Allies convened at Versailles to debate the future of the German nation and to hammer out what many have since recognized as a vindictive peace treaty. Four years spent in a losing cause had taken Germany to the brink of bankruptcy, forcing her to sue for peace and accept any terms offered. The Allies gathered in the French palace with the mutual goal of eliminating the military and economic strength of Germany through the Treaty of Versailles, which was signed in June 1919.

The German people were impoverished and gravely short of food and all other necessities of life. Their nation's few remaining military assets included a still-sizeable Naval force, the Army and the Flying Corps. One aim of the representatives at Versailles was to end Germany's military aviation capability. Resurrection of the German Flying Corps would be prohibited. Under the monitoring of the Allied Control Commission, the Germans were compelled to turn over all of their aircraft and aeronautical material to the governments of the Allied powers during 1920. This amounted to the surrender of more than 15,000 aircraft and 27,000 aero engines. The framers of the treaty, however, did not include a long-term provision to prevent the manufacture and mass production of civilian aircraft. This oversight resulted from the Allies' failure to recognize the potential of civil aviation in the years to come.

In spite of all the restrictions, limitations and prohibitions of the treaty, the Germans capitalized on the civil aviation loophole and plunged head-long into the development of commercial airlines, flying and gliding clubs and aviation training schools. They trained pilots and pursued the design, engineering and construction of many new and conceptually advanced aircraft. Their efforts formed the nucleus of the clandestine German Air Force.

Adolf Hitler and Hermann Goering did not found the German Air Force. It was General Hans von Seeckt who began to plan for the new *Luftwaffe* in 1920, even while the German Flying Corps was being eliminated. Von Seeckt was Chief of the Army Command at the German Defence Ministry and was able to create and staff a small sub rosa group of regular officers within his department to deal exclusively with special aviation matters. The Allies would come to regret their negligence in not breaking up the surviving and highly effective core of the German Army Staff, for from it came the members of von Seeckt's special aviation department, including Hugo Sperrle, Walther Wever and Albert Kesselring, who would rise to principal commands in the *Luftwaffe* during World War Two.

In the 1920s, the German aircraft makers Heinkel, Junkers, Dornier, and Focke-Wulf were formed, followed by Messerschmitt. Their development of new and varied aircraft (ostensibly for civil use), laid the groundwork for equipping a new German Air Force and, in 1924, von Seeckt arranged future cooperation between the Civil Aviation Department of the Ministry of Transport and his Defence Ministry by securing the appointment of a colleague to head the CAD. Thereafter, German civil aviation would develop under clandestine military control.

The year 1926 saw the establishment of *Deutsche Lufthansa*, the German State airline and, with it, the development and construction of many large airfields. The chairman of *Lufthansa* was Erhard Milch, who would become the production chief for Hermann Goering's *Luftwaffe* in the next world war. Milch oversaw the pioneering developmental work in flying instrumentation and radio navigation and his airline rapidly became the best in Europe. Its pilots and navigators would form the basic training organization of the new *Luftwaffe*.

While *Lufthansa* was growing, so, too, was the *Deutscher Luftsportverband*, an organization of more than 50,000 members whose involvement in sport flying and gliding had been encouraged by von Seeckt's Defence Ministry as another way around the restrictive clauses of the Versailles Treaty. Von Seeckt had determined to make Germany air-minded and in another clandestine move, an agreement with the Soviet Union was entered into, giving service personnel military flying instruction at the Lipetsk training centre. Thus, by the 1933 accession of Adolf Hitler and the Nazi Party to power in Germany, the foundation of the new *Luftwaffe* was firmly in place.

Barely two years after Hitler took power, he openly flaunted the Treaty of Versailles, announcing a major rearmament programme. In it he called for development of a *Reichsluftwaffe* which would put a 'steel roof over Germany'. By 1935, Germany had a frontline air strength of eight squadrons – three of fighters and five of bombers. They were, of course, illegal under the terms of Versailles. Hitler even embellished his annual mass rallies at Nuremberg with low-level flypasts by these aircraft which now wore the black cross insignia of the *Luftwaffe*. The propaganda message for the rest of the world was clear and intentional. Goering's man, Erhard Milch, was quietly generating production miracles, raising the annual manufacturing output of the German aircraft industry from a few hundred to thousands of planes. Gone from the inventory of the young *Luftwaffe* were the old, obsolete machines that had been purchased for training. They had been replaced by a range of powerful, all-metal monoplane types of superb and advanced design and capability.

During the Spanish Civil War in the mid-thirties, when Hitler offered

Germany's assistance to the Franco government of Spain, the new *Luftwaffe* was given an ideal opportunity to try out its latest weaponry in combat conditions. Many of the future aces and leaders of the World War Two *Luftwaffe* – men like Adolf Galland, Gunther Lützow and Werner Mölders had their first taste of air combat.

This book considers the air force careers of Galland, Mölders, Eric Hartmann, Gunther Rall, Johannes Steinhoff and Hans-Joachim Marseille – all of them high-achieving aces and outstanding leaders, and, each in his own way, a pioneer in aerial warfare.

CHAPTER ONE

Adolf Galland

Probably the best known and arguably the greatest all-round German fighter pilot of the Second World War was Adolf Galland. Greatest because Galland was much more than a superb, high-achieving aerial hunter; he was a brilliant fighter leader, a dynamic visionary and a singular figure among very few officers at that time who stood up to *Luftwaffe* chief Hermann Goering and said what he believed needed saying. In their book *Horrido!*, Trevor Constable and Raymond Toliver wrote:

> Galland . . . became General of the Fighter Arm before he was thirty. He is probably the only man to handle high command and acedom simultaneously. He meets the two basic criteria of genius: capacity to probe deeper and see further than his contemporaries and ability to give effect to this insight in a practical way. He will be as long remembered for his battles on the ground as the advocate of the fighter pilots in high councils as he will for his 104 confirmed aerial victories – all of them scored against British- and American-flown aircraft. Only a few German pilots lived to score one hundred victories on the Western Front.

In Galland's opinion, and that of many others among the elite of the fighter force, Goering represented an utterly outdated First World War mindset about aerial combat, tactics, strategy and planning. Goering had been a fighter pilot in that war and, according to Galland, had lost contact with the realities of aviation development. The idea that the Bf-109, that excellent front-line weapon of the *Luftwaffe* fighter force through most of the Second World War, could be flown in air combat with the same sort of manoeuvrability as the fragile, wood and fabric aeroplanes of the earlier conflict, was absurd to Galland. He knew from experience that the far greater speed and wing-loading of the 109 meant that it, and its opponents, could not be operated in that way. It was but one of many delusions of the *Luftwaffe* high command relating to the utilization of the fighter. Eventually, Goering would relent to some extent, purging the air force of most of its First World War pilots and leaders, but that was merely a palliative and not a cure.

Galland recalled the fateful pattern of sluggishness in developing the 109 and its nominal successors, the Focke-Wulf Fw-190 and the jet Me-262, citing as an example the monthly production of the 109 which in 1940 averaged around 125, rising slowly to around 300 in 1942, 1,000 in 1943 and, under Reich Armaments Minister Albert Speer, peaking at 2,500 in late 1944, when the Germans had already lost the war. Galland believed that if German fighter production in 1940, or even 1941, had reached the 1944 level, the German Air Force would have achieved air supremacy over the British and the tide of the war would have taken a very different course.

Adolf Galland was born in Westerholt, Westphalia, in March 1912. There his father served as a land manager to the Graf von Westerholt. The Galland family were Huguenots who had fled religious persecution in France, resettling in Westphalia in 1742. Adolf followed his early interest in aviation, learning to fly a glider from a heath near Westerholt. He quickly became proficient and was made an instructor. Later he was one of thousands of applicants for the *Lufthansa* school for airline pilot training at Brunswick and one of only 20 who were accepted. He graduated in 1932 and joined the then sub rosa German Air Force, receiving training in Italy and later at Dresden. During the training he suffered an eye injury in a crash. He was in a coma for three days and had a skull fracture and a broken nose. A year later he crashed an Arado Ar-68 and was back in hospital. His earlier eye injury was aggravated but he managed to pass his next physical examination having memorized an eye chart. Galland and two of his three brothers would serve as fighter pilots in WWII. Both the brothers were killed in action.

It was a time of rapid expansion for the *Luftwaffe* under the new German Chancellor, Adolf Hitler. When Germany offered to assist Generallisimo Francisco Franco in the Spanish Civil War, Adolf Galland signed to serve with the Condor Legion, the German Volunteer Corps, sailing from Hamburg in 1937. The 370 German airmen of the Corps were dressed as civilians pretending to be members of a 'Strength-Through-Joy' tourist group. While in Spain, Galland wore the uniform of a Spanish Air Force Captain. But unlike his colleague Werner Mölders, he was not to become famous there as a fighter pilot. He was placed in *Jagdstaffel* 3 (JG 3), a unit assigned to provide close air support through the strafing of ground targets. The unit flew the slow, obsolescent Heinkel He-51 fighter, a biplane that was certainly no match for the Polikarpov Rata and Curtiss fighters of the Loyalist opposition, and Galland made it his policy to avoid all dogfights. Confining his activities to ground support of Franco's troops, he and the others of his unit gained valuable knowledge about the role which would prove extremely useful to the *Luftwaffe* in the coming world war.

Galland first met Mölders at the Hotel Christina where they were billeted in Seville. There was a coolness between them, but it soon thawed when Galland observed the other man's skills as a fighter pilot and fighter leader. They would become fast friends and friendly rivals over time while they both established themselves as phenomenal aces at the sharp end of the German fighter arm. It was in Spain that Galland first painted Mickey Mouse on the side of his aircraft. The cartoon character had a cigar in his mouth and a hatchet in one hand. He painted Mickey on at least one of his Bf-109s in World War II. When this author asked Galland why he had put the mouse on his aircraft he replied: "I like Mickey Mouse. I always have. And I like cigars, but I had to give them up after the war." Galland left Spain in 1938 and was replaced as commander of JG 3 by Mölders. While flying in the Spanish war, Galland had written a series of reports on his direct ground-support operations based on his more than 300 sorties. Collectively, the reports amounted to a kind of operations manual and they attracted the attention of the *Luftwaffe* top brass in Berlin. The reports were highly regarded by Johannes Jeschonnek, who was soon to become Chief of the *Luftwaffe* General Staff. Jeschonnek championed dive-bombing and the dive-bomber as the means to *Luftwaffe* success in small-target bombing, and his view was shared by the bulk of the General Staff officers. Unhappily for Galland, who like most fighter pilots wanted to fly and fight, the praise for his ground-support 'manual' resulted in his assignment to a desk job in the German Air Ministry. There he was tasked with implementing his own procedures and recommendations. Soon, however, he was reassigned to head the organization, training and equipping of two new ground-support wings to participate in the 1938 invasion of the Sudetenland. While back in action of sorts, his new wings, which were to be equipped with obsolescent Heinkel 45, Heinkel 51 and Henschel 123 aircraft and their pilots, had to be moulded into units able to combat effectively the Czech Army, should that be necessary. He got the job done but in the end, the Munich Pact of 1938 obviated the need for the units he had prepared.

With the Blitzkrieg on Poland in 1939, Galland's remaining *Schlachtgeschwader* group and its Hs-123 biplanes was brought into action in the *Luftwaffe*'s initial test of direct-support air power. It proved highly effective, destroying most of the Polish Air Force on the ground in just under a month of dive-bombing and strafing attacks on the Polish infantry, cavalry and transport elements. The experiences of Galland and his pilots in Spain were paying big dividends. In the campaign, he flew as many as four sorties daily for 27 days and contributed mightily to its success. For his effort he received the Iron Cross, Second Class. But the campaign also served to crystallize his thinking about his future in the air force. He desperately wanted to fly frontline fighters and get away from direct-support operations and their second-rate aircraft. He was a hunter by nature and he had to follow his instinct.

To that end, he indulged in a little ploy. After the Polish campaign, he 'developed' a case of painful rheumatism and the group doctor sent him to a clinic in Wiesbaden for treatment. At Wiesbaden a friendly, sympathetic doctor provided the medical judgement Galland was looking for: 'No more flying in open cockpit aircraft.' It was his ticket out of direct-support aircraft and into the state-of-the-art *Luftwaffe* fighters. Then, in a serendipitous meeting in Wiesbaden, he happened on Werner Mölders whom he had not seen since a Condor Legion parade in Berlin after the Spanish war. Mölders' unit was operating with great success in the area where the borders of Germany, France, Luxembourg and Belgium meet and by this time he had numerous Allied aircraft to his credit. Galland remembered: 'Mölders taught me how to shoot in the air and bring down aircraft.' Galland felt that his time had come. He was soon posted to Krefeld where he would fly with JG-27 under the command of Colonel Max Ibel. Again, however, Galland was disappointed. He was made Operations Officer, which in this case meant an administrative ground job. He literally had to sneak away to fly on the occasional combat mission, relying on tricks and ruses to get away with it.

Finally, on 12 May, 1940, Adolf Galland achieved the first of his 104 aerial victories. It happened near Liége, Belgium, and it was the first of three kills he would score that day, all of them Hawker Hurricane fighters of the Royal Air Force. For a long time he had believed that the three Hurricanes were aircraft of the Belgian Air Force, but many years after the war he learned from contacts with pilots of the RAF squadron involved that his victories that day were indeed British. In his superb book *The First and The Last*, Galland recalled:

On the morning of 12 May when I flew in company with another plane over the front, our troops had already penetrated deep into Holland and Belgium. During those first days of the campaign in the west, together with the 8th Flying Corps, we gave fighter cover to the German advance at Maastricht.

It is true to say that the first kill can influence the whole future career of a fighter pilot. Many, to whom the first victory over the opponent has been long denied either by unfortunate circumstances or by bad luck, can suffer from frustration or develop complexes they may never rid themselves of again. I was lucky; my first kill was child's play.

We did not see much of the English in those days. Occasionally we met a few Blenheims. The Belgians for the most [part] flew antiquated Hurricanes, in which even more experienced pilots could have done little against our new [Messerschmitt] ME-109E. We outstripped them in speed, in rate of climb, in armament, and above all in flying experience and training.

Therefore it was not particularly heroic when some five miles west of Liége my flight companion and I dived from an altitude of about 12,000 feet on a flight of eight Hurricanes flying 3,000 feet below us. The route had been practised innumerable times. The Hurricanes had not yet spotted us. I was neither excited nor did I feel any hunting fever. 'Come on, defend yourself!' I thought as soon as I had one of the eight in my gun sight. I closed in more and more without being noticed. 'Someone ought to warn him!' But that would have been even more stupid than the strange thoughts which ran through my head at that moment. I gave him my first burst from a distance which, considering the situation, was still too great. I was dead on the target. The poor devil at last noticed what it was all about. He took rather clumsy avoiding action which brought him into the fire of my companion. The other seven Hurricanes made no effort to come to the aid of their comrade in distress, but made off in all directions. After a second attack my opponent spun down in spirals minus his rudder. Parts of the wings came off. Another burst would have been a waste of ammunition. I immediately went after another of the scattered Hurricanes. This one tried to escape by diving, but I was soon on his tail at a distance of 100 yards. The Belgian did a half-roll and disappeared through a hole in the clouds. I did not lose track of him and attacked again from very close quarters. The plane zoomed for a second, stalled, and dived vertically to the ground from a height of only 1,500 feet. During a patrol flight that afternoon I shot down my third opponent out of a formation of five Hurricanes near Tirlemont.

I took this all quite naturally, as a matter of course. There was nothing special about it. I had not felt any excitement and I was not even particularly elated by my success. That only came much later, when we had to deal with much tougher adversaries, when each relentless aerial combat was a question of 'you or me.' On that particular day I had something approaching a twinge of conscience. The congratulations of my superiors and my comrades left an odd taste in my mouth. An excellent weapon and luck had been on my side. To be successful the best fighter pilot needs both.

On that day Adolf Galland had opened his account and through the remaining days of the Battle of France more kills accrued to it. Then in June 1940 he was posted to command the 3rd Group of JG-26, or III/JG-26. JG-26 would later become renowned as a very special, elite unit of the German Air Force. With their yellow-cowled 109s they met and were feared and respected by the bomber airmen of the Eighth United States Army Air Force in the skies of the Western Front. The Yanks referred to them as 'the Abbeville Kids' and the 'Yellow-nosed Bastards' and whenever an American air gunner managed to score hits on an aircraft of JG-26, he took considerable pride in the accomplishment.

Galland arrived on the squadron and immediately indicated the sort of leader he intended to be by downing two enemy fighters during his first day there. Throughout the previous winter months and the period of time known by some as the 'Sitzkrieg', the pilots of JG-26 spent much of their time fighting boredom as they yearned for combat action. While other units, Werner Mölder's JG-53 in particular, were more active, with Mölders himself scoring ten kills during the period, it was a matter of location. His unit was based near the French-German border, whereas JG-26 was stationed near the Channel coast. Its pilots could only count the days until the beginning of the coming spring campaign. In that waiting time they speculated among themselves about what sort of opponent the highly-touted British Spitfire would make. The only RAF fighters the Germans had encountered in France thus far were Hurricanes and they had been proven inferior to the Bf-109E-3 that equipped the squadron.

When Galland arrived to take command of III/JG-26, the French campaign still raged. His impression of the little airfield that hot summer day was less than favourable. The facilities were primitive and he noted that no one was there in a welcoming capacity. In his flying gear he walked across the runway to where a few ground crewmen were standing by an old well. Being both thirsty and in need of a bath, he politely asked if a pail of water might be provided. One of the ground men responded: "Certainly. The whole well is full, only you'll have to wind it up yourself." Not realizing they were addressing their new commanding officer, the men went on with their casual conversation while Galland drew the pail of water for himself. He said nothing more to them and went off to locate his quarters. That afternoon he took off on his first sortie as group CO and promptly bagged two enemy aircraft.

Hauptman Ernst Freiherr von Berg was replaced by Adolf Galland as *Gruppenkommandeur* (commanding officer) of III/JG-26 and Galland swiftly began implementing some significant changes in group procedure. He observed the methods and tactics then in place and made adjustments according to his own views and his hunting instincts. The first of these was to bring his pilots down from the 20,000-foot altitude where they had been regularly patrolling, to far lower levels where he thought they should be. One of his wingmen, Gerhard Schoepfel, remembered that Galland was not easy to fly with. He often led the group over the south of England at 1,500 feet where the flak was 'terrible.' It was a nerve-wracking experience for Schoepfel (who would account for 29 kills in the Battle of Britain) and the other pilots, but they considered Galland an outstanding fighter leader and were well motivated to follow him wherever he chose to take them.

By July 1940, Galland had been promoted to the rank of Major and was bringing JG-26 into the most active and lethal days of the Battle of Britain, when he would raise his own tally to 40 confirmed kills. He had become one of the greatest aces of the *Luftwaffe* and in relatively quick succession was awarded the Knight's Cross to his Iron Cross, followed in September by the award of the Oak Leaves to the medal. He was only the third German soldier to have received the award.

From the perspective of the German leadership, the strategic necessity for the operation known historically as the Battle of Britain arose from its inability to reach an agreement with the British government to end the war. As they saw it, the tasks of the German Air Force in the Battle included the blockade of the British Isles in cooperation with the German Navy through attacks on ports and shipping, and the mining of sea lanes and harbour entrances; the achievement of air supremacy over England and the Channel preliminary to a German invasion (Operation Sea Lion); and possibly even the annihilation of England through total air warfare.

Leading up to the Battle, the Germans had determined that the British possessed 3,600 war planes of which about 600 were fighters. They saw themselves at a numerical disadvantage with 2,500 available aircraft, but judged their fighters technically superior to those of their enemy. They had great faith in the Messerschmitt Bf-109 as being the best fighter plane in the world at that time. In Berlin the leaders of the Reich were revelling in their early *Blitzkrieg* successes. Hitler was especially intrigued with the possibility of crushing his enemies from the air by bombing them into submission. He and many of his High Command generals believed that the bomber was of utmost importance to their plans of conquest and saw their fighter force as clearly subordinate, a concession to the unpopular act of defence. In their minds attack was all that mattered; the enemy air force must be destroyed, preferably on the ground in surprise attacks. But such raids could only be carried out safely through providing the bombers with ample fighter support and protection. With the bomber seen as the all-important number one priority in German military aircraft production, only one-third of the entire warplane manufacture for Germany in the first year of the war was fighters. In 1940, of the entire German warplane output, just one-quarter was fighters. In terms of personnel too, the emphasis heavily favoured the bomber arm, with most of the best pilots in 1938 and 1939 being drained away from the fighter force to fly the Dornier Do-17 and Heinkel He-111 twin-engined bombers.

In Adolf Galland's view, the emphasis on bombing, particularly on dive-bombing by the Ju-87 Stukas, was misplaced and its effect on the Battle of Britain highly overrated. While the Stuka was certainly able successfully to attack relatively small, difficult targets such as bridges, power stations, and ships, it was clear to Galland that truly effective and long-lasting results could only be achieved with saturation or 'carpet bombing' by horizontal bombers flying in tight formations at high altitude. Also, a primary draw-back of the Stuka dive-bombing attack was that the aeroplane was required to leave its formation and dive very low and directly into the range of the enemy anti-aircraft defences, making itself a rather easy target for the AA guns and the enemy fighters.

The German fighters were required to provide cover for the attacks of the bomber and Stuka formations on shipping and convoys vital to Britain's survival. It was in these attacks that the slow speed of the Stukas in the dive became a major drawback. The suspended external bomb-load of the Ju-87 dictated a 150 mph maximum speed in its dive, which had to be started at between 10,000 and 15,000 feet. This slow, rather lengthy dive allowed many Hurricanes and Spitfires to catch and dispose of the German planes, often before they dropped their loads. The fighter pilots of the RAF quickly realized that the Stukas were nearly defenceless and quite vulnerable from the moment they peeled away from their formation to dive individually towards their targets, until they had rejoined their formation. Substantial fighter protection was needed for the Stukas; an extremely challenging task for the Bf-109s. As the 109 had no dive-brake it was not possible to dive and stay with the Stukas in their relatively slow descent. The Stukas simply could not be adequately protected throughout their dives. Predictably the Stukas suffered enormous losses before their entire dive-bomber force was finally withdrawn from participation in the Battle. And it was the German fighter pilots who were blamed by their High Command for the failure of the Stukas in that Battle.

The concept behind the Stuka came from the United States, where a small, light dive-bomber had been developed to perform pinpoint attacks. Ernst Udet and then *Luftwaffe* chief Major General Johannes Jeschonnek were attracted to the idea because of the apparent efficiency in its acquisition and performance, a new weapon that would provide the most bang for the buck, a prime consideration in the resource-poor Germany of the late 1930s. The Stuka did, in fact, perform with great efficiency throughout the war, both in support of the German Army and against enemy armour. But in the Battle of Britain it failed spectacularly.

Galland:

This did not deter the German Command from continuing with the idea of the Stuka. The accompanying fighter pilots were blamed for the painfully high losses, although the limitations of the Stuka in action were obvious enough in the Battle of Britain. The fighter pilots were blamed, not the designers who continued to base their entire production of medium and heavy bombers on the Stuka idea. They not only went on to produce a twin-engined Stuka, the Ju-88, and the Do-217, but demanded full diving performance from all subsequent types of bombers, including the four-engined He-177, which entailed high stability, the fitting of dive-brakes, automatic pull-out apparatus, Stuka target-sighters, etc. Because of this blockheaded-ness – one cannot call it anything else – the development and production of the German long-range bomber was seriously delayed. To the claim that at the beginning of the war, four-engined bombers operating 500 miles to the west of Ireland accounted for no less than half the shipping losses in the North Atlantic, the famous North American air force expert P. de Seversky, replied, 'Luckily Hitler allowed himself to be talked out of the idea of long-range bombers . . .' He should have added, ' . . . and got all excited about the strategic Stuka idea.'

In its rather narrow bomber-oriented mindset, the German High Command continued to relegate its fighters to a strictly tactical agenda which included local air defence, the achievement of air superiority over the front and, if need be, assisting the army in conjunction with the *Luftwaffe*'s ground-support aircraft.

Though discontented by the top level mismanagement of the air war, Galland continued to manage his own and his unit's participation in the Battle efficiently and successfully. Then, after roughly a month of action on the Channel coast, he was ordered to attend a war conference at Carin Hall, Goering's estate in the March of Brandenburg. On arriving in Berlin, he was struck by the contrast between his recent days filled with air combat, and the calm, serene lifestyle being enjoyed in the German capital, where the war seemed to be making little difference. Most people continued to patronize theatres, cafés, restaurants and cinemas. Galland found the contrast deeply depressing. At the Carin Hall meetings he and Mölders were drawn aside by Goering at one point and were presented with bejewelled gold Pilot Medals, after which the *Reichsmarschall* told the pair in no uncertain terms of his profound dissatisfaction with the performance of the German fighter force to date, with particular reference to bomber protection. He urged them to greater effort and told them of his intention to replace many at the command level of the force with younger, more aggressive and successful fighter pilots, beginning with the two of them. Galland protested at the change, stressing his desire to remain on combat operations and not be tied to a desk job. Goering reassured him that a key element of his plan called for the fighter squadrons to be led in the air by his new commanders.

By 1 November Galland had been promoted to *Oberstleutnant*, Lieutenant Colonel, and was made commander of JG-26, replacing *Oberst*. Gotthardt Handrick, an older man whose prior claim to fame was having been a 1936 Olympic champion. His dismissal was in line with Goering's programme replacing most of the World War One-era group and wing commanders with bright young stars like Mölders and Galland. The leading lights among the new crop of fighter aces would be rewarded and saddled with rank and responsibility not normally imposed on officers still in their twenties.

Two weeks after the Carin Hall conference, Goering visited Galland and Mölders on the Channel coast. The *Luftwaffe* was within days of beginning large-scale bombing attacks on British cities and targets and the *Reichsmarshall* registered his displeasure that the air supremacy needed for these raids had not been achieved. While RAF Fighter Command had suffered great losses to date, it was anything but beaten, and the German Stuka and fighter forces had suffered considerable losses of their own in personnel, aircraft and morale. Goering roundly condemned his fighter pilots for lacking both confidence and spirit, reproaching them in the harshest terms. He demanded adherence to the close and rigid protection of the bombers. He and Galland argued over the comparative offensive and defensive capabilities of the 109 and the Spitfire, and he continued to berate Galland. At the end of the tirade he seemed to mellow a bit and asked what Galland and Mölders required for their squadrons. Mölders requested a new series of 109s equipped with more powerful engines. "And you?" he asked Galland. "I should like an outfit of Spitfires for my squadron." Goering was speechless. He stamped off in a rage.

From the first days of the Battle of Britain it was obvious, to Galland at least, that the *Luftwaffe* would not have its way with the pilots and planes of RAF Fighter Command, as it had with the air forces of the countries the Nazis had already overrun. He believed that the British fighter arm had a considerable advantage over the *Luftwaffe* fighter force, being numerically stronger. It had superior control through Britain's more advanced radar capability and the further advantage of fighting within relatively easy reach of its own airfields which, with very limited range and the need to frequently refuel to and rearm, was a real plus. He was also greatly impressed by the fighting spirit of the RAF airmen.

To Galland there appeared to be confusion in the German High Command as to which of its three strategic requirements was primarily behind the order to the *Luftwaffe* to achieve total air supremacy through large-scale air battles. Whether it was the blockade of England, the invasion, or annihilation by air, was unknown to him. As the Battle went on, the generals in Berlin stressed them all in turn. It seemed to Galland that the High Command had no clear strategy for the further pursuit of the war in the west. He felt that Hitler saw the campaign against Britain as merely a necessary evil. The real enemy lay to the east in the Soviet Union.

In Berlin the top generals were divided over the need to attack England and the importance of invading and occupying her. As Germany did not possess a strategic heavy-bombing capability, it seems unlikely that Hitler or any of his general staff would have anticipated the sort of massive bombing effort that would be coming his way from the British, and the Americans (who were not even in the war yet). So the necessity for German occupation of England would certainly have been arguable. But Goering continued to exercise great influence over Hitler and temporarily persuaded him that everything necessary would be achieved by his *Luftwaffe*.

Down at the operational level, the initial phase of the Battle of Britain was concluded on 24 July and thereafter, until 8 August, a great fighter struggle ensued. On the first day of this second phase, *Oberst*. Galland led his squadron in action over England for the first time. As they approached the Thames Estuary they encountered a flight of Spitfires that was protecting a convoy. His Bf-109s had a height advantage over the British fighters and fell on them unobserved. Galland manoeuvred his plane in tightly behind a Spitfire on the left flank of the British formation and fired a single long burst. The Spitfire fell vertically and Galland followed it down until he saw the cockpit canopy come off and the enemy pilot bale out. He watched as the pilot fell all the way down to the sea, his parachute having failed to open. In the engagement, the German pilots downed three of the Spitfires, but lost two of their own aircraft and pilots. It was a sobering experience for Galland and his comrades, leaving them in no doubt that the fighter pilots of the Royal Air Force would be a serious, determined adversary in the dramatic weeks to come.

Now the Battle was truly joined and the heat was on. JG-26 and other German fighter units operating from fields near the Channel coast were in virtually continuous action, with the pilots flying three sorties a day as a rule. The assignment: free chase over southeast England. Galland recalled the very high fatigue factor of his pilots in the situation; the extreme mental and physical strain they were under and the strain placed upon the ground personnel and the aircraft.

It used to take us roughly half an hour from take-off to crossing the English coast at the narrowest point of the Channel. Having a tactical flying time of only 80 minutes, we therefore had about 20 minutes to complete our task. This fact limited the distance of penetration. German fighter squadrons based on the Pas de Calais and on the Cotentin peninsula could barely cover the southeastern parts of the British Isles. Circles drawn from these two bases at an operational range of 125 miles overlapped approximately in the London area. Everything beyond was practically out of our reach. This was the most acute weakness of our offensive. An operating radius of 125 miles was sufficient for local defence, but not enough for such tasks as were now demanded of us. With additional fuel tanks, which could be released and discarded after use, as employed later by both sides and which we had already tried successfully in Spain, our range could have been extended by 125 to 200 miles. At that time this would have been just the decisive extension of our penetration. As it was, we ran daily into the British defences, breaking through now and then, with considerable loss to ourselves, without substantially approaching our final goal.

Our fighter formations took off. The first air battles took place as expected and according to plan. Due to the German superiority these attacks, had they been continued, would certainly have achieved the attempted goal, but the English fighters were recalled from this area long before the goal was reached. The weakened squadrons of the RAF left their bases near the coast and used them only for emergency landings or to refuel. They were concentrated in a belt around London in readiness for our bomber attacks. Thus they evaded the attack in the air in order to counter more effectively the attack from the air, which would logically follow. The German fighters found themselves in a similar predicament to a dog on a chain who wants to attack the foe but cannot harm him, because of the limitation of his chain.

As long as the enemy kept well back, our task could not be accomplished. Rather aptly we called the few bombers and Stukas, which from now onward accompanied our roving expeditions, 'decoy ducks.' Only with bombers was the war from the air over England a possibility, and to prevent such a development was the decisive aim of the British Command. To this end the RAF called out the fighters again, but the German hope of attracting them into annihilating combats was never realized.

In the opening encounters the English were at a considerable disadvantage because of their close formation. Since the Spanish civil war we had introduced the wide-open combat formation in which great intervals were kept between the smaller single formations and groups, each of which flew at a different altitude. This offered a number of valuable advantages: greater air coverage; relief for the individual pilot who could now concentrate more on the enemy than on keeping formation; freedom of initiative right down to the smallest unit without loss of collective strength; reduced vulnerability, as compared to close formation; and, most important of all, better vision. The first rule of all air combat is to see the opponent first. Like the hunter who stalks his prey and manoeuvres himself unnoticed into the most favourable position for the kill, the fighter in the opening of a dogfight must detect the opponent as early as possible in order to attain a superior position for the attack. The British quickly realized the superiority of our combat formation and readjusted their own. At first they introduced the so-called 'Charlies': two flanking planes following in the rear of the main formation, flying slightly higher and further out, on a weaving course. Finally they adopted our combat formation entirely. Since then, without any fundamental changes, it has been accepted throughout the world. Werner Mölders was greatly responsible for these developments.

From the very beginning the English had an extraordinary advantage which we could never overcome throughout the entire war: radar and fighter control. For us and for our Command this was a surprise and a very bitter one. England possessed a closely knit radar network conforming to the highest technical standards of the day, which provided Fighter Command with the most detailed data imaginable.

Thus the British fighter was guided all the way from take-off to his correct position for attack on the German formations.

We had nothing of the kind. In the application of radio-location technique the enemy was far in advance of us. It was not that British science and technics were superior. On the contrary, the first success of radar must be recorded on the German side. On 18 December, after the RAF had previously tried in vain to attack Wilhelmshaven on 4 September 1939 – the day following the British declaration of war – a British bomber formation approached the German Bight, making for the same target. An experimental Freya radar set sighted their approach in time for German fighters to intercept and practically destroy the enemy task force which flew without fighter protection; the attack was defeated. After this defensive success thanks to timely radio location, the British bombers never returned without fighter protection.

There could be no more singular proof of the importance of high-frequency technique for defence against air attacks. However, since the German Command was predominantly occupied with offensive plans, not enough attention was given to this technique. The possibility of an Allied air attack on the Reich was at the time unthinkable. For the time being we were content to erect a few Freya sets along the German and later along the Dutch, Belgian, and French coast; they had a range of 75 miles but gave no altitude reading.

Under the serious threat for England arising from the German victory in France – no one described it more forcefully than Churchill in his memoirs – the British Command concentrated desperately on the development and perfection of radar. The success was outstanding. Our planes were already detected over the Pas de Calais while they were still assembling, and were never allowed to escape the radar eye. Each of our movements was projected almost faultlessly on the screens in the British fighter control centre, and as a result Fighter Command was able to direct their forces to the most favourable position at the most propitious time.

In battle we had to rely on our own human eyes. The British fighter pilots could depend on the radar eye, which was far more reliable and reached many times farther. When we made contact with the enemy our briefings were already three hours old, the British only as many seconds old – the time it took to assess the latest position by means of radar to the transmission of attacking orders from Fighter Control to the already-airborne force.

Of further outstanding advantage to the English was the fact that our attacks, especially those of the bombers, were, of sheer necessity, directed against the central concentration of the British defence. We were not in a position to seek out soft spots in this defence or to change our approaches and to attack now from this direction, now from that, as the Allies did later in their air offensive against the Reich. For us there was only a frontal attack against the superbly organized defence of the British Isles, conducted with great determination.

Added to this, the RAF was fighting over its own country. Pilots who had baled out could go into action again almost immediately, whereas ours were taken prisoner. Damaged English planes could sometimes still reach their base or make an emergency landing, while for us engine trouble or fuel shortage could mean a total loss.

Morale too and the emotions played a great part. The desperate seriousness of the situation apparently aroused all the energies of this hardy and historically conscious people, whose arms in consequence were directed toward one goal: to repulse the German invaders at any price!

Failure to achieve any noticeable success, constantly changing orders betraying lack of purpose, and obvious misjudgement of the situation by the Command, and unjustified accusations had a most demoralizing effect on us fighter pilots . . . We complained of the leadership, the bombers, the Stukas, and were dissatisfied with ourselves. We saw one comrade after the other, old and tested brothers in combat, vanish from our ranks. Not a day passed without a place remaining empty at the mess table. New faces appeared, became familiar, until one day these too would disappear, shot down in the Battle of Britain.

Galland:

In summer and autumn of 1940 I shot down 21 Spitfires, three Blenheims and one Hurricane. The battle was tough but it never violated the unwritten laws of chivalry. We knew that our conflict with the enemy was a life and death struggle. We stuck with the rules of a fair fight, foremost being to spare the life of a defenceless opponent. The German Air Sea Rescue people therefore picked up any RAF or American pilot they found floating in the Channel as well as the German airmen.

To shoot a pilot parachuting would have seemed to us an act of unspeakable barbarism. I remember the circumstances when Goering mentioned this subject during the Battle of Britain. Only Mölders was present when this conversation took place near the *Reichsmarshall*'s train in France. Experience had proved, he told us, that especially with technically highly developed arms such as tanks and fighter aircraft, the men who controlled these machines were more important than the machines themselves. The aircraft which we shot down could easily be replaced by the English, but not the pilots. As in our own case it was very difficult, particularly as the war drew on. Successful fighter pilots who could survive this war would be valuable not only because of their experience and knowledge but also because of their rarity. Goering wanted to know if we ever had thought about this. 'Jawohl, Herr *Reichsmarshall!*' He looked me straight in the eyes and said, 'What would you think of an order to shoot down pilots who were baling out?' 'I should regard it as murder, Herr *Reichsmarshall*,' I told him, 'and I should do everything in my power to disobey such an order.' 'That is just the reply I had expected from you, Galland.' In World War One similar thoughts had cropped up, but were just as strongly rejected by the fighter pilots.

Sir Hugh C.T. Dowding, Commander-in-Chief, RAF Fighter Command, during the Battle of Britain:

This is perhaps a convenient opportunity to say a word about the ethics of shooting at aircraft crews who have baled out in parachutes. Germans descending over England are prospective prisoners-of-war and, as such, should be immune. On the other hand, British pilots descending over England are still potential combatants. Much indignation was caused by the fact that German pilots sometimes fired on our descending airmen (although, in my opinion, they were perfectly entitled to do so), but I am glad to say that in many cases they refrained.

Group Captain Peter Townsend, RAF fighter pilot:

By the rules of war it was justifiable to kill a pilot who could fight again. But few of us could bring ourselves to shoot a helpless man in cold blood.

Captain Jack Ilfrey, Eighth U.S.A.A.F. fighter pilot:

Ethics went out the window. The principles of right or good behaviour – the rules and standards of conduct certainly did not – could not apply to the combat fighter pilot's profession. This is where the beast came out, self protection ruled – get that S.O.B. before he gets you

Lt Colonel Robert M. Littlefield, Eighth U.S.A.A.F. fighter pilot:

Ethics in war? The object of war is to kill and wound as many of the enemy as one can and to destroy all his supplies and communications in as short a time as possible. However, at the time I was there, it was an unwritten gentleman's agreement between the fighter pilots of the *Luftwaffe* and the U.S. Army Air Force not to shoot an airman in a parachute.

Wing Commander Douglas Warren, RAF fighter pilot:

I never thought about ethics in regard to air combat. I had decided that even if the opportunity arose I would never shoot at a man in his parachute. Why I thought that way, I am not sure. It just didn't seem the right thing to do.

Flight Lieutenant Charles M. Lawson, RAF fighter pilot:

I think war brings out the best and the worst in people. We did hear of cases where German pilots allegedly fired at Allied airmen who had baled out and were floating in parachutes. I recall one of the pilots on my squadron, a very nice guy, who claimed that if he saw a German airman floating in a rubber dinghy after being shot down, he would attack him from the air. His rationale was that total war pulled no punches. Personally, I would not have done that, but I guess there are two sides to every coin.

Ira Jones, World War One Royal Flying Corps fighter pilot:

My habit of attacking Huns dangling from their parachutes led to many arguments in the mess. Some officers, of the Eton and Sandhurst type, thought it was 'unsportsmanlike' to do it. Never having been to a public school, I was unhampered by such considerations of form. I just pointed out that there was a bloody war on, and that I intended to avenge my pals.

Captain Eddie Rickenbacker, World War One American fighter pilot:

Resolved today that hereafter I will never shoot at a Hun who is at a disadvantage, regardless of what he would do if he were in my position. Just what influenced me to adopt that principle and even to enter it into my diary I have forgotten. That was very early in my fighting days and I had then had but few combats in the air. But with American fliers the war has always been more or less a sporting proposition and the desire for fair play prevents a sportsman from looking at the matter in any other light, even though it may be a case of life or death. However that may be, I do not recall a single violation of this principle by any American aviator that I should care to call my friend.

Pilot Officer Roger Hall, RAF fighter pilot:

I watched the Hurricane turn over on its back and fall away. The pilot himself was on fire as he fell away from the machine. As the

Hurricane went into a shallow dive, he released his parachute but, as it opened, its shrouds caught fire. The pilot, who had now succeeded in extinguishing the flames on himself, was desperately trying to climb up the shroud lines before they burnt through. I witnessed this scene with an hypnotic sort of detachment, not feeling myself able to leave it as I circled above. I was thankful to see the flames go out and the parachute behave in a normal manner. I felt a great surge of relief well up inside me, but it was to prove short-lived.

Two 109s appeared below me coming from the north and travelling very fast towards the south as though they were intent upon getting home safely to France.

I disregarded the pilot hanging from the parachute and diverted my attention to the 109s, which appeared to be climbing slowly. I felt I should get my first confirmed aircraft now and I turned on my back to dive on them. When I was in the dive I laid my sights well in front of the forward 109 with lots of deflection, for I was coming down upon them vertically. The leading 109 was firing and I looked to see where he was firing at but could see no other aircraft near him. Then I saw it all in a fraction of a second, but fraction that seemed an eternity. He was firing at the pilot at the end of the parachute and he couldn't possibly miss.

I saw the tracers and the cannon shells pierce the centre of his body, which folded before the impact like a jack-knife closing, like a blade of grass which bends toward the blade of the advancing scythe. I was too far away to interfere and now was too late to be of any assistance. If to see red is usually a metaphorical expression, it became a reality to me at that moment, for the red I could see was that of the pilot's blood as it gushed from all the quarters of his body.

I expected to see the lower part of his body fall away to reveal the entrails dangling in mid-air but by some miracle his body held together. His hands, but a second before clinging to the safety of the shroud lines, were now relaxed and hung limp at his sides. His whole body was limp also, like a man just hanged, the head resting across one shoulder, bloody, scarlet with blood, the hot rich blood of youth which had traversed and coursed through his veins for perhaps not more than nineteen or twenty years. It had now completely covered and dyed red an English face which looked down on but no longer saw its native soil.

Captain Richard E. Turner, Eighth U.S.A.A.F. fighter pilot:

I saw ahead of me the parachuting pilot of the 109 I had shot down a few minutes before. Pointing the plane at him, I flipped the gun switch to 'camera only' to get a picture, but the thought crossed my mind that this circuit had been known to foul up and fire the guns, so I restrained my desire to get a confirming picture of my victim. Instead, I turned aside, passing within 30 feet of him. I suppose when he saw me point straight at him, he fully expected to be gunned down, for he had drawn himself up and crossed his arms in front of his face as if to ward off the bullets, and when he saw me turn aside without firing, and waggling my wings as I passed, he started waving his arms and grinning like a Cheshire cat. I thought as I climbed that, since he had provided me with my tenth victory, he deserved a break. I just hoped he'd live to spread the word that Americans didn't shoot helpless pilots in parachutes. Maybe the Germans would follow suit.

Galland remembered with a smile how loudspeakers all over the greater German Reich in those days used to shatter the air with the song *Bomben auf En-ge-land*, and how his pilots hated it. The Germans were now into the third phase of the Battle of Britain. It would last from 8 August to 7 September 1940 and its theme would be the complete destruction of the British air force on the ground by waves of German bombers overhead. Here again, in Galland's view, the Germans were disadvantaged by the very limited range of their fighters, pointing out that the actual air battle over Britain was confined to an area representing less than ten per cent of England. This left ninety per cent of the country in which aircraft could be built and repaired, pilots trained, reserves built up and new squadrons formed to rearm and replenish the British air force virtually without German interference. And to get them into action the RAF needed only to vector its units and support to a relatively limited area around London. The lack of an efficient German long-range bomber exacerbated the difficulties of the *Luftwaffe* in trying to carry out their mission. Had such a plane been available to the Germans they would have been able to strike in large numbers at targets anywhere in Britain, preventing the RAF from restoring itself. The positive side of the German aircraft range limitation was that the part of the country the *Luftwaffe* could reach, the southeastern corner, included the capital. London, one of the world's great cities, came within range of the German bomber attacks with fighter protection, and as a major port, armaments and distribution centre, as well as the centre of the British High Command, it was a most tempting target.

On 7 September the fourth phase of the Battle began. Hermann Goering again visited the Channel coast to give the order that would launch more than a thousand aircraft, horizontal bombers, Stukas, fighters and destroyers, the largest air armada ever assembled, in the first major mission on London. It was the first of 38 such large-scale raids on the British capital and the targets were dock installations and oil storage facilities on the Thames. In the subsequent raids the total weight of bombs released in each attack averaged about 500 tons and it was normally delivered by a bomber

force of between 50 and 80 aircraft being shepherded by one fighter wing.
Galland:

> The assembly of the bombers and fighters took place in the vicinity
> of our fighter bases over some landmark on the coast at a pre-
> determined altitude and zero hour. It happened more than once that
> the bombers arrived late. As a result the fighters joined another
> bomber formation which had already met its fighter escort and thus
> flew doubly protected; while the belated formation had either to turn
> back or make an unescorted raid usually resulting in heavy losses.
> Radio or radar guidance for such an assembly was not available; even
> our intercom did not work most of the time. These difficulties
> increased with the deterioration of the weather in the autumn and
> finally assumed the proportions of a tragedy.
>
> All formations had to take the shortest route to London, because
> the escorting fighters had a reserve of only ten minutes' combat time.
> Large-scale decoy manoeuvres or circumnavigation of the British AA
> zone were therefore impossible. The anti-aircraft barrage around
> London was of considerable strength and concentration and
> seriously hampered the target approach of the bombers. The balloon
> barrage over and around the capital made low-level attacks and dive-
> bombing impossible. The bulk of the English fighters were sent up to
> encounter the German raiders just before they reached their target. I
> know of no instance in which they managed to prevent the bombers
> from reaching their target, but they inflicted heavy losses on them and
> the German escort fighters.

While returning from London on one such raid, Galland spotted a flight
of twelve Hurricane fighters north of Rochester and attacked from 2,500
feet above and behind them. At extremely close range he fired on an aircraft
at the rear of the formation, ripping large sections from the plane. His
greater speed carried him right over the top of the flight of Hurricanes and
down the length of their formation. He dropped his nose slightly and fired
into another of the enemy fighters. He received no return fire and as he
broke away he noticed two pilots descending in their parachutes.

When Galland was summoned to Berlin to receive the Oak Leaves to his
Knight's Cross, the award was presented to him by Adolf Hitler in the new
Reich Chancellery. The two had met once before, but the other occasion
had been on Galland's return from Spain with the Condor Legion. That
had been a large reception, but this was a private meeting of just the two.
Galland remembered it being a lengthy conversation. 'The first time I met
him I was not very impressed with him . . . short, grey-faced and not very
strong. He did not allow me to smoke, nor did he offer anything to drink.
He had little understanding of the air force, and for air combat none at all.
He couldn't think in three dimensions. He was an army man.' He recalled

expressing to Hitler his admiration for the British enemy and mentioning his disdain for the fallacious and insidious commentaries and representations that were being made on German radio and by the press, that referred to the Royal Air Force in a condescending manner. He anticipated an angry response or contradiction from Hitler when he offered the Nazi leader his own very different impressions. But Hitler just listened intently and then told Galland that the comments confirmed his own beliefs. He told the fighter leader that the decision to launch the campaign against Britain had been especially difficult in view of his own admiration for the British. He referred to it as a 'world historical tragedy', saying that it had been impossible to avoid the war 'despite all his sincere and desperate attempts' and how, if Germany won the war 'a vacuum would be created by the destruction of Great Britain, which it would be impossible to fill.' According to Galland, Hitler expressed his 'sympathy for the English race and his admiration for the class of political and industrial leaders which down the ages had developed on a much broader base than anything that had so far existed in Germany. In their political development, favoured by different circumstances, the English were a hundred years ahead of the Germans.' He thought that 'all the virtues an eminent race had developed over long periods became manifest during critical phases in its history, as England was going through then.'

Following his session with the Nazi leader, Galland flew to see Goering at the *Reichsmarshall's* hunting lodge in the *Rominterheide*. At the estate he met Werner Mölders who told him that Goering had detained him there for three days and how anxious he was to get back to his command, the 51st Fighter Wing on the Channel coast, to resume his combat flying. He said that Goering had promised to detain Galland at least as long. Soon Goering appeared, dressed, as Galland described, 'in a green suede hunting jacket over a silk blouse with long puffed sleeves, high hunting boots, and in his belt a hunting knife in the shape of an old Germanic sword.' He noted that the *Reichsmarshall* was in a good mood, with the unpleasant memory of their last meeting, and his concerns about the *Luftwaffe*'s progress in the Battle of Britain, seemingly forgotten. He then granted Galland permission to hunt one of his royal stags, a *Reichsjägermeister*-stag, and admitted having promised Mölders to keep Galland there for at least three days, thus giving Mölders an advantage in the German ace race. By ten the next morning, however, Galland had bagged his stag and there was no real reason for him to stay on at the lodge. But Goering kept his word to Mölders, compelling Galland to remain there for the three days, during which the *Reichsmarshall* received the latest Battle reports from his 2nd and 3rd Air Force Group commanders. They were not happy reading, reporting especially heavy losses in the most recent major raid on London. Disheartened, Goering relented, allowing Galland to return with his stag to the war front.

In November 1940 the Soviet foreign minister, V.M. Molotov, was in

Berlin for talks with Hitler about his government's claims for a 'free hand' in Finland and the Baltic States, along with the occupation of Rumanian territories, the whole of Bulgaria, and access to the Bosporus. Hitler saw the demands as throwing open the door for Bolshevism to the Western world. He could not accede to Stalin and he would not allow the campaign in the west for air supremacy over Britain to interfere with his main objective in the war, the total destruction of Bolshevism, and he turned the bulk of his attention to the east.

The conclusion of the fourth phase of the Battle of Britain came on 20 October with the ending of the main day-bombing campaign and the beginning of the night blitz. It was to be another testing time for the German fighter force, elements of which were to be converted to 'fighter-bombers'. This decision was based, according to Galland, on the *Luftwaffe* High Command rationale that, as the fighter arm had been unable to provide sufficient protection to the German bombers, it should be required to deliver bombs to England on its own account. The fighters were being asked to do this job as a stopgap measure while preparations for a major night-bombing campaign against England were being made. Galland felt that this use of fighters as bombers could only be a political rather than a military policy decision. And, while he saw the value of the fighter-bomber in certain contexts, assuming the availability of a surplus of fighter aircraft, this to him was merely a weakening of the fighter force when it should have been strengthened to help achieve the essential German aim of air superiority over England.

Each of the seven German fighter wings then participating in the Battle of Britain were now ordered to equip either one squadron per wing, or one flight per squadron, as fighter-bombers, which translated into the conversion of one-third of these fighter-wing aircraft into fighter-bombers. It would be perhaps the most severe test of *Luftwaffe* fighter pilot morale in the entire war. Galland believed that the pilots had done all they could to keep up with and surpass their very capable and aggressive British counterpart. They had never ceased their demands for long-range fuel drop-tanks which would have greatly enhanced their ability to escort effectively their bombers and engage the RAF fighters for longer periods over England and now they had to operate at only two-thirds of their former fighter strength. And the entire German fighter-bomber force for use over Britain numbered fewer than 250 aircraft.

In the effort, the converted Bf-109 carried a single 500-pound high-explosive bomb, while the Me-110 carried two 500-pounders and four 100-pound bombs. The pilots knew that these light loads would achieve little in destructive results, and probably even less for the fact that there was almost no time to train them to drop bombs. Most would drop their first live bomb during an actual raid on London or another British target.

At the start of these operations, the fighter-bombers flew together in ordinary bomber formations with their separate wing escort fighter protection, but this soon proved unsafe with the fighter-bombers too vulnerable to the attentions of the enemy fighters. Thereafter the fighter-bombers were dispersed through the escort fighter formation. Doing so hampered the performance of the escort fighters more; their speed, rate of climb, and manoeuvrability reduced to that of the far-heavier fighter-bombers to whom they were tied operationally. Goering was, of course, wholly unsympathetic with his fighter pilots. He took the view that they had failed in the job of adequately protecting his bombers and they now opposed him over escorting his fighter-bombers, a task that had resulted from their own inability to do the first job. He made it known that, if they were not up to escorting the fighter-bombers, it would be better to disband the fighter force entirely. The deteriorating relations between the fighter pilots and the *Luftwaffe* Command became much worse now. The superb and courageous pilots had fought brilliantly and with deadly effect for several weeks in the murderous battle, chalking up many victories and suffering devastating losses. Many of the young pilots were now openly critical of the *Luftwaffe* leadership.

The fighter-bomber operations amounted in the end to little more than nuisance raids. That, and the increasingly foul weather over the Channel and England as the autumn wore on brought an end to the six weeks of daylight raids on London. The night blitz was about to begin. The German fighter force would not take part in the night raids and many of the bombing attacks ranged far beyond the capital, with targets in Birmingham, Liverpool, Manchester, Southampton, Edinburgh, Glasgow and others on the receiving end. There was no delay for crew training in night bombing technique as the German bomber crews had already received such instruction in their pre-war training. Day crews became night crews flying the same aircraft they had used in daylight raids. They were soon delivering upwards of 1,000 tons of bombs a night per target.

Most of the raids were made at altitudes between 9,000 and 18,000 feet. Bombing accuracy was rarely good owing to the frequently poor weather conditions in the target areas. Precision bombing was still in the future. Navigation was fair but uneven. There was no nightfighter opposition at this stage, but the anti-aircraft guns, especially those positioned to defend the London area, threw up a lot of steel and frightened the German crews, even if few of the raiders were actually brought down by the AA. The Germans considered the losses they took in aircraft and crews due to both the weather and the ground defences during this final phase of the battle to be reasonable. The raids were continued into April 1941 when they were reduced to a minimum.

The telephone rang on Galland's desk in the early evening of 10 May, 1941. A clearly agitated Goering was ordering him to take off with his entire wing immediately. As it was nearly dark and there had been no reports of enemy aircraft on the way in to the French coast, and he said as much to the *Reichsmarshall* who shouted: "What do you mean, flying in? You are to stop an aircraft flying out! The deputy Führer has gone mad and is flying to England in an Me-110. He must be brought down." Galland asked about the time the aircraft had taken off and its probable course. Goering demanded that Galland call him back personally on his return. The first problem Galland faced was that darkness was imminent and he knew that a number of Me-110s were in the air, on service trial and test flights ahead of night sorties. There was simply no way that he and his pilots could distinguish which 110 Rudolf Hess was flying. He elected to have each squadron leader send up one or two planes in a token effort.

Galland had been told that Hess had taken off from the Messerschmitt factory at Augsburg. Hess had been a pilot in the First World War but Galland thought the chances of the Deputy Führer actually succeeding in reaching the British Isles from Augsburg were slim. He said as much to Goering in his phone call reporting the failure of his interception mission, adding that if Hess did manage to cross the Channel, the Spitfires were bound to get him. Around the time of the call to Goering, the Me-110 that Rudolf Hess was flying ran out of fuel near Paisley in Scotland. Hess baled out and was greeted by a farmer with a pitchfork.

Two days later an official Nazi Party communication was issued:

Party member Rudolf Hess recently managed to obtain an aircraft against the Führer's strict orders forbidding him to fly on account of an illness which had been growing worse for years. On 10 May at about 6 p.m. Hess took off from Augsburg on a flight from which so far he has not returned . . . A preliminary check on the papers he left behind seems to indicate that he harboured the illusion that he could bring about a peace between Germany and England by a personal intervention through certain English acquaintances.

There was no clear-cut final shot. The Battle of Britain was over. The *Luftwaffe* was by no means defeated, but the young fighter pilots of the Royal Air Force had persevered and saved their country from invasion and conquest. Or had they? In the spring of 1941 Hitler, Goering, and the *Luftwaffe* had moved on to other areas of interest. In the third week of May the Germans invaded Crete, with the air force heavily involved. They considered the operation a brilliant success and back in Berlin Dr Goebbels, the propaganda minister, was proclaiming the Crete conquest as a dress rehearsal for the 'imminent invasion of the British Isles.' In Paris, meanwhile, *Reichsmarshall* Goering spoke at a briefing of all the *Luftwaffe* commanders based in France. He told them that the Battle of Britain had been only an overture to the final subjugation of the British enemy. He said that the operation would be implemented through 'an immensely increased rearmament of the air force, an intensification of the U-boat war, and would be brought to a conclusion by the actual invasion itself.' Galland and the other commanders were to believe that the Sea Lion operation, or an updated version of it, was still on. After the speech Goering took Galland and Mölders aside and, rubbing his hands gleefully, told them that everything he had said in it was a lie; a ruse intended to mask the real High Command plan: the imminent invasion of the Soviet Union. To Galland this was the worst possible news: war on two fronts; starting a war with the Soviet Union, with its enormous natural resources and immense manpower pool, and at a point when it had only recently been shown that Germany's military might was insufficient to conquer the British.

The watchword of every fighter pilot has always been 'check six', always be sure there is no enemy behind you. This was and still is fundamental. Galland thought then of what Hitler had said to him, and of what the Führer had said in his Christmas address to the men of JG-26: 'Avoid war on two fronts and eliminate one enemy after another.' Yet on the positive side, the Soviet air force, while strong in numbers, was utterly inferior to the *Luftwaffe* in technology and personnel. The prevailing view in the *Luftwaffe* then was, as Galland expressed it, "It would only be necessary to shoot down the leader of a flight for the remaining illiterates to lose themselves on the way home. We could shoot them down like clay pigeons". But he was visibly shocked and horrified about the invasion plan. "And what about England?" he asked Goering, who only waved his hand disdainfully. This business in the east would be concluded in two or three months, he informed Galland. Initially, Mölders would take his wing out there for the first four to six weeks. The 2nd and 26th Fighter Wings would then go east to relieve Mölders. Galland and Mölders were then sworn to silence about the real plan. Galland returned to his base near the Channel, deeply worried but forbidden to discuss his concerns with anyone.

The RAF had started what it called the 'Nonstop Offensive', in which it began fighter sweep attacks on Continental German targets. The offensive soon developed into bombing raids with fighter escort. The attacks appeared to Galland to have no particular strategic purpose but clearly, roles were reversed. The enemy was on the offensive and the Luftwaffe on the defensive. In this time JG-26 achieved its 500th victory and Galland received the congratulations of *Feldmarshall* Sperrle. By year's end the number would double, but with the transfer of much of the German fighter force to the eastern front, the Channel front was rather weakly defended and the Royal Air Force saw the opportunity to gain air supremacy in the sector.

Around noon of 21 June, a warm, sunny day on the Channel coast, German radar was reporting the approach of a large formation of enemy aircraft. The raid was made up of a force of Bristol Blenheim bombers with an escort of about fifty Spitfires and Hurricanes and they were heading for a target, the airfield at Arques near Saint-Omer. Galland immediately scrambled all three of his squadrons to meet the enemy formation. In the battle both sides incurred heavy losses.

Galland led the primary unit of the wing into the air at 12:24 and soon spotted the British formation, which had just bombed the airfield. With a height advantage on the enemy bomber force, he dived through the British fighters to manoeuvre in close for a shot at a Blenheim in the lower rear row of the formation. The bomber erupted in flame and Galland saw a few of the crew bale out. It was eight minutes since he had taken off. This was his 68th victory.

He got in position for a second attack and this time his target was a bomber in the front row of the formation. He fired from close range and the starboard engine of the Blenheim began pouring flame and thick black smoke as the bomber slowly broke away from the other Blenheims. Two of its crew fell away and their parachutes blossomed – number 69.

Before he could recover from this combat, Galland saw tracer bullets shooting past his canopy. He threw the 109 into a tight downward turn in an effort to lose his attacker. But bullets from the Spitfire had already ruined his right radiator and smoke or coolant trailed his plane. In what seemed only seconds his engine seized and stopped. But his luck held. He saw that he was right over the Calais-Marck airfield and was able to put the Messerschmitt down in a fairly gentle crash-landing. Unhurt, he was delivered safely back to his own field 30 minutes later.

The excitement of the day continued. At four in the afternoon the alarm sounded again. Another large enemy formation was approaching from the Channel. Galland and the pilots of all air-worthy JG-26 fighters took off to intercept the raiders. This time though, he was flying without his regular wingman who, like himself, had been shot down during the mid-day action. Unlike Galland, though, the wingman had not returned to base as yet. In the air Galland joined up with the aircraft of I/JG-26 south-east of Boulogne and they immediately encountered a flight of Spitfires. Galland bounced one of the graceful British fighters, sending it down in flames for his 70th victory. With no wingman to witness the kill, he decided to follow it down to register it for himself. The decision was a bad one.

Something hard hit my head and arm. My aircraft was in bad shape. The wings were ripped by cannon fire. I was sitting half in the open. The right side of the fuselage had been shot away. Fuel tank and radiator were both leaking heavily. Instinctively I banked away to the north. Almost calmly I noticed that my heavily damaged ME still flew and responded tolerably well with the engine cut off. My luck has held once more, I was thinking, and I will try to glide home. My altitude was 18,000 feet.

My arm and head were bleeding. But I didn't feel any pain. No time for that. Anyhow nothing precious was hurt. A sharp detonation tore me out of my reverie. The tank, which up to then had been gurgling away quietly, suddenly exploded. The whole fuselage was immediately aflame. Burning petrol ran into the cockpit. It was getting uncomfortably hot. Only one thought remained: Get Out, Get Out, Get Out! The cockpit roof release would not work – must be jammed! Shall I burn alive in here? – I tore my belt open. I tried to open the hinged top of the roof. The air pressure on it was too strong. Flames all around me. I must open it! I must not fry to death in here! Terror! Those were the most terrible seconds of my life. With a last effort I pushed my whole body against the roof. The flap opened and was torn away by the air stream. I had already pulled her nose up. The push against the joy stick did not throw me entirely clear of the burning coffin, which a few minutes before was still my beloved and faithful ME-109. The parachute on which I had been sitting was caught on the fixed part of the cockpit roof. The entire plane was now in flames and was dashing down to earth with me. With my arm around the aerial mast I tugged, I pushed against anything I could find with my feet. All in vain! Should I be doomed at the last moment although I was already half freed? I don't know how I got free in the end. Suddenly I was falling. I turned over several times in the air. Thank God. In my excitement I nearly operated the quick harness release instead of the cord. At the last moment I noticed that I was releasing the safety catch. Another shock! The parachute and I would have arrived separately. A jerk and like a pendulum I was suspended from the opened parachute. Slowly and softly I floated down to earth.

Below me a column of black smoke marked the spot where my ME crashed. By rights I should have landed in the Forest of Boulogne like a monkey on a tree, but the parachute only brushed a poplar and then folded up. I landed rather luckily in a soft, boggy meadow. Up to now I had been under high tension of nerves and energy. I collapsed. I felt as wretched as a dog. Shot and bleeding profusely from head and arm, with a painfully twisted ankle which started to swell immediately, I could neither walk nor stand up. Suspicious and unfriendly French peasants came at last and carried me into a farmhouse. The first Germans I saw were men of the Todt Organization from a nearby building site. They packed me into a car and took me back to my base at Audembert.

Another of Adolf Galland's most memorable experiences centred around the arrival in that hot summer of 1941 of RAF Wing Commander (later Group Captain) Douglas Bader, the famous legless ace, who had been shot down in a dogfight over the Pas de Calais. On being captured by the Germans, Bader was eager to know who had shot him down. As both the British and the Germans had many non-commissioned officer pilots in their squadrons, he later told Galland that the idea that he might have been brought down by an NCO was intolerable to him [an interesting parallel to the view of so many downed German pilots in that time who preferred to believe that a Spitfire had got them rather than a Hurricane]. Galland, who himself had shot down two aircraft in the encounter with Bader's wing the day the Englishman was downed, felt sure that Bader had indeed been shot down by one of the young German officers. But, as there was no way of establishing who had scored the victory, Galland, the good host, chose not to offend Bader and selected one of the participants in the Bader combat, a good-looking young flying officer and introduced him to Bader as his victorious opponent. Bader seemed pleased to meet the young German.

Galland and his staff were delighted that the legendary Douglas Bader had literally fallen into their hands and enjoyed briefly hosting the enemy fighter leader before sending him off to prison camp. In their early conversations, Bader described his combat on the day he was downed:

> I saw pieces flying off my crate. The nose dipped. I looked round – the tail unit had practically gone . . . nothing else to be done but to get out as quickly as possible. That was easier said than done, especially as the plane dived vertically and began to spin. I pulled myself up with my hands. I had already got one leg outside. The other one, the right one, was wedged inside. I tugged and the plane tugged too. Then I was shooting through the air minus my right leg. That was going down with the aircraft . . . !

Bader was, of course, referring to the artificial legs he had been fitted with following the disastrous plane crash he had survived in 1931. When his parachute deposited him quite firmly onto the French landscape he suffered great pain as the force of the impact jammed his remaining artificial leg up into his body. On his arrival at the Saint-Omer Hospital he asked about his artificial limbs. The right leg was there by his bedside and he requested that a search be made in the wreckage of his Spitfire for the missing leg. The Germans found the limb but it was badly damaged. Galland had one of his mechanics straighten it and soon the Englishman was practising walking in the hospital ward. He had been placed in a private room but asked to be moved to the ward to be with other downed British pilots.

When Bader was well enough to travel, Galland sent his large staff car to bring him to the fighter base in style. There he had tea with the officers and commanders of JG-26. Galland recalled that Bader was charming and had good manners, but was always on his guard against giving even a hint of any military information. He needn't have worried. Galland and his officers were strictly forbidden to interrogate any prisoners in their charge. Still, Galland had instructed his personnel before Bader's arrival, to ask the RAF pilot no questions of a military nature.

Gradually, Bader relaxed and loosened up a bit in the company of his

German hosts and agreed when Galland offered him a tour of the installation. Bader asked Galland if he would have a message dropped over England to tell his wife that he was well and to put a package together for him containing his spare pair of legs, a better uniform, some tobacco and a pipe. On the tour they came to where Galland's own fighter was parked and Bader asked if he might be allowed to sit in the cockpit. Galland agreed and when he was settled in the seat he showed great interest as Galland explained every detail. Then he asked the German: "Will you do me a great favour?"

"With pleasure if it is in my power" the Galland replied.

"At least once in my life I would like to fly a Messerschmitt. Let me do just one circle over the airfield" said Bader.

Galland looked him in the eye and said: "If I grant your wish, I'm afraid you'll escape and I should be forced to chase after you. Now we have met we don't want to shoot at each other again, do we!"

They both laughed and Bader was returned to the hospital.

Later Galland called Goering and told him of Bader's request for the spare set of legs, and Goering agreed that the request should be honoured. He told Galland to contact the RAF on the international SOS wave length and offer safe conduct to a British plane which could land on an airfield near the coast and unload the package for Bader. The radio contact was made and the request was confirmed with the British.

Douglas Bader tied bedsheets together and escaped out a window of the Saint-Omer hospital to the embarrassment and concern of Galland. The British, meanwhile, did visit the French coast, Galland's airfield and a few others, and they dropped the box containing Bader's spare legs and the other items, along with a great many bombs. Chivalry in war had probably lost whatever significance it may have had for the British during the incessant bombing of London. When the box was found it bore a large red cross and, in German, THIS BOX CONTAINS ARTIFICIAL LEGS FOR WING COMMANDER BADER, PRISONER OF WAR. Bader was soon recaptured but later made several more abortive escape attempts in Germany.

If Douglas Bader was famous among the pilots of the *Luftwaffe*, Adolf Galland was his counterpart among the pilots of RAF Fighter Command. Photos of Galland in dress uniform with all his decorations had been widely seen in Britain and the German's taste for cigars, fine food and wines was well known. The British saw Galland as somewhat of a dandy and nicknamed him 'The Fighting Fop'. On one occasion, the birthday of Major General Theo Osterkamp on 15 April, 1941, (Osterkamp had become an ace in both world wars), a party was arranged at Le Touquet. Galland was invited and flew to Brest where he loaded a basket of champagne and lobsters in his fighter and took off for Le Touquet. He was accompanied by his current wingman, First Lieutenant Westphal. Their route took them rather near the English coast and they happened to encounter a flight of Spitfires near Kent. The Spitfires had apparently been sent to meet the approaching enemy aircraft. Galland engaged and quickly destroyed one of the British planes and moved on to attack another, not realizing that his wingman was experiencing a technical problem with his aircraft and could not assist him should he require help. The odds quickly shifted in favour of the Spitfires and it was all Galland could do to escape to the French coast with the precious cargo. Once again the Galland luck held and he was able to pull away from the chasing enemy fighters. Now Galland was having second thoughts about his original choice of route to Le Touquet, feeling that a straight line from Brest might have been a better way, and his wingman was not in sight. As Galland approached the field to land at Le Touquet he noticed a show of red flares bursting over the landing strip and animated ground staff waving frantically at him. He went around to make a second approach and was again met with a show of flares and this time he realized that his undercarriage must be up. He must have accidentally lowered it during his escape dash and then, thinking the landing gear was retracted as he approached the field, 'lowered' it, but actually retracted it. It occurred to him that landing without wheels was no way to treat a cargo of champagne.

In the bleak, dreary afternoon of 17 November 1941, Adolf Galland heard the radio announcement from General Forces Headquarters: 'The *Generalluftzeugmeister* of the *Luftwaffe, Generaloberst* Ernst Udet had a fatal crash this morning while testing a new type of plane. The Führer has ordered a state funeral.' Within the hour Galland received orders to proceed immediately to Berlin.

Galland remembered Udet, his popularity with the fighter pilots, his charismatic charm and pleasant disposition, his great flying skill and his 62-victory score in the First World War. He recalled how in 1933 Goering had overcome Udet's resistance and talked him into helping in the rebuilding of the *Luftwaffe*. At first Udet served as an inspector of the fighter force. In 1936 he became Chief of the Technical Department of the Air Ministry and in 1938 was promoted to *Generalluftzeugmeister*, responsible for rearming the German aircraft industry. With the war in Europe Udet, like Galland, was convinced that the *Luftwaffe*'s emphasis on medium bombers was wrong and what was needed was fighters by the many thousands. He had the power and position to achieve much, but lacked the organizational skills to succeed in the role. The load was too great for him. The warmth and charm went out of Udet and was replaced by deep depression. He had not died in a plane crash. He had shot himself in his home.

Werner Mölders was riding as a passenger in a Heinkel He-111 bomber en route from the Crimea to join the honour guard at the funeral of Ernst Udet. The Heinkel crashed in bad weather killing Mölders, a mechanic travelling with him, and the pilot of the bomber. Two others, Mölders' aide-de-camp and the radio operator, survived the crash and provided the information needed to reconstruct the accident in detail. Two days after Udet's funeral Galland was attending that of his friend, Mölders. After the service Goering took him aside and promoted him to be General of the Fighter Arm. Galland: 'Mölders was the best man the *Luftwaffe* had. He was a good man, very strict with his own conduct and expected the same of his men. He was a wonderful man.' Becoming a General Staff officer, a 'brass hat', was probably the last thing Galland wanted. He was the hunter, the fighter leader, and that was what mattered most to him. He vowed never to lose contact with his men.

In January 1942 the 28,000-ton German battle cruisers *Scharnhorst* and *Gneisenau*, and the 10,000-ton cruiser *Prinz Eugen*, lay in the French port of Brest. Since the beginning of the war they had collectively sunk more than a million tons of British shipping, including the aircraft carrier *Glorious*, and the battleship *Hood* (which the *Prinz Eugen* and the battleship *Bismarck* had sunk). They had been at Brest since the spring of 1941, acting as a 'fleet in being', a static little German armada serving to tie up a portion of the British Royal Navy without leaving port. This forced the British to maintain heavy sea forces on alert to protect their convoys in the English Channel, and to suspend the deployment of the naval force intended to operate in the Mediterranean against German and Italian supply ships for the North African campaign. As such, the mighty German warships at Brest were ripe targets for attacks by the RAF, generally ineffectual raids in the course of which the British lost 43 aircraft and 247 airmen. Though damage to the *Scharnhorst* in one attack was heavy, both battle cruisers were readily repaired.

The Soviet Union, meanwhile, which was now allied with Britain and the United States against Germany, was demanding the opening of a second front against the Germans. Believing that the new front might be launched in Scandinavia, concerned about the success of his own coming offensive against the Soviets, and considering the experiments with heavy water then being conducted in Norway in relation to potential atomic weapons development, Hitler decided to move the three German warships from their berths at Brest to Norway via Germany.

Transferring the German naval vessels from the French port meant the choice of two routes. The first, around Scotland, would have brought a potentially disastrous encounter with the British Home Fleet, stationed at Scapa Flow, with at least three battleships and two aircraft carriers, an option the German Navy considered impossible and would not entertain. The only other possibility was a southern route through the English Channel, which would expose the German vessels to the might of the Royal Air Force, to British naval units and the British coastal gun batteries. The Germans saw this 'Channel Dash' as easily the better choice, particularly if effectively supported by the *Luftwaffe* fighter force on the Channel.

Johannes Jeschonnek, Chief of the *Luftwaffe* General Staff, briefed Galland on the ship movement mission, which was to be called Operation Thunderbolt. A meeting with Hitler was to be held shortly to discuss the operation and Jeschonnek was certain that the naval representatives there would demand 'close, continuous escort, with full air cover by a sufficient strength of fighters.' Jeschonnek was adamently opposed to such a demand as the entire *Luftwaffe* fighter force on the Channel numbered less than 250, of which many were part of training units. Jeschonnek and Galland were required to attend the meeting. Goering would not be there as he knew he could not say no to the Führer, though he also knew that the available fighter strength on the Channel was inadequate for the job. Jeschonnek would propose that Galland, as commander of the Channel fighter force, assume responsibility for the planned operation.

The meeting was set for 12 January at Hitler's Wolf's Redoubt bunker. Those attending were the Führer, Field Marshal and Chief of the High Command Keitel, Grand Admiral Raeder, Vice-Admiral Ciliax, Commodore Ruge, the commanders of the battleships, Jeschonnek, Galland, the aides-de-camp and a stenographer. Hitler began by summarizing the thinking behind his decision to transfer nearly the entire German fleet to Norwegian waters. Ciliax then covered the main points of the Admiralty plan for the mission: 1. The movements of the ships must be reduced to a minimum before the start of the operation. 2. The ships must leave the port of Brest by night, so that when passing through the Channel they could use the daylight for the most effective defence. 3. The ships must be escorted from early dawn to twilight by the strongest possible fighter force. The Navy continued with an additional demand for raids on British torpedo aircraft bases, with Raeder insisting that the success or failure of the operation would depend solely on the efforts of the *Luftwaffe*. Jeschonnek said it would be difficult to provide permanent escort with 250 planes, but that he would also employ some nightfighters in the dawn and dusk hours. Hitler then ordered the *Luftwaffe* to do everything possible to ensure the safety of the warships. Jeschonnek repeated that he could not guarantee continuous protection with the fighter resources available. The meeting ended. The operation would proceed as planned.

At the Thunderbolt meeting, Hitler had demanded that absolute secrecy be adhered to as a prerequisite for success. He had a document prepared that all in attendance had to sign pledging to keep the secrets of the mission. At the close of the session Hitler asked Galland in private if, as everything depended on the air cover for the naval units to make the dash successfully, he believed it could succeed? Galland gave a well considered response:

It all depends on how much time the English have to mobilize the RAF against the ships. We need complete surprise, and a bit of luck in the bargain. My fighter pilots will give their very best when they know what is at stake.

Under a blanket of strict secrecy, planning and preparations for Thunderbolt began in earnest. Outwardly, it was to appear to be preparations for a new and imminent large-scale offensive against England. The German Navy referred to the coming mission with the code word Cerberus, to disguise their preparations for it. For them, the efforts were to look like getting ready for a new major deployment to the Atlantic. Supporting these ruses was a plethora of misleading radio messages. Hitler even participated in the scam by joking that he would tell Mussolini that the warships at Brest were soon to sail for the Pacific in aid of the Japanese. He said that giving the message to his Italian partner would be the quickest and safest way of getting such information to the British Admiralty.

Tactical command of the German battleships fell to Vice-Admiral Ciliax, as commander of the vessels. To facilitate the most efficient teamwork during the operation, liaison officers were exchanged between the naval and air force commands. Single practise trial runs were conducted between 22 January and 10 February, with 450 fighter escort sorties being flown. In the period, RAF bombers attacked Brest harbour nearly every night but failed to damage the three warships preparing to make the dash.

The escorting fighters would have to operate from several fields in order to minimize the distances they had to fly to the ships and maximize their time in the air over the vessels. The fields ranged from Abbeville, Lille, Calais, to Le Touquet, Cherbourg, Caen, Le Havre, to Schiphol, Jever and Wilhelmshaven. Galland's headquarters would be connected by special ultra-short-wave and long-wave radio links to the various sector airfields and to the flotilla in the Channel. New and relatively untried methods of interference and deception with the enemy radar system were to be employed as well. To enable the flotilla to achieve the greatest possible speed through the Channel and to avoid mines, it was decided to plot a course approximately in the middle of the waterway. Marking boats were stationed to assist in the navigation of the warships. A fleet of 80 minesweepers was employed to clear more than 100 mines along the route. All of these activities were conducted by night.

Galland's plan for the air cover of the vessels called for successive waves of 16 planes each to arrive and maintain station in the area of the ships for approximately 35 minutes. If they encountered enemy aircraft during that period they could remain in the area for a further 10 minutes. Each relieving wave of fighters would arrive 10 minutes before the time to relieve the current escort aircraft, thus for a period of at least 10 minutes, the flotilla would have the benefit of 32 fighters protecting it during every changeover. The already efficient ground crews of the fighter units trained specifically to cut the down time for refuelling and possibly rearming the fighters to just 30 minutes.

The fighter pilots had orders to intercept attacking enemy aircraft and if any such aircraft should penetrate the German fighter cover to make a direct attack on the warships, it was to be put out of action by all available means, including if necessary, ramming. The Germans were told to avoid fights with enemy aircraft that were leaving the combat area. All that mattered was the successful protection of the warships.

In scheduling the actual date for Thunderbolt, the considerations included the essential surprise element which meant taking advantage of the long winter nights which became shorter after February. Thus the mission had to be launched before the end of that month. Another factor was the water and tidal conditions which were most favourable between the 7th and 15th of the month. Finally there was the weather to consider based on the best available information the Germans could obtain. It was up to General-Admiral Sallwachter, the German C-in-C of Navy Group Command West, to decide the date of Thunderbolt and he chose 11 February with a departure time from Brest at 8 p.m.

As it happened, the British intelligence network functioned at least well enough to alert the RAF to the impending German warship movement around 11 February and during the preceding days British aircraft had dropped 1,100 magnetic mines between Brest and the Frisian Islands off northern Germany. Still, the RAF was anticipating the Channel dash of the German vessels at night and had prepared for a nighttime encounter somewhere between Dover and Calais in the narrow straight.

So the British knew something was up with the Brest warships, but not when. At nightfall on the 11th seven German destroyers gathered near the Brest harbour entrance to form a perimeter guard for the capital ships, which left their berths at 8 p.m. as planned. Almost immediately, however, an air raid alarm warning sounded and the three ships were returned to their berths. An RAF raid was approaching and the Germans immediately threw a smoke screen over the harbour. As the enemy bombers neared, the harbour flak guns roared into action and searchlights panned the night sky looking for the intruders. Preceded by their engine noise, about 20 British bombers appeared over the harbour at an altitude of between 6,000 and 9,000 feet and released their bomb loads. As the bomb explosions erupted around the port, the guns of the warships joined the party. Again, the German vessels escaped damage and, at 11 p.m. they sailed from Brest to begin the Thunderbolt-Cerberus mission.

The naval formation rounded Ushant west of Brittany and set its Channel course at 13 minutes after midnight in complete radio silence. They steamed at some 30 knots and were soon making up the time lost to the air raid. They would reach their intended position at dawn as planned. As the ships passed Cherbourg a group of German torpedo E-boats joined it to enhance the perimeter guard. The E-boats would be relieved by a similar force as the flotilla entered each sector along the route. By 9 a.m. the warships were off the Cotentin peninsula and the destroyer fighters were flying down near sea level to keep below the English radar detection capability. Then, off Dieppe, an area of uncleared mines was discovered in the path of the flotilla, and minesweepers were ordered in to clear a route through the mine field. All the ships passed through it without incident.

Now there was an overlap in the protective air cover. The Me-110 nightfighters that had been flying to the left (enemy) side of the flotilla were joined by the first wave of dayfighters. All pilots had been ordered to fly as low as possible and maintain total radio silence. For safety Galland had kept between 25 and 30 fighters standing by on the various sector airfields. The pilots sat in the cockpits and the aircraft were ready to take off instantly if needed. At 11 a.m. the nightfighters were released and landed on airfields in the Dutch sector. They were then prepared to return to the escort duty that evening. For 2 hours the German flotilla had been approaching the narrowest point in the Channel, the straight between Dover and Calais in broad daylight.

Just as the nightfighters left the flotilla, German radio operators intercepted a radio message from a Spitfire pilot alerting his base that a large German naval formation consisting of three capital ships and about 20 other warships was steaming at high speed towards the Strait of Dover. A light rain was falling, the cloud ceiling was down to about 600 feet and visibility, though poor, revealed the white English coastal cliffs. In a brilliant tactic, Galland held his radio silence order for as long as he dared, thus gaining an extra 35 unmolested miles for the flotilla just as it was passing through the narrowest part of the Channel. Nearly 2 hours passed between that first RAF sighting and the initial British attack on the German ships. Luck stayed with the Germans and as the warships passed opposite Boulogne an additional 15 E-boats joined the flotilla, further expanding its security guard. The fighter pilots of the Channel-based JG-2 and JG-26 were still reasonably fresh and looking forward to the seemingly inevitable air battle to come.

The first action began at 1:16 p.m. when British coastal gun batteries opened fire on the *Prinz Eugen* and almost at the same moment a battle sparked between German and British motor torpedo boats, as the battle cruiser *Scharnhorst* reported being under artillery fire from 400 yards to her port. As fate would have it, the flotilla was steaming at its closest point to Galland's fighter sector bases in the area and he was able to add to the fighter cover moments later when six British Fairey Swordfish torpedo bombers and their Spitfire escort approached the flotilla in a low-level attack. Fighter radio control on one of the warships broke radio silence at that point to direct the Messerschmitts and Focke-Wulfs onto the attackers. Most of the German fighters engaged the escorting Spitfires while the remainder, in cooperation with the warship gunners, shot down every one of the Swordfish bombers. The lid was off now and Galland cancelled the order for radio silence and low-level flying.

For more than 5 hours air and sea battles raged around the German warships. Galland's pilots and the guns of the vessels brought down more than 60 enemy aircraft of various types including Spitfires, Swordfish, Blenheims, Wellingtons, Hampdens and Whirlwinds. During the mêlée, at about 3:30 p.m., the flotilla flagship *Scharnhorst* struck a mine and was heavily shaken. Her lights went out and her radios were silenced. She was stopped and was leaving a slick of oil astern. The German destroyer Z-29 was immediately dispatched to her side to take aboard the commander and the fighter control liaison officer. Now the weather was worsening rapidly with the ceiling down to below 500 feet and visibility just over ½ mile. The flotilla proceeded with *Gneisenau, Prinz Eugen*, and most of the destroyers and motor torpedo boats. By 6:45 p.m. *Scharnhorst* had got under way again and was steaming at full speed trying to catch up with the flotilla.

Shortly after 9 p.m. *Gneisenau* slammed into a mine and shook violently under the force of the explosion. Her engines stopped but in a little while she was under way again, having suffered only superficial damage. An hour later *Scharnhorst* hit another mine but was able to continue though at a reduced speed of 15 knots. Early on 13 February, *Gneisenau* and *Prinz Eugen* arrived at Kiel. At 10:30 a.m. *Scharnhorst* reached Wilhelmshaven.

Galland recalled:

The weather position developed almost dramatically for fighter action. In the Pas de Calais (No I) take-off and landing were still unaffected. The approach to the flotilla in the Channel could only now be made in low-level flight. But the distance of 120 miles was now so far that after 30 minutes' escort flight, a return to the starting base was out of the question. The fighters therefore had to land on Dutch territory (No II). But there the weather was at its worst. Over large stretches the clouds were at ground level. It was no easy decision for me to send the fighters into the bad-weather zone to land after their fourth sortie on this day of a major battle, but I had no alternative. In fact there were quite a few emergency landings outside the airfields, some of which ended in crashes. But most of the pilots landed safely. On their own initiative, without waiting for orders, a few determined flight lieutenants and squadron leaders took off again with small formations before darkness fell after rapid servicing and refuelling. They were conscious that everything was at stake here. No scruples about safety existed on that day. The fighter pilots had done more than their duty. They were carried away by the grandeur of the operation and showed an enthusiasm I did not think would have been possible any more after the long and hard struggle the squadrons had waged on the Channel, after the heavy losses they had sustained, and after so many bitter disappointments.

As 1943 came to a close the fortunes of Germany's war had turned on her, in Russia, at El Alamein, and elsewhere, the Germans were racking up more defeats than victories, their armies in retreat, and Hitler, always a believer in finding scapegoats to take the blame for his many failed strategies, was blaming the *Luftwaffe* more and more. The inadequacies, drug addiction and incompetence of Goering were suddenly spotlighted. The *Reichsmarshall* squirmed, as did Jeschonnek under the same treatment from the Führer, whom he had long revered. The disaster of Stalingrad, where the *Luftwaffe* had been unable to resupply the surrounded German troops, had brought the wrath of Hitler down on Jeschonnek. He broke under it and committed suicide.

Galland was receiving more than his share of the heat and blame from Goering as things went from worse to much worse for the air force and the Reich. Galland, the fighter leader, the hunter, believed now more than ever in his basic philosophy of the fighter: unrelenting aggressive tactics even on the defensive. With the British and American air forces growing daily in their capability to deliver massive, crushing raids not only on German Continental targets but now on German cities as well, Galland was determined to defend Germany in the air through those same aggressive tactics.

As many events in 1944 were to demonstrate, however, in most of the European air battles that year it was the Germans who would suffer the most crippling losses on the ground and in the air. But there were exceptions. In several daylight attacks on German targets by American bombers in February and March, sixty or more heavy bombers were brought down by fighters or flak with each occasion costing the U.S.A.A.F. upwards of 600 highly trained men. And on the night of 30 – 31 March, when a force of more than 800 Royal Air Force bombers attacked Nuremberg, more than 90 of their aircraft were shot down by German nightfighters. In another example of *Luftwaffe* success, a force of 169 B-17 bombers on a strike at Brunswick 10 February were initially hampered by deteriorating weather, causing them to miss their rendezvous with their escort fighters on the withdrawl from the target area. That day the Germans had been able to assemble a force of some 350 fighters which located the enemy bomber stream and attacked it taking full advantage of the thick white contrails of vapour forming behind the bombers' engines. The German planes were able to hide among the contrails in their attacks on the bombers, eventually destroying 29 of the B-17s, and eight of the escort fighters, while damaging 111 of the remaining bombers.

But the Americans and the British had long since determined to build up sufficiently balanced and broadly capable air forces which would ultimately destroy Germany. In the course of that effort they both made mistakes, learned from them, and continued to grow in numbers and capability. Whereas, the *Luftwaffe*, as Galland saw it, had now reached a critical stage with an insufficient fighter force in numbers and performance and it was these insufficiencies that he was asked to discuss with the *Reichsmarshall* at Schloss Veltenstein in the autumn of 1943.

They talked as they walked around the courtyard at Veltenstein. Galland was, by this time, quite used to having the blame for *Luftwaffe* fighter failures heaped upon him by the increasingly reproachful Goering, but was never shy about defending his beliefs, his policies and his actions. He persistently made the case for strengthening the fighter force with better aircraft and training, and whenever he disagreed with the positions of the *Reichsmarshall*, he challenged him. As they talked, Goering became more and more agitated. Finally, they came to a sensitive subject involving the Führer. Hitler believed that a large-calibre, long-distance cannon was needed as essential armament for a destroyer aircraft, the ME-410. He had criticized Goering for lagging behind both the army and the navy in the development of such a weapon. The navy had a similar gun for use against distant targets; the army had one on its latest tanks enabling them to shoot accurately at enemy armour up to 3,000 yards away. Only the air force had thus far lacked such a weapon and still had to get within 400 yards of an enemy plane [i.e. an American bomber in a large, well-protected formation] to be able to hit it. The Führer's demand resulted in an aircraft armed with a cannon that weighed 2,000 lb, was reconstructed to be an automatic weapon with a magazine that held fifteen shells, and a rate of fire of about one shell per second. The barrel of the weapon projected nearly 10 feet out in front of the plane, making the aircraft handle less well than a conventionally-armed version. When fired, the cannon invariably jammed after about five shots and could not be fired with accuracy at 3,000 yards, nor even at 1,000 yards. 400 yards was still the maximum range with any hope of hitting the target, and that possibility was often negated by the difficulty of flying the plane when using the cannon.

In a carefully detailed, well reasoned explanation, Galland spelled out the problems with the weapon system in the view of the air force engineering specialists, the crews and himself. But Goering was now too angry to listen much less be drawn into rational debate. As he had done on many previous occasions, he accused the fighter pilots of cowardice. As always, Galland defended them, risking his career and his life in doing so. Goering loudly berated Galland for constantly protecting the fighter arm and sabotaging the orders he as *Reichsmarshall* gave after deep and careful deliberation. Galland, for his part, found the order to implement the wide deployment of the ME-410 irresponsible and deplorable, and the continuing furious criticism and demands by Goering intolerable. He told Goering that he could not reconcile his conscience with what the *Reichsmarshall* was demanding of him and he formally requested that he be relieved of command as General of the Fighter Arm and sent back to the front. The shocked Goering was momentarily silent and then responded: "Granted!"

Two weeks after the heated exchange at Veltenstein, Galland asked

Goering who would be succeeding him as General of the Fighter Arm and when that person would be arriving to take over? He was told that no order had been issued yet and he would be informed in due course. Two weeks after that Galland was told that he was to stay at his post. Weeks later, the *Reichsmarshall* apologized to Galland, asking him to take into account the stress he had been under at the time.

March 1944. With the operational entry of the North American P-51 Mustang as the ultimate long-ranging escort for the American daylight bomber forces, Goering's old boast that no Allied bomber would ever appear over Berlin, returned to haunt him on a monumental scale. Now the enemy bombers could hit targets anywhere in Germany with un-interrupted fighter protection and greatly improved odds of survival. In one of his reports of April 1944, Galland wrote:

> The ratio in which we fight today is about 1 to 7. The standard of the Americans is extraordinarily high. The day fighters have lost more than 1,000 aircraft during the last four months, among them our best officers. These gaps cannot be filled. During each enemy raid we lose about 50 fighters. Things have gone so far that the danger of a collapse of our arm exists.

So desperate had the situation become for the *Luftwaffe* that a new form of interceptor force had to be created, the 'storm' fighters. As Galland wrote:

> It was typical of the spirit of the German fighter pilots that they did not put up with the enemy's superiority, that they did not resign them-selves, that they proposed to attack the death-dealing bombers to the point of self-sacrifice. In this way at the end of 1943, in addition to many other suggestions from the front, the following was brought to me: to ram the heavy bombers and in particular the leading aircraft. This idea was undoubtedly inspired by the example of the Japanese kamikaze pilots, who in order to destroy especially im-portant targets dived their aircraft into them. Such self-sacrifice was rooted in the beliefs, the traditions, and the concept of heroism of the Japanese race. We Europeans could marvel at it, but it was foreign to our nature. Therefore I had to reject this idea of self-sacrifice on principle. On the other hand these ideas, whose keenest champion was Major von Kornatzki, gave rise to the formation of special elite units of fighters. Instead of ramming, they were to attack in tight formation as close as possible to the bombers. With more powerful armament they would have a better chance of a kill. Ramming was unnecessary. But it was imperative to wade right in and get as close as possible. The aim was to shoot the heavy bomber down at any

price. If during such a storm attack their own aircraft was heavily hit, they could always ram and bale out.

Testing of the storm fighter concept was conducted by an experimental flight. This was followed by a call for volunteers to fly with the new units, which resulted in a strong and enthusiastic response. The storm fighters were equipped with specially modified Focke-Wulf Fw-190 aircraft armed with cannon. The pilot was protected by extra armour. The first such squadron to be formed was IV(Sturm)/JG 3/Udet and it soon proved a success, achieving impressive results while suffering acceptably low losses. Galland intended to add one such squadron to each of the nine fighter wings defending the Reich.

> I took part in a fighter operation of the Reich's defence together with the Inspector of the Day Fighters, East, *Oberst* Hannes Trautloft. A Fat Dog (a large formation of enemy heavy bombers) was reported to be approaching the Dutch coast. We were following this, as we always did, from my little control room in Hottengrund. I ordered two Focke-Wulfs to be warmed up on the Staaken airfield and invited Trautloft to accompany me. He sprinted across the 50 yards to the plane that was waiting with the engine running. Ten minutes later we took off from Staaken. Course west; climb to 25,000 feet.
>
> On the Reichs-fighter wavelength we received details of location, course, altitude, and other information concerning the major formation of about 800 B-17s and the other oddments which were flying in advance or safeguarding the flanks. We had just crossed the Elbe north of Magdeburg when we first caught sight of the enemy. We let the American formation pass at a respectful distance of from 5 to 10 miles. Eight hundred bombers went by, 2,000 tons of death, destruction, and fire inside their silver bodies, flying to their appointed targets in the heart of Germany. Something had to be done. Wave upon wave, endless formations of four-engined bombers! Right and left above them, with and without vapour trails, a vast pack of Mustang fighters. "The range of the enemy's fighter escort does not extend beyond the Elbe!" according to the General Staff. They had stopped talking about the Ruhr long ago, but they still refused to see what was written in realistic letters in the German sky.

To illustrate the fallen state of the *Luftwaffe* fighter force at the time of the Allied D-Day landings at Normandy on 6 June 1944, the German 3rd Air Fleet had fewer than 100 fighters available to confront the more than 6,000 Allied aircraft participating in the invasion. The entire German Air Force on all fighting fronts had a total of just 3,222 aircraft, of which only 40 per cent were serviceable. Only two German fighter wings remained on station in France. The majority of the fighter force was in use for the defence of the Reich. Even during the days and nights surrounding the Normandy landings, the Americans and the British continued to operate their combined bombing offensive against Germany and their prime objectives were the destruction of the German fighter aircraft industry and the weakening of the German fighter defence.

Towards the end of 1944 Goering had lost virtually all the influence he had enjoyed with Hitler, along with whatever respect the pilots of the *Luftwaffe* ever had for him. The incompetence of his leadership as head of the air force, and his many errors of commission and omission, had finally caught up with him. To fill the void left through his failure, small groups of officers formed in clandestine bids for position and influence. Morale among the air force officers was precariously low and, as word of the unrest reached the *Reichsmarshall* he reacted by calling a meeting near Berlin of several fighter and nightfighter leaders. At the gathering Goering lost all self-control and descended into a raving tirade of insults that aroused bitter rebellion in his audience. Galland:

> We fighter pilots were indeed prepared to fight and to die, as we had proved often enough, but we were not prepared to let ourselves be insulted or blamed for the disastrous situation in the air over the Reich. Most unnecessarily Goering ordered on top of all this that his impossible speech should be recorded. The record was to be played at intervals to the pilots at action stations.

Late in January 1945 General of the Fighter Arm Adolf Galland was officially relieved of his command. A successor had not yet been appointed and Galland was suddenly sent on leave. His absence spurred a wave of unrest among the fighter force. Some of the now openly rebellious fighter officers approached *Obersts* Hannes Trautloft and Gunther Lützow, having decided that things could no longer go on as they were. They tried to gain an audience with Hitler to press him for a radical change, Lützow acting as their spokesman. It was denied, but a delegation headed by Lützow was received by Goering. Once the *Reichsmarshall* had been impressed with the seriousness of the situation, he called another meeting, this time with all the commodores of the fighter wings. There he asked for a summary of their grievances and Lützow presented a memorandum with all the grievances of the fighter arm: the overwhelming influence of the *Luftwaffe* Bomber Command on the fighter force; the equipment of bomber instead of fighter squadrons with the new ME-262 jet; the impossible demands for bad-weather operations; insults to the fighter arm and doubts about its fighting spirit expressed by the Commander-in-Chief; distrust of the *Reichsmarshall*'s influential advisers; and the dismissal of the General of the Fighter Arm. As many of these themes had been the subjects of Galland's prior conversations with him, the *Reichsmarshall* immediately singled out Galland as the probable instigator behind the memorandum.

In a fury, Goering ended the meeting, calling the action of the pilots mutiny. He stormed from the room, pausing to threaten Lützow with a court-martial. Instead, the courageous *Oberst* was exiled from Germany and sent to Italy as a Fighter Leader. He was also forbidden to contact Galland or any other fighter pilots except on operational matters. The next morning Galland was told to leave Berlin that day, to report his where-abouts, and to keep himself in readiness for orders. He did leave but later returned to the capital without permission and, while there, was ordered to report at the Reich Chancellery where one of Hitler's aides informed him that the Führer had not known of the measures taken against Galland, but now that he knew about them, had ordered 'a stop to all this nonsense at once.'

Goering later contacted Galland, invited him to Carin Hall and magnanimously declared that no further actions would be taken against him in view of his past services to the fighter arm. He then told Galland that he was to have the chance to prove the worth of the ME-262 jet fighter by forming and leading a new unit of the planes. He would be entitled to select his own pilots, recommending the choice of some of the more re-calcitrant fighter officers, including Lützow. Galland's replacement, the new General of the Fighter Arm, would have no jurisdiction over the new jet unit – all of this at Hitler's order. Galland was delighted.

Early in the morning of 22 May 1943, Adolf Galland had joined Willy Messerschmitt on the latter's testing airfield at Lechfeld, near the Messerschmitt works at Augsburg. Accompanying them were technicians, designers, engine experts, the Commander of the *Luftwaffe* Testing Station, Rechlin, and his chief test pilot. As they drove out to the runway, Galland spotted the two ME-262 jet fighters, extreme designs with two engine nacelles slung beneath the swept wings, and no propellers. Galland would fly one of the strange new planes today.

After the chief test pilot made a brief demonstration flight in one of the planes, it was refuelled and Galland climbed in and listened to some instruction. As the mechanics started the turbines one of the engines caught fire. Galland got out quickly, the fire was doused and he climbed into the second plane. All went smoothly in the start sequence. Taxiing out to the take-off runway, his view was hampered by the fact that, unlike later production models, these early 262s had tailwheels, which meant that the nose of the plane blocked the pilot's forward vision during the take-off roll until the tail came up. As the little fighter passed 120 mph, it gently lifted from the runway.

For the first time I was flying by jet propulsion! No engine vibrations. No torque and no lashing sound of the propeller. Accompanied by a whistling sound, my jet shot through the air. Later when asked what it felt like, I said, 'It was as though angels were pushing.' On landing

I was more impressed and enthusiastic than I had ever been before. Feelings and impressions were no criteria, but the performance and characteristics were ascertained. This was not a step forward; this was a leap!

To *Feldmarshall* Erhard Milch, second in command of the *Luftwaffe*, Galland sent this telegram:

'The aircraft 262 is a very great hit. It will guarantee us an unbelieveable advantage in ops., while the enemy adheres to the piston engine. For air worthiness it makes the best impression. The engines are absolutely convincing, except during take-off and landing. This aircraft opens up completely new tactical possibilities'.

After flying the ME-262 jet, Galland knew that with this fastest of all aircraft, the fighter pilots of the *Luftwaffe* could beat any other fighter plane. In a conference with other fighter leaders, there was unanimous agreement that full advantage must be taken of this unique opportunity. The group proposed the immediate construction of 100 ME-262s for combined technical and tactical testing, to shortcut the normal lengthy process by which new aircraft finally reached the production assembly lines. Through this early testing, all necessary changes that cropped up could be implemented on the first actual production series of aircraft. A formalized version of this suggestion was brought by Galland to Goering at Burg Veltenstein. Goering agreed entirely with the thinking of the fighter leader group and telephoned Milch about the suggestion. Milch too concurred. Now it was up to Hitler to sanction the action. Several days passes with no word from the Führer and Galland worried that Hitler's ever-increasing distrust of Goering and the *Luftwaffe* had led to a rejection of the accelerated jet manufacture. Hitler then held his own conference of aeronautical experts, pointedly omitting any member of the *Luftwaffe*, but including Willy Messerschmitt. In the meeting Hitler dominated the conversation, demanding guarantees about the aircraft that the engineers, constructors and executives could not give. In the end, the Führer denied the suggested plan and ordered that only technical testing of a few prototype 262s be continued, while expressly forbidding preparation for mass production of the plane. Goering had no say in the decision.

By the end of 1943, however, when the fortunes of Germany and the German Air Force in the air war with the Allies were far worse than they had been in the spring, the High Command suddenly became interested in the ME-262 again. Full mass production was demanded and an armaments high priority was assigned to the programme. In early November Goering visited Willy Messerschmitt at the Augsburg works and asked him, on behalf of Hitler, about the possibility of the new jet carrying one or two bombs. Messerschmitt replied that it was, of course, possible to fit the plane for carrying a few light bombs, like any other fighter, but at a loss of performance. Later, at a demonstration of the jet at Insterburg in East Prussia in December, Hitler asked Goering if the plane could carry bombs. The Reichsmarshall answered: "Yes my Führer, theoretically yes. There is enough power to spare to carry 1,000 pounds, perhaps even 2,000 pounds." But Galland knew that the 262 had no bomb sight nor any fixtures for releasing bombs and that it was highly unsuited aerodynamically for aimed bomb release. Its high speed obviated dive or glide bombing. At very high speeds the aircraft became uncontrollable and at low altitudes the fuel consumption was so high that the range was unacceptably short. For the plane to succeed at high altitude bombing, the target would have to be at least the size of a large town. Hitler commented: "For years I have demanded from the Luftwaffe a 'speed bomber,' which can reach its target in spite of enemy fighter defence. In the aircraft you present to me as a fighter plane I see the 'Blitz bomber,' with which I will repel the invasion in its first and weakest phase. Regardless of the enemy's air umbrella it will strike the recently landed mass of material and troops creating panic, death, and destruction. At last this is the Blitz bomber! – Of course none of you thought of that!"

Despite the Führer's wishes, Galland assigned a group of highly experienced fighter pilots, in cooperation with the Messerschmitt works, to test a number of the 262 jets in real action against deHavilland Mosquito daylight reconnaissance aircraft over Germany. Soon the jets were scoring victories over the British planes. These successes did not go unnoticed by General James Doolittle, Commander of the U.S. Eighth Army Air Force in England, who immediately realized that, if the Germans could produce their new jet fighter in sufficient quantity it would soon make the American daylight raids on Germany impossible. What followed in February 1944 was called 'Big Week,' a campaign of precision bombing against the German aircraft industry with particular attention to the Messerschmitt factories at Augsburg and Regensburg, greatly delaying the completion and delivery of the first 100 ME-262s. On 24 April another American raid, this time on the Messerschmitt final assembly works at Leipheim, heavily damaged the first batch of the new jets.

Galland desperately needed the ME-262 in large numbers if there was to be any chance of redressing the balance between the enemy air forces' capability and that of the *Luftwaffe*. He called for production of 1,000 of the jet fighters a month within three months of the start of mass production, but Hitler rejected the call, in his persistent refusal to think in terms of air defence. Work on the plane continued, until the day that the Führer suddenly asked Milch how many of the newly completed jets could carry bombs. Milch, who had not been present at Insterburg when Hitler had offered his thoughts about the 'Blitz bomber,' answered truthfully, "None, my Führer; the ME-262 is being built exclusively as a fighter aircraft." The

Nazi leader flew into a rage, lambasting Milch, Goering and the *Luftwaffe*, calling them disobedient, unreliable and unfaithful.

Within hours Galland, Milch, Messerschmitt and the commander of the testing stations were summoned by Goering who informed them that Hitler had ordered the readjustment and rearming of the entire series of ME-262s as bombers, henceforth no one was allowed to refer to the plane as a fighter, or even a fighter-bomber, but only as the 'Blitz bomber.' Hitler's intention was to wreck the coming Allied invasion with the Blitz bomber by raiding the embarkation points in England and bombing the landing craft, tanks, and troops on the landing beaches. Galland and Messerschmitt railed at the decision, but Goering made it clear that there was to be no further debate or discussion of the matter. The final hope of the fighter arm for the defence of the Reich was now dashed and on top of that, the entire programme of testing, training and preparing for action was removed from the control of the General of the Fighter Arm and given to the General of the Combat Fighters (bombers).

In the weeks leading up to the Allied invasion of Normandy, the American and British bomber commands concentrated their efforts on the destruction of German armament factories, transportation facilities, synthetic oil plants, towns and cities. The *Luftwaffe* fighter force tried gallantly to defend these vital targets but were overwhelmed by the enormity of the task. The General of the Combat Fighters, meanwhile, strived to turn the 262 into a bomber, making numerous modifications and training pilots in bombing and tactics. By the time of the invasion in early June none of the jets was ready to be put into action against the invaders. It wasn't until August that the first of the aircraft was operating against the Allied armies which had by then advanced considerably through France. As bombers, though, they made little impact.

Thus, the fighter arm of the *Luftwaffe* was left without what they saw as the one possible means to tip the balance in the air back in Germany's favour. Worse still, the bomber units being equipped with the Blitz bomber were now also ordered to fly it as a fighter, in an additional affront to the fighter force. Galland tried his best to persuade Goering of the folly in the decision, pointing out that only the best and most experienced of fighter pilots could be effective in the ME-262, that bomber pilots could not be quickly transformed into fighter pilots, that they must first receive intensive training on ordinary piston-engined fighters, that by virtue of being bomber pilots by experience, their ability to see the enemy in the air could not possibly match that of real fighter pilots, and that, even if they were able to spot and approach the enemy they would not be able to aim and hit their target because of the great speed of the jets they flew. All of this was ignored by Goering. Galland then tried for a compromise asking that equal numbers of ME-262s be built as fighters and bombers. Combat action would then show which of the types would achieve the best results. Again the *Reichsmarshall* said no. Utterly frustrated, Galland made a final suggestion. In view of how poor the results of the present plan were undoubtedly going to be, it would be better to send the entire fighter force on a skiing holiday in the Bavarian mountains until the end of the war. Predictably, his forecast was accurate. To the end of the war relatively few of the German jets were operated successfully, either as fighters or Blitz bombers.

With the continuing sympathetic support of Reich Armaments Minister Albert Speer, Galland was able to maintain operation of a small fighter test unit of ME-262s that Speer was able to provide, a challenging task because at that point Hitler had personally taken charge of German turbojet production. Checking weekly production figures personally, the Führer actually involved himself in the disposition of individual aircraft. Galland, through all of this turmoil, continued to stress to both *Luftwaffe* and armaments leaders the importance and urgency of defending the Reich by employing all the new jets as fighters as quickly as they came from the assembly lines.

Through the summer and into the autumn of 1944 much of the entire German military effort in the war was virtually paralysed by the extreme fuel shortage. Speer, on his own initiative, stopped the enormous bomber production activity of the German aircraft industry. The failed Blitz bomber experiment left the participating units with few remaining aircraft as replacements could no longer be provided. And when a large contingent of American bombers approached the Messerschmitt works at Augsburg and the nearby airfield at Lechfeld, Galland was only able to send up a token resistance of six jet fighters to engage the attackers. It was nowhere near the kind of reception required to prevent the 60 ME-262 Blitz bombers on the ground there from being destroyed by the American bombs.

Finally, and far too late for Germany in the war, Galland received an order in October from Goering to form a pure jet-fighter unit at Lechfeld for action in the west. It seemed that Hitler was beginning to be impressed with the 262 as a fighter plane and the production allocation for the jet as a fighter was increased substantially. With the appearance of the first Arado A-234 jet bombers the Führer had relented to the extent of allowing one ME-262 fighter to go to the fighter force for every A-234 that was delivered to the bomber and reconnaissance units.

The renowned German ace Walter Nowotny, with a record of 250 enemy aircraft destroyed, had been ordered by Hitler to form the first ME-262 pure fighter unit at Achmer near Osnabruck. While coping with several aircraft losses due to accidents, servicing and technical problems, Nowotny got his jets into action in a matter of days and within a few weeks his pilots had managed to bag 50 enemy planes.

Galland visited Nowotny at Achmer on 8 October and the next morning the station alarms sounded. An American formation of heavy bombers was approaching the field as a number of ME-262s taxied to take off for the intercept. Their take-off was to be protected by a flight of propeller-driven German fighters, but these were already engaged in combat with Mustangs and Thunderbolts of the American bomber escort force. The German jets all took off safely. In the fighter control centre Galland listened to the attack commands of Nowotny as the jets met the incoming enemy bombers and fighters. Nowotny shot down an enemy aircraft and then reported to fighter control that one of his engines had just failed and that he was trying to get back to the field. Galland left the room and went outside where the visibility was only fair. He soon heard the turbine whine of a 262 and then the sounds of cannon and machine-gun fire somewhere overhead. In seconds an ME-262 emerged in a vertical dive from the cloud layer and crashed onto the airfield. A dense black smoke plume marked the site. Later, Nowotny's left hand and bits of his Diamonds decoration were found in the wreckage.

With the death of Nowotny, his squadron was ordered to form the basis of a new jet fighter wing, JG-7 under the command of Johannes Steinhoff, and near the end of November it seemed that, at last, the German jet fighter was about to join the defence of the Reich on a significant scale.

In one of the most bizarre plans of the entire war, discussions of the German High Command were held near Rastenburg in late September regarding the implementation of the 'Volksfighter', an entirely new single-engine jet fighter plane intended to be flown by sixteen to eighteen-year-old boys of the Hitler Youth. This was to be the absolute last-ditch attempt to defend the Reich. Over the intense objections of Adolf Galland, the Volksfighter plan was put through and the production of the new plane was ordered without delay. The People's Fighter concept called for a mass-produced little plane that could be built using the least amount of material in the fewest possible man-hours. All signs pointed to a finished aircraft designed and built to minimum standards of construction and performance; in all likelihood a nasty little weapon as dangerous to the pilot as to the enemy. Most of Germany's major aircraft firms generated designs for the fighter and Heinkel's design was selected. It was designated HE-162. When assessed by Galland, Messerschmitt, and Kurt Tank, the brilliant designer from Focke-Wulf, there was agreement among them that the specifications and requirements set for the plane could only result in complete failure. Galland was particularly disturbed by the diversion of effort and resources from the ME-262 programme to that of the Volksfighter at a time when the 262 was so desperately needed in the fighter force.

So, at the eleventh hour for the Reich, teenage boys were hurriedly to be trained on gliders and sent off in absurd aircraft against the now awesome might of the American and British bomber and fighter commands to save the day for Germany.

In just 2½ months the prototype HE-162 was completed. It flew for the first time on 6 December 1944. Days later the plane was demonstrated at

Vienna-Schwechat to a large gathering of aviation experts. To their horror, the aircraft began to disintegrate in the air as the test pilot attempted an over-ambitious loop. The right wing separated from the craft in flight and he died in the resulting crash. By March 1945, two months before the war ended with Germany's unconditional surrender, 200 Volksfighters had been produced and were ready to become operational. In the final weeks of the conflict, the advancing Russian forces seized detailed production information and several examples of the aircraft, some of which also came into the possession of the Western Allies.

Galland began the formation of JV-44, his final fighter unit command of the war, in January 1945. He had selected Johannes Steinhoff to take charge of the new ME-262 jet operation. Steinhoff went to all the major fighter bases of the *Luftwaffe* and lured the elite of the fighter force to the unit, including Gerhard Barkhorn, Heinz Bar, Erich Hohagen, Günther Lützow, Walter Krupinski, and Wilhelm Herget. Many of them reported without consent or transfer orders. All had been wounded and had been in action since the first day of the war. Most wore the coveted Knight's Cross and all were eager to begin the adventure that Galland was planning.

JV-44 was stationed at Munich-Riem in March. It was a squadron of expert fighter pilots comprised of one lieutenant general, two colonels, one lieutenant colonel, three majors, five captains, eight lieutenants and eight second lieutenants. Short on adequate intelligence reports about the American bomber and fighter operations, strengths, etc., and subject to technical and supply problems that at times seemed insurmountable, the pilots of JV-44 were also subjected to the almost constant attentions of American aircraft in low-level attacks on the airfield. The ensuing bomb craters kept hundreds of workers busy repairing the runway. The jets began combat operations flying in small units. Because of the incessant enemy raids, the take-offs were always high-risk and on landing the 262s had to be dispersed and completely camouflaged around the perimeters. In the midst of this chaos, Galland was asked to visit Reichsmarshall Goering at Obersalzberg. It would be their last meeting and he was flabbergasted by Goering's cordiality and candour as he admitted that Galland had been correct in his views through all the many clashes of opinion they had had in the preceding months.

In the final weeks of the war Galland's jet pilots were given a new tool to ply their trade – underwing rocket racks that held 24 R4M 5-cm rockets, each of which was capable of knocking down a heavy bomber. The rockets enabled the pilot to remain beyond the effective range of the enemy defensive machine-gun fire. When properly aimed a salvo of the rockets could theoretically hit several bombers. It was, of course, far too late to really matter, but at last fighter pilots of the *Luftwaffe* had a practical means of breaking up the enemy bomber formations.

As the end neared for the Reich, Galland called his officers together. It was 25 April. American and Russian troops met on the banks of the Elbe and the last of the 2,755,000 tons of Allied bombs had fallen on Europe. He told them:

Militarily speaking the war is lost. Even our action here cannot change anything . . . I shall continue to fight, because operating with the ME-262 has got hold of me, because I am proud to belong to the last fighter pilots of the German *Luftwaffe* . . . Only those who feel the same are to go on flying with me.

Now, as what remained of the German command structure was collapsing, Galland began receiving the coveted ME-262s of the bomber, reconnaissance, combat fighter, nightfighter, and test units, for his use. In all he had 70 jets available.

With scattered clouds at varying altitudes and $^3/_{10}$ visibility on 26 April, Galland led six jets into action against a formation of Martin B-26 Marauder medium bombers. He was the first of the pilots to spot the enemy planes, near Neuburg on the Danube. The pilots of the 262s may have had rockets, but they also had the problem of judging their approach to the far slower enemy aircraft. With their great speed, the jets had to be ready for action far sooner than in their former prop-driven planes. Galland brought his small flight into a reasonably good position relative to the bombers and found that, even at a considerable distance out from the B-26s, his jets were already receiving defensive fire from them. At first, in the excitement of the moment, he neglected to release a safety catch for his rockets and when he was in perfect firing position, they did not go off when he pressed the tit. But his cannon were working and a one-second burst sent one of the Marauders out of the formation on fire. It soon exploded, falling through the formation and colliding with another B-26. Galland moved on to attack another of the bombers, this one in the lead of the formation, heavily damaging it. In the action his own aircraft had taken a few hits from the defensive fire of the bombers.

Galland climbed steeply to the left over the bombers, never seeing the enemy fighter that peppered his jet with .50-calibre rounds. His canopy and instrument panel were shattered as was his right knee. He noted too that the engine cowling under his right wing had been hit and was flapping in the wind. And then his left engine was taking machine-gun hits and the little fighter was becoming uncontrollable. The knee was agony.

He thought about escaping from the wrecked jet but also about the possibility of being machine-gunned by an enemy fighter pilot as he descended in his parachute. He discovered that he could still steer the jet, albeit with some difficulty, and managed to bring it down through a break in the cloud cover. Then he saw Munich in the distance and located his airfield to the left of the city.

* * *

James Finnegan was a P-47 Thunderbolt pilot with the 50th Fighter Group, Ninth US Army Air Force. He had arrived in the European Theater of Operations on 20 May 1944 and had flown his first combat mission on D-Day, 6 June. Throughout May and early June Finnegan's group attacked bridges, roads, vehicles, railways, trains, gun emplacements and railway marshalling yards during the Normandy campaign. On 26 April, 1945, he was leading the top cover flight of P-47s escorting a formation of B-26 bombers into a German target when he looked down and spotted two fast-moving objects hurtling up through the bomber formation. Almost simultaneously, two of the bombers exploded and Finnegan realized that the objects he had seen must be the new German jet fighters he had been hearing about. At that point he was roughly 3,000 feet above the bombers and, as one of the climbing jets veered into a left bank, he dived towards it and got to within 100 yards. Through luck as much as skill, he was able to position the big Thunderbolt for a shot at the jet and got in a single three-second burst. He estimated his own speed in the encounter at 450 mph and watched as his bullets tracked across the right wing and engine of the green and brown camouflaged ME-262 fighter. He later reported the combat and claimed a 'probable' kill.

In the 1970s, a Japanese-American student at San Jose State University read Adolf Galland's book, *The First and the Last*, for a class he attended. On graduating, the young man was given a present by his parents, a trip to Japan and there he met some former Japanese fighter pilots who asked if he would look up U.S. Air Force records of their air combats in the Pacific Theater of WWII, as all such Japanese records had been destroyed. The young man did the research for the Japanese pilots and was greatly impressed by the detail in the records he received. Remembering Galland's book, he contacted the German and asked if Galland would like to know who had shot him down on 26 April, 1945. Galland replied that he certainly would, and the student requested the combat reports for the American fighters escorting the B-26s near Munich on the 26th. By deduction he then determined that Galland had been Finnegan's 'probable' that day. James Finnegan and Adolf Galland then began a correspondence and jointly pieced together the mission they had shared. They finally met at an Air Force Association meeting in San Francisco in 1979 and became friends.

With one of his engines refusing to react to the throttle, Galland was forced to cut the power of both engines as he rushed towards the edge of the airfield. As he drifted across the threshhold he noticed that the field was under attack by P-47 Thunderbolt fighter-bombers. In the combat his radio had been destroyed and he had not been able to hear a warning from the fighter controller on the airfield that the base was under attack. Committed now, he touched down at 150 mph. The nose wheel tyre had been shot up and was flat. The brakes were not effective but at last Galland brought the craft to a halt, scrambled out and dived into the nearest bomb crater. In the height of the furious attack by the Thunderbolts, an armoured tractor arrived to rescue him. In the action Galland and his pilots had accounted for five enemy aircraft destroyed, for no German losses. He was driven to a hospital in Munich where his knee was treated and the leg put in a cast.

Galland began and ended the war as a squadron leader, but at the end he was also a Lieutenant General. He became a prisoner of war and was held in military custody for two years until 1947. He resided near Kiel in northern Germany for a year, after which he was offered and accepted a four-year contract from the Argentine government to assist in the building of their air force. There he established a tactical training programme. Kurt Tank, the designer of the Focke-Wulf Fw-190, was a part of the German team of fighter experts in Argentina and it was he who convinced President Juan Peron to bring Galland into it. His initial four-year term was followed by a second contract, which kept him in South America until the end of 1954.

In his 705 combat missions Adolf Galland achieved 104 aerial victories, all of them on the Western Front. They included: 53 Spitfires, 31 Hurricanes, 1 P-38 Lightning, 1 B-24 Liberator, 3 B-17 Flying Fortresses, and 4 B-26 Marauders. Seven of his victories were achieved in the ME-262 jet fighter.

Galland died in 1996 at the age of 83. He is remembered by most who knew him as modest and soft spoken, careful and deliberate in his choice of words, and always pleasant and patient with the many people who wanted his time, his views and his autograph. A gentleman and a true knight.

CHAPTER TWO

Werner Mölders

In March 2005 more than 100 retired German military officers signed an open letter to newspapers protesting the intention of the German Defence Minister to enforce a 1998 law banning the award of any honours to German volunteers who served with the Condor Legion during the Spanish Civil War. One such airman was Colonel Werner Mölders, referred to by the retired officers as 'a model soldier and fighter pilot.' The officers also paid tribute to the members of German Air Force Fighter Squadron 74, named 'Mölders' in his honour. Members of Fighter Squadron 74 were required to remove the armbands bearing the name Mölders from their uniforms, ending a 50-year tradition and raising the question of who counts as a war hero for modern Germans and for the many others around the world who percieve the life and career of Werner Mölders in a more objective light.

The German fighter ace Ernst Udet achieved 62 aerial victories during the First World War. With the rank of Major-General in the Second World War, Udet was appointed Head of the Office of Air Armament where he served until the autumn of 1941. It was then that *Reichsmarshall* Hermann Goering laid blame on Udet for the failure of the *Luftwaffe* in the Battle of Britain. The pressure became more than Udet could stand and he 'chose' to commit suicide on 17 November. That act was followed by Goering summoning the celebrated war hero and General of the Fighter Arm Werner Mölders back to Berlin from Chaplinka on the Eastern Front to participate in Udet's funeral as a pall bearer and member of the Honour Guard. Mölders was able to arrange his return to the German capital as a passenger aboard a Heinkel He-111 bomber on the morning of 22 November. The plane took off in a severe thunderstorm and, near Breslau, one of the Heinkel's two engines failed. Shortly thereafter, the second engine quit and the bomber crashed killing Mölders and the pilot. With the death of Mölders, the *Luftwaffe* lost one of its greatest aces and leaders.

*   *   *

"You are not fit to fly, Lieutnant Mölders." That was the verdict of the German doctor who had just examined the nauseated twenty-two-year-old who sat in the centrifugal test chair in 1934. Mölders had just applied to transfer from the Army to the *Luftwaffe* in order to enter pilot training. "You will do much better to stay in the Army" warned the doctor. The determined Mölders, sick as he was, set out to prove the physician wrong.

As a child Werner had been taken up for an aeroplane ride by an uncle and from that day he had wanted to be a military pilot. That first attempt to become one in 1934 had identified his motion sickness problem and caused him to train himself to overcome it. He then returned to the centrifugal chair to try the test again. This time he did not vomit though he did feel just as sick as he had after the first test. He was, however, granted permission to enter flying training.

Mölders began the course at the *Deutsche Verkehrsflieger Schule* in Brunswick and, for the first month, his flying brought him little satisfaction, a lot of vomiting, severe headaches and giddiness. He was almost constantly in distress, but adamently refused to give up. In time, the illness and headaches diminished and finally, he overcame the problem completely. Once freed from it he quickly progressed as a pilot and air leader.

Within a year of beginning his *Luftwaffe* flying training, he was instructing new pilots on the base at Wiesbaden, a position he held for nearly two years.

With the German involvement in the Spanish Civil War, through its famous Condor Legion of Luftwaffe volunteers, Mölders got the chance he had been waiting for to experience at first hand the adventure of aerial combat. In Spain he flew with and got to know a number of the *Luftwaffe*'s future aces and leaders, Hannes Trautloft, Walter Oesau, Edu Neumann, Wilhelm Balthasar, and Adolf Galland.

Werner Mölders arrived in Spain at Cadiz on 14 April, 1938, carrying a cardboard suitcase and dressed in the civilian garb of a 'strength through joy' tourist. Galland was somewhat cool towards him when they first met, but that reaction soon changed to one of approval as Galland became familiar with the flying skills and leadership potential of Mölders. As he left Spain for a new appointment, Galland's last report on Mölders as his new commander of Fighter Squadron 3 included: '*Lieutnant* Mölders is an excellent officer and splendid pilot, with brilliant and precise leadership.'

Within weeks of taking command of the squadron, Mölders' spectacular career literally took off when his unit was re-equipped with the latest model Bf-109 fighters. He was well suited to the 109 and would quickly become one of the *Luftwaffe*'s most successful aces in it. With the 109, his unit suddenly gained the advantage over the Russian Polikarpov I-15 and I-16 Rata fighters then being flown by the Spanish Loyalists.

On 15 July 1938, he encountered a flight of I-16s which he quickly pursued. With the exagerrated eagerness of a newcomer, he concentrated on getting well positioned before opening fire on one of the Russian-built planes. When he did fire he was astonished and greatly disappointed at how badly he had misjudged his attack. He had missed his prey by a wide margin and vowed to do better. Almost instantly, he was able to line up on another of the Ratas. This time he pressed his attack and gained on the I-16 until it seemed to fill his windscreen. He fired and was rewarded as the enemy aircraft appeared to collapse under the impact of his machine-gun rounds. It fell away to crash on the barren countryside below as he watched. It was the first of fourteen aerial victories Mölders would score in Spain.

But as good as he was as a pilot and shooter and as a leader and organizer, probably his greatest achievement in that period was as a tactician. Together with a few of his fellow squadron pilots, he developed and put into practice the 'Finger Four' fighter formation. Formation flying as a fighter tactic was introduced by Oswald Bölcke and Manfred von Richthofen for the Germans in the First World War, ushering in the era of air battles between formations and mass dogfights.

The Finger Four has been used by fighter pilots in air forces the world over since the Spanish Civil War. After the end of the Second World War the U.S. Air Force began referring to the German-invented Finger Four as the Double Attack System.

In the First World War and the years between it and the Second World War, the basic fighter flying formation was the three-plane 'V', called the 'Vic' by the British and the 'Kette' by the Germans. In the First World War, pilots of both sides had tended to extend their distance from one another in the formation, to make their aircraft more difficult to spot and to avoid collision. Between the wars, however, with the proliferation of air displays like the Hendon Pageant, the various air forces tightened their formations to breathtakingly close tolerances. In Spain the German pilots came in flying the old V formation. Initially, however, they had a shortage of the new Bf-109s and were forced to fly them in pairs when escorting bombers on their raids so as to provide fighter protection on all sides of the bombers.

German fighter pilots now flew in pairs with each pair called a '*Rotte*'. Mölders' idea was to put two pairs of aircraft together into a new formation called a '*Schwarm*', or two pair operating together. Ultimately this was accepted universally as the Finger Four as its alignment was based on the positions of the four finger-tips of an outstretched hand. Each pair consisted of a leader and a wingman. All four aircraft flew fairly wide apart, with the two leaders scanning the sky ahead and the two wingmen watching the sky behind and to the sides to make sure no enemy aircraft could sneak up on the *Schwarm*. The leader in each *Rotte* is the attacker, with his wingman protecting him from behind, freeing the leader to concentrate solely on the enemy aircraft. In the *Schwarm* formation the *Schwarm* leader and his wingman are the attackers and they are protected by the other pair.

The altitudes of the four aircraft of the *Schwarm* are staggered eliminating the intense pressure of holding precise formation. In the First World War the fighter pilot was constantly distracted in his efforts to keep in formation while simultaneously scanning to spot the enemy. By the dawn of the Second World War technology was forcing a change from the old ways when large areas of sky were obstructed from each pilot's view by the wings of the other aircraft in the close formation.

The secondary pair would fly slightly behind the first pair and stepped up, away from the sun. The leader's wingman would fly slightly behind and below him. It was the coming of fast, all-metal, low-wing, high-performance aircraft equipped with radios for air-to-air communication that made the new formation possible. Flying it as a loose formation with ample distance between the aircraft made spotting them much more difficult. The leader would only call for them to close the distance between them when flying through heavy cloud. Operationally, a two-aircraft formation is easier to control than three aircraft. The Finger Four allowed all four pilots to have an unobstructed view of the sun to guard against a potential enemy aircraft obstructed by it. The pilots in a Finger Four were able to scan a much larger area of sky than pilots in the old formations. Their efficiency in spotting, sighting and downing enemy aircraft was greatly improved by the new formation, and in putting more space between the aircraft in the *Schwarm*, Mölders made them all less vulnerable to enemy attack. Crucially, initiative, the essential advantage of every successful fighter pilot, was given back to him with the advent of the Finger Four. The new-found efficiency of the Finger Four effectively gave the equivalent of an increase in the numerical strength of the squadron. It is a tribute to the genius of Mölders that the formation is still central in fighter tactics to this day.

At the end of the Spanish Civil War Mölders was the highest scoring German pilot of the conflict and wore the award of the Spanish Gold Cross with Swords and Diamonds. His reputation in Germany was further enhanced by his renown as a leader and *Luftwaffe* tactician with a maturity beyond his years. He had been raised in a strict Roman Catholic tradition which had equipped him with a fundamental decency and morality that was missing from the character of those airmen who were philosophically comfortable with German National Socialism. His open opposition to the Nazi doctrine of hatred was well known to his fellow pilots as was his objective appreciation of the good qualities he discerned in both his friends and foes. As the *Staffelkapitän* (commander) of No. 1 Squadron, JG-53 at Wiesbaden-Erbenheim, his uniquely balanced maturity soon earned him the nickname '*Vati*' (Daddy) Mölders, an affectionate expression of the respect and appreciation his men felt for him as their leader.

Hartmann Grasser, Mölders' adjutant with JG-51 during the Battle of Britain period, remembered him as a highly intelligent and well-educated man of exceptionally good character. So good was his character that most who knew him perceived his honour as his personal guarantee in all situations. Brilliantly analytical, Mölders direct thought processes and reason made him an exceptional leader and mentor. Understanding and sensitive, he ruled his command with appropriate discipline as well as principled conduct. One example of his command methods is the occasion during the Battle of Britain when one of his pilots made a strafing attack on a train in England. Mölders was disgusted by the act and gave the man a lecture he would never forget on the difference between military and civilian targets.

Grasser:

> He was an outstanding teacher and instructor. He could teach you to fight in the air. His special personal attention was given to every new pilot who came to the wing. He would take these young men to himself and introduce them to the conditions and demands of aerial fighting. His credo was, 'The most important thing for a fighter pilot is to get his first victory without too much shock'. He had a gift for tactics, an outstanding tactical imagination. He was mature beyond his years, an analytical thinker, a practical man and with it all a humanist. I owe my life entirely to Werner Mölders. He not only showed me how to fight in the air, he showed me how to stay alive and come back from a fighter operation. His men were devoted to him. I think that if Mölders had lived, he was a man with the character and intellectual capacity to get his ideas through against the leadership – against the politicians.

A French Curtiss 75A fighter became Werner Mölders' first victory of the Second World War on 21 September 1939, and on 1 November he was made *Gruppenkommandeur* (commander) of III/JG-53, the third unit of Fighter Wing 53, which was also based at Wiesbaden-Erbenheim. On 27 May, 1940, Mölders achieved his twentieth aerial victory, another Curtiss 74A, this time south-west of Amiens, after which he was promoted to the rank of *Hauptmann* (Captain) and awarded the coveted Knight's Cross.

On 5 June, Mölders had shot down two French aircraft during a fighter sweep over the Chantilly Forest when he himself was the victim of a perfect out-of-the-sun bounce by a French Dewoitine D.520 fighter flown by *Sous Lieutenant* René Pommier Layragues. Mölders was completely surprised when his Bf-109 was riddled with cannon shells and machine-gun bullets. His fighter was fast becoming uncontrollable. He was unhurt but, with smoke from his engine pouring back into the cockpit, he had to get out of the aircraft without delay. He baled out, wondering as he began to fall, if the French bullets had also riddled his parachute pack. They had not and when he landed in French territory, he was captured by French Army personnel. Within two weeks the French surrendered to the Germans and Mölders was released and went back to Germany where he was soon to become *Kommodore* of JG-51 and the youngest Wing Commander in the *Luftwaffe*.

On Sunday morning, 28 July, No. 74 Squadron, RAF flew down from their Hornchurch base to Manston on the North Sea coast to be ready for immediate action. The weather of the previous days had been stormy and thoroughly unpleasant but Sunday had dawned clear and blue. It was well after lunch though before the phone finally rang sending 12 pilots of No. 74 running for their Spitfires. With Adolf 'Sailor' Malan in the lead, the Spitfires got into the air at 1:50 p.m. and as they climbed Malan heard from the controller that the enemy raid was heading towards Dover at 18,000 feet. The German bombers were to be engaged by Hurricanes. The job of the Spitfires was to take on the enemy fighters accompanying the bombers. When Malan spotted the first of the Messerschmitt 109s, the Germans were heading towards a flight of Hurricanes. He led the Red Section pilots into a gentle turn behind the 109s. The Germans had not yet seen the Spitfires. As the British planes closed on the 109s Malan got close enough to fire on one, spraying it with a series of two-second bursts from about 100 yards and the German fighter sloped off into a gentle descending right-hand turn. It was Werner Mölders' first sortie with his new unit and he had just downed a Spitfire 1 in the Dover area, flown by RAF Flying Officer A.D.J. Lovell of No. 41 Squadron. It was then that Sailor Malan eased up behind Mölders and stayed there expending his ammunition into the aircraft of the German fighter leader. Mölders was severely wounded in the legs and barely managed to nurse his crippled plane across the Channel to make an emergency landing on the airfield at Wissant, France.

He was put in hospital and out of combat action for the next month. He then returned to the fight with a savage intensity. On 20 September he shot down his 40th kill, a Spitfire over Dungeness and was awarded the Oak Leaves to his Knight's Cross the next day. By 12 October, had scored a total of 45 Second World War victories in 196 combat missions. On 22 October he shot down three Hurricane fighters to become the first *Luftwaffe* pilot with 50 aerial victories. It was during this period that Mölders committed his only instance of less than rational behaviour as a fighter pilot. Suffering from severe influenza, he had been grounded by the Wing medical officer on 11 November and was feverish as he learned that a friend of his, a First Lieutenant Claus, had been shot down on a fighter sweep over the Thames Estuary. Mölders ordered a seemingly impossible effort by his air-sea rescue units and when they were unable to execute his order, he had his own fighter and that of another JG-51 pilot, made ready for immediate flight. Against the pleas of his staff, they took off and crossed the English Channel to make their own futile search for the downed pilot whose Messerschmitt would have long since sunk. Still feverish, Mölders led the other pilot around the Estuary, exposed to the threats of RAF Fighter Command aircraft and anti-aircraft fire. They found no trace of the downed German pilot, and returned to their French base. By the end of 1940, Mölders had raised his total of air victories to 55.

Mölders and the pilots of JG-51 continued to fight the RAF over the Channel Front until early May 1941, when his score reached 68 enemy aircraft destroyed. The first day of German action on the Eastern Front in Operation Barbarossa, he shot down four Russian aircraft and was then awarded the Swords to his Knight's Cross and on 30 June he became the first pilot to surpass von Richthofen's First World War record of 80 kills, downing five Russian bombers in a single day.

In mid-July Mölders was the first pilot in history to achieve 100 aerial victories. The accomplishment brought him the award of the Diamonds to his Knight's Cross, the first German soldier so honoured. With the award came the order from *Reichsmarshall* Goering expressly forbidding Mölders from flying any further air combat missions. He did continue to fly them, but infrequently. And at the age of twenty-eight he was promoted to *Oberst* (Colonel) and appointed General of the Fighter Arm on 7 August. Thereafter he devoted much of his time to the development of the forward air controller concept, another pioneering idea he had devised.

At the time of Ernst Udet's suicide, Werner Mölders was commanding a Battle Group on the Eastern Front comprised of fighters, Stukas and ground-attack aircraft. As then Major Günther Rall recalled:

> Every morning Mölders flew a Feiseler Storch aircraft right over the front. He had his own radio and he would land the Storch and hide in a foxhole and then talk on the radio to the pilots in the air. He became a Forward Air Controller, in effect, and directed us accurately on to enemy positions. In the evening he would fly back and have a commander's conference where he would review the day's operations telling us what we had done right and where we had gone wrong. This was a period of intense, critical fighting. Three days before he left for the Udet funeral he was having serious support problems. He wasn't getting enough ammunition, fuel, or spare parts and he wanted to fly back to Germany and tackle the high command about it.

Oberleutnant Kolbe, like Mölders a veteran of the Conder Legion in the Spanish Civil War, was at the controls of the He-111 bomber on the flight from Chaplinka to Berlin. Kolbe was an excellent pilot, thoroughly capable of handling the bomber in the treacherous weather predicted for their route to the German capital. Mölders was determined to get back to Berlin as soon as possible and would not be budged as Kolbe urged him not to continue the flight after they had been forced to land at Lemberg by the deteriorating weather conditions. They flew on, fighting an extreme headwind and Kolbe had to pour fuel to the engines to make even slow progress. The fuel gauges of the Heinkel registered low quantities and an engine quit as they neared Breslau. Relying on the power of the remaining engine, Kolbe struggled to control the big plane as it descended through the thick cloud and rain. The second engine then failed and the bomber crashed heavily near the Breslau airfield. Both Mölders and Kolbe died in the impact. Mölders' aide-de-camp and the radio operator of the Heinkel both survived and were able to describe the final moments of the flight. Mölders flew a total of 330 missions and accumulated a score of 115 aerial victories.

In their fine book *HORRIDO!*, Trevor J. Constable and Colonel Raymond F. Toliver stated:

Galland and Mölders would probably have to rank as the two outstanding personalities of the *Luftwaffe* fighter force in the Second World War. Perhaps the worthiest tribute to Mölders is the respected place he occupies in the minds and memories of his contemporaries, and the posthumous fame he still enjoys. The authors, as externes to German wartime affairs, have had abundant opportunity to meet in recent years numerous German aces and fighter leaders. From this it has been possible to build up an objective comparison of Mölders and Galland which may prove of interest to the reader.

Mölders actively sought and desired the challenges inherent in following in Bölcke's footsteps. Galland by contrast was the archetypal aerial hunter – a fighter first, last, and always to whom the thrill of the chase and victory in a fair fight was the elixir of life. Mölders approached the problems of high command with zeal and zest. Galland never wanted high command, hated paper work and desk flying, and resisted being taken off operations; he returned to aerial fighting whenever possible.

Mölders was serious and quiet, a man who seldom smiled and rarely laughed. He took his responsibilities right to heart and poured his energy into his work. Galland was an ebullient young leader, dashing, gallant, and arresting in appearance. Galland had a superb sense of humour; he was a wit and a man who could laugh.

Mölders maintained his equilibrium and sustained his seriously energetic approach to life from a strong religious base. He was in no sense a religious propagandist, but he lived with a quiet Christian dignity that no inferior individual could breach. Mölders' inner strength, combined with his formidable flying, tactical, administrative, and leadership skills, made him a practical man in the true sense of the term.

Galland's equilibrium stemmed from his sense of humour. Yet his amiability, friendliness, and warm heart in no way diminished the razor-sharpness of his intelligence. He was a far better General than he himself thought he was. Mölders was perhaps more of a humanist, but Galland had to steel himself to ruthless decisions involving men's lives from which Mölders may have recoiled.

Werner Mölders' strength of character, his quiet dignity, his self-discipline, religious upbringing, and perhaps more than anything else, his humane concern for the men he commanded, certainly made him outstanding among the leaders and top aces of the *Luftwaffe*. But what made him extraordinary and exceptional was that he combined those characteristics with the skills and capabilities required of a great fighter pilot in a way that few others in aviation history have done. Unlike nearly all great fighter pilots, Mölders was a true team player, utterly unselfish and a powerful role model for those who served with him.

Gunther Rall

Many years after the end of the Second World War, *General-leutnant* Gunther Rall can still 'see' every one of his aerial victories, and he was credited with 275 enemy aircraft destroyed in that long conflict. He has no need to hype or embellish his descriptions of aerial combats; he is able to 'replay' them with clarity and great detail, just as they actually happened:

These combats are simply burned into my memory like movie films. When you enter aerial combat, you have absolutely nothing else on your mind. Every iota of your consciousness is concentrated on that particular action in which you are fighting for your existence. You just never concentrate with such intensity on anything else in life, and the vividness of the memory is in proportion to the degree of concentration. I am not able to separate the victories in my mind numerically. I cannot tell you about a certain victory and say, 'This was number 26 or 57.' But in each action I can tell you exactly what my position was, where the sun was, and the relative movements of myself and the enemy aircraft with which I fought.

Gunther Rall had shown no particular interest in aeroplanes, flying or aviation while attending classes at the German War College (*Kriegschule*) in Dresden during 1937. He had completed his ordinary schooling the previous year, had immediately entered the German Army and was training to be an infantry officer when a friend, a cadet at the *Luftwaffe* Officers' School in Dresden, began telling him about his flying adventures and the advantages of life for young men in the German Air Force. Rall was captivated by the idea, especially compared with his current existence and future prospects as an infantryman. He was both intrigued by the possibility of flying and attracted to the notion of a less muddy, more gentlemanly role in the military, and soon transferred to the Air Force. There he began pilot training at the Neubiburg *Luftwaffe* school in the summer of 1938. He finished the course and graduated as a pilot a year later. Initially he was posted to the German Fighter Weapons School north of Berlin at Werneuchen in 1939. At some point in their careers, virtually all the *Luftwaffe*'s highest-achieving fighter aces and leaders would attend the course at Werneuchen. There Rall was to come under the tutelage of Gunther Lützow, a fighter ace who had earned that distinction while flying with the German Air Force in the Spanish Civil War during the mid-1930s. Lützow had received his fighter pilot training clandestinely on a German base at Lipetsk in Russia before transferring to the fledgling and still low-profile *Luftwaffe* in 1934. In Spain he had served operationally as *Staffelkapitän* of II/JG 88 of the Condor Legion. There, over the spring and summer of 1937, he achieved the five victories that qualified him as an 'ace,' one of them being the first ever made in a Messerschmitt Bf 109. For it he was awarded the Spanish Cross in gold with swords and diamonds. In November 1938, Lützow was assigned as an instructor at *Jagdfliegerschule* 1, based at Werneuchen, where he mentored the young Gunther Rall. Of Lützow, the German Fighter General Adolf Galland said: "He was a great leader and a true knight – a gentleman."

Gunther Rall had been born in the Black Forest village of Gaggenau in the German state of Baden on 10 March, 1918. The son of a merchant, he grew up in the worst years of the Great Depression. In his youth he was active in the Boy Scouts and the YMCA, where he learned about self-reliance and developed a strong sense of fair play and common decency. Of medium height and build, the sandy-haired Rall's first squadron posting after his year at the Fighter Weapons School was to II/JG-52 at a base near Stuttgart, as a Second Lieutenant. In early 1940, he was the youngest officer in the wing and was somewhat frustrated by the lack of action at that time. The Germans were unsure about the will and capability of the French to go on with the war, and the units of JG-52 were ordered to fly patrols along the German border with France, but not to enter French airspace. Now and then a French reconnaissance plane would overfly the border into German territory. These flights were attacked by Rall's unit, but he had not yet participated in any such missions and was eager for the experience and adventure.

It came on 12 May during the Battle of France. Rall had been transferred into a newly organized group within JG-52, then operating from Mannheim. On that fine spring day his group was assigned to rendevous with and escort a *Luftwaffe* reconnaissance plane that was returning from a flight into France. He sighted the recce aircraft over Diedenhoven at an altitude of 26,000 feet. The German plane was under attack by twelve Curtis P-36 fighters of the French Air Force and the fighters of Rall's unit fell on the P-36s in a combat that would result in Gunther Rall's first aerial victory, of which he recalled: 'I was lucky in my first dogfight, but it did give me a hell of a lot of self-confidence . . . and a scaring, because I was also hit by many bullets.'

*   *   *

Further missions followed in quick succession, adding to Rall's early operational experience. Soon he was sent with his unit to a North Sea base where they received vital training in ditching and survival techniques. It was at this base that many of the German Air Force's (GAF) Bf-109s were then being modified for the requirements of operating over the North Sea and the English Channel, which they would soon be doing in the Battle of Britain.

Rall's unit, III/JG-52, was now flying from a base near Calais on the Channel coast. He recalled: "We were facing the Spitfires in very rough dogfights every day." He was concerned about their operational techniques, most especially their having been ordered to fly as close escort for the German bombers, particularly the extremely slow Ju-87 Stuka. This tactic, he believed, made sitting ducks of Rall and his fellow fighter pilots, dishing up a clear advantage to the Spitfires of the Royal Air Force which took every opportunity to bounce the 109s from a higher altitude and shoot them up. JG-52 suffered in these early Battle of Britain combats. In its first four missions to England, Rall's unit lost its commanding officer and two key squadron leaders, a devastating leadership loss, but one which presented a rare opportunity for the twenty-two-year-old Rall, who was made a squadron leader.

Gunther Rall and the pilots of his unit continued their daily struggles with the men of the RAF until October, when his outfit was withdrawn to Germany to rebuild its personnel with replacement pilots. As the days wore on, Rall and the other pilots grew restless and weary of the inaction. They yearned to get back to the excitement of the Channel coast. But it was not to be. The intense aerial activity of the Battle of Britain had diminished considerably by late October. With the inability of the *Luftwaffe* to gain air superiority, much less air supremacy, over England and the Channel, what plans the Germans may have had for invading England were shelved. They turned the bulk of their attention eastward towards the Soviet Union, effectively abandoning England and the essential bases it would ultimately provide for both the RAF and the American Air Force to launch their massive combined strategic bombing offensive against Germany.

Rall's outfit was moved down to a base near Vienna, and further to Pipera/ Bucharest in Rumania where they were tasked with protecting the Rumanian drilling rigs, refineries and oil installations as well as the bridges across the Danube River to Bulgaria. His pilots were also responsible for the defence of Constanza Harbour. After several weeks of such operations, Rall's squadron received orders to fly in support of the German attack on

Crete in what would be recorded as history's first opposed landing by parachute troops. Rall and the JG-52 pilots flew these close-support missions from bases in the Peloponnesus, opposing British, Australian and New Zealand troops in spring 1941. Rall:

> The battle for Crete was grim and deadly, and horrible even from the air. It was some of the most bitter fighting of the war. Our support work with the troops was extremely difficult. As well as paratroops, our planes also dropped boxes of guns, supplies and ammunition. The boxes also contained German flags and the idea was for our men to lay the flags out on the ground so we could see them and tell where the front lines were. But the New Zealanders recovered many of these flags and spread them out on their positions, thus providing excellent protection for them and creating total confusion for us in the air, making ground attack very difficult.

With the fall of Crete Gunther and his squadron returned to Rumania, where they were switched to the 109E (Emil type), which featured a more powerful engine and rounded wing tips. Just two days into the Russo-German campaign, the airmen of JG-52 were sent again to the Constanza region. Soviet bombers were pounding the Rumanian oil refineries, which were protected by relatively few flak batteries. Rall brought his squadron into the area to a bare grass field which he then used as a fighter base. The conditions were primitive and the situation challenging. Ju-52 transports brought in a small amount of aviation fuel and a small quantity of spare parts. There were no buildings or facilities of any kind on the 'base'. Rall remembers it: "We had nothing to eat, almost no fuel, no shelter and, after a few sorties, no spares. Still, in these primitive conditions, we were heroes to the Rumanians. Antonescu came to comgratulate us. We even felt a bit like heroes." In the circumstances, Rall and his pilots managed to bring down many Russian bombers in two weeks, ending the Soviet attacks against the oil fields.

JG-52 was then re-equipped with the new Messerschmitt Bf-109F (Friedrich type) fighter and was soon posted to the southern part of the Eastern Front just after the start of the German-Soviet conflict. Rall and his comrades now found themselves operating over the Caucasus, and in action over Stalingrad. They fought in the Crimea and in the large-scale actions around Rostov. His score of victories was steadily growing. But the winter, one of the worst on record, was closing in and it was one that Rall would never forget.

> The cold was savage. We had no clothing or equipment for contending with it. The temperature fell dramatically from the mildness of autumn to 40 degrss below zero Centigrade in just a few

days, and it stayed down. Getting our fighters started in the morning required a major effort. We had to put open fires under the aircraft and let them burn all night, disregarding all safety regulations. It was the only way we could get them going in the morning.

At this point Rall had been credited with 36 confirmed victories. And then came the mission of 28 November. Rall:

> I was flying between Tagaenrog and Rostov. In those days it was very cold. I was flying an afternoon mission, what we would today call a fighter sweep, when my wingman and I ran into Russians. It had just started getting dark, and I had a dogfight with a Russian and shot him down. He landed with a mighty burst of flame. Watching this spectacular crash in the very late light not only distracted me from combat with the other Russians, but also temporarily blinded me with its brilliance. Another Russian came in behind me and got on my tail. He shot my engine dead and I went down. We were over Russian territory so naturally I tried to reach the German lines. There was not a solid line, but I saw some German tanks. I was flying westward and I decided to try to make a belly landing, but I saw that I was heading into what they call a baikal, a little canyon just across my flight direction. I touched down at too high a speed. The aircraft hit and jumped up again. I bounced over a little canyon and pushed my stick forward. I watched petrified as the valley wall rushed up at me out of the gloom. I then bellied in and crashed on the other side. The last thing I knew, there was a big bang and I was knocked out.

The crew of a nearby German tank rushed to the crash site, pulled the injured, unconscious Rall from the wrecked fighter and called for assistance. Late that night he awoke in a burnt-out school in Tagaenrog. The school was being used as a medical aid station but no significant medical treatment was available there and no X-Ray capability. Rall couldn't move his legs and was in great pain. He was soon evacuated to a properly equipped hospital in Bucharest where he was examined and diagnosed: back broken in three places.

The doctors told him that he was finished as a combat pilot; no more flying. He was put into a full body cast and, just after Christmas 1941, was transferred by train to the University Hospital in Vienna, after a tortuous eight-day crawl through the Carpathian Mountains. And there he met a pretty blonde doctor named Hertha who would eventually become his wife.

Over the following nine months Rall gradually recovered, regaining partial mobility at first and refusing to accept that he could never return to flying.

With Hertha's considerable help and encouragement, and his own strong will and determination, he began to overcome his physical and psychological problems. One day he was visited by an old friend, the commander of a nearby fighter school, who was sympathetic and agreed to let Rall try to fly again in an old biplane. It was the chance he needed to re-familiarize himself with the mechanics of flying; to test his physical and mental skills in the air and re-evaluate his capability as a pilot. He had been kept apprised of the aerial successes being achieved by his fellow JG-52 aces, which motivated him to get out of the hospital and back to the front at the earliest opportunity.

In August 1942 Rall managed to get himself released from the hospital and reassigned to JG-52 back at Tagaenrog where he would resume his combat career with renewed spirit. He was then as much as 60 victories behind some of his squadron mates in the ace race and was determined to catch and surpass them. By November he was back to operating at a maximum effort pace. He had raised his score to 101 and was averaging two kills every 3 days, a pace he maintained for a 3 month period. On 3 September, he had been awarded the Knight's Cross and just 7 weeks later, the Oak Leaves was presented to him by Adolf Hitler.

Among Gunther Rall's most vivid memories of the Russian campaign are the battles that were fought in the Kuban Peninsula and around Novorossisk, where his unit first encountered Spitfires being flown on the Russian Front. The usual mount of many Russian squadrons in the area was the P-39 Bell Airacobra and it probably came as a shock to the German fliers, seeing the excellent Lend-Lease-provided British fighter opposing them in Soviet skies for the first time. Rall's recollection:

The quality of the Lend-Lease aircraft was important, but pilot quality was important too. The machine can only respond to a man, when all is said and done. In my experience, the Royal Air Force pilot was the most aggressive and capable fighter pilot during the Second World War. This is nothing against the Americans, because they came in late and in such large numbers that we don't have an accurate comparison. We were totally outnumbered when the Americans engaged, whereas at the time of the Battle of Britain the fight was more even and you could compare. The British were extremely good. But not the Russians, not at the ordinary level. The Russians, however, had special Red Banner Guards units where experts were concentrated. These Guards pilots were more like the British, real fighter types – not flying masses like the others. They fought the fighter battle and they were good. So the value of Lend-Lease aircraft depended on who got the aircraft on the Russian side.

Rall recalled another occasion, in 1943:

> This was just when the Fw-190 was appearing on the Russian Front.
> I had never seen one before. The Russians were using German for-
> mations in that sector a lot, flying in *Rotte* and *Schwarm* formations
> much of the time. The aircraft I spotted below me looked very much
> like the Fw-190 photos and silhouettes I had seen, so I wanted to
> make sure before shooting them down. I couldn't see the colour and
> insignia on the other aircraft, only the silhouette, so I chased him at
> high speed, pulled up, and at that moment saw the aircraft against
> the ground instead of against the sun. The Red Star was glaring back
> at me from his fuselage. I couldn't turn away, because otherwise he
> would have just turned too, and shot me down like a duck. I turned
> back from the left and down, pulled the trigger, and there was an ear-
> splitting, terrifying crash. Collision! I bounced on this Russian from
> above. I cut his wing with my propeller, and he cut my fuselage with
> his propeller. He got the worst of it, because my propeller went
> through his wing like a ripsaw. Losing his wing, he went into a spin
> from which he had no hope of recovering. I was able to belly in before
> my fuselage gave way, but I will never forget the sound and impact
> of the mid-air collision.

Eight times in his long and colourful career as a fighter pilot Gunther Rall
was himself shot down, the victim of skilful adversaries. On one of these
occasions he was able to bale out, but in each of the others he had to execute
belly landings, and in all of those, other than the time in which his back was
broken, he was able to walk away with only minor injuries. On 12 May
1944, he experienced what was probably his most dangerous and bizarre
aerial encounter. He was leading a new command, II/JG-11, assigned on
the Western Front for *Reichsverteidigung* or Home Defence. Their job was
to engage the Allied fighters that were escorting the heavy bombers of the
American Eighth Air Force, while their bigger brothers, the twin-engined
German day fighters, attacked the enemy bombers. In the fight near Berlin,
Rall's 109 was hem-stitched by .50 calibre machine-gun rounds from a P-47
Thunderbolt fighter. One of the bullets slammed into his cockpit, slicing
off his left thumb, but the rapidly deteriorating condition of his aircraft
allowed him no time to deal with his injury. He scrambled to leave the
crippled plane, hoping, as all fighter pilots in such situations did, that none
of the enemy bullets had found his parachute pack. Floating down to earth
from the high altitude air battle, Rall now had plenty of time to reflect on
the experience and plenty of time to feel the agonizing pain of his hand
wound. He realized that he was going to come down in a farm field and
when he hit the ground he had only seconds to get out of his parachute
harness before being accosted by an obviously furious German farmer
armed with a frightening pitchfork. Aware of the extreme hatred many

German civilians felt for the Allied '*terror fliegers*' or '*luftgangsters*', as they referred to them, Rall, though in great pain from his wound, tried desperately to calm the angry farmer. "I am German!" he told the countryman, but the farmer continued to move toward him, all the while menacing him with the pitchfork. It didn't take much imagination for Rall to envision his own inglorious end at the hands of the enraged rustic, and this after surviving more than 5 years of intense air combat. It was then that Rall fired a salvo of German invective, cursing the farmer vehemently in their common language and causing the man to relent. Rall was then able to arrange a trip to a hospital for treatment of his hand. But his troubles were just beginning.

In the hospital Gunther Rall contracted a diphtheria infection which would keep him there until November, a period during which he again suffered paralysis for a while. When finally allowed to return to the Air Force, he was ordered to report to Adolf Galland's staff where he was given command of a school for squadron leaders, which combined operational and training duties. He ran the unit at Koenigsburg-Neumark until early 1945, when the advancing Russians compelled a move. Now Rall was, for the first time, in command of a unit flying the long-nosed Fw-190, JG-300. The unit was known as the Ram Fighters (*Rammjaegers*) and it would be his final command of the war.

In another example of his astounding wartime exploits, Rall described a fight with a P-39 Airacobra on the Russian Front:

> My adjutant was flying with me and I spotted the enemy aircraft below us. I initiated the first attack out of the sun, and they didn't see me. I had this Airacobra in my reticle, and suddenly he turned just a little bit to the left. It was a very slight turn and the full side of his aircraft was exposed. I pulled hard and pressed the triggers. There was a blinding sheet of fire in the air as the fuel burned right in the tanks. He didn't explode. It was just the fuel that burned. This gigantic sheet of flame was at least 100 metres long, and I had no option but to rush right into it at high speed. At that time the ailerons on the Bf-109 were fabric, and when I came out on the other side of that fantastic fireball there was no fabric in the ailerons any more – just the metal structure remained. The paint on my aircraft was blistered off as though a blowtorch had been turned on it from nose to tail. The Airacobra was about four thousand metres high, and he went down like a brick. He crashed upside down, flat on his back, and just lay there. A wisp of smoke curling up was all that remained of what had been a formidable fighter plane only moments before. That aircraft completely burned out in the air.

Rall may not be quite as celebrated a marksman as a few of the other Second World War *Luftwaffe* fighter aces, but he is unquestionably one of very best aerial shooters of all time. He makes no claim to any particular system or method of shooting as the reason for his success.

I had no system of shooting. It is more in the feeling side of things that these skills develop. I was at the front five and a half years, and you just get a feeling for the right amount of lead. Fritz Obleser was my witness in many victories. He flew with me often and I used to tell him to look at me and I will show you how to do it. He was surprised and incredulous that you could kill an aircraft from such positions as are possible to one who has the feel for deflection shooting. Sometimes Obleser would be literally shouting with surprise at some of the victories. I couldn't always turn around directly on their tails. In some cases, an attempt to do so would have put them on my tail and allowed them to shoot me down. Sometimes, I would put the nose up and with that feeling for the lead which I have described, press the triggers at the moment my intuition and experience told me was right. Boom! The other aircraft flies right into that hail of bullets and shells. I had no system and do not consider myself a genius fighter pilot. It was just hard work and experience that gave me my success.

The fighter pilots of the *Luftwaffe* were occasionally afforded a chance to fly one or more of the captured Allied fighter planes that had been repaired and repainted with German Air Force insignia. Of the types available to them, including the North American P-51 Mustang, the Supermarine Spitfire, the Republic P-47 Thunderbolt, and the Lockheed P-38 Lightning, most of the pilots thought that the P-38, with its centre-mounted guns was the best gun platform and offered a further advantage in that its guns jammed less often when subjected to the excessive G-forces of air combat. Gunther Rall was among the keenest of the German fighter aces to fly and experience the capabilities and limitations of the planes of his adversary. He agreed that concentrating the guns in the centre of the aircraft, along the longitudinal axis, was the preferable design. His own experience with the Bf-109 and the Fw-190 had convinced him that this sort of gun platform (as provided in the 109), was better, even though the Fw-190 had four guns as opposed to the three guns of the 109. He felt that the concentration of fire from the 109, coupled with the explosive power of the excellent German ammunition, was more effective and deadly. Of the Allied fighters that he had an opportunity test, he favoured the Spitfire, as, of course, did most RAF fighter pilots. But his preferred combat mount was the one he had flown most and been most successful with, the Messerschmitt Bf-109. Flying the captured enemy aircraft gave the *Luftwaffe* fighter pilots valuable experience and insight into their qualities and characteristics. In the period when Rall commanded the Squadron

Leader's School, he frequently flew as an 'American' or 'British' pilot in practice aerial combats against his students. This early 'Top Gun' activity proved useful in teaching the students about exploiting the weaknesses they discovered in the enemy aircraft.

Astute, sober and deadly serious, the modest Rall is remembered by some of his fellow aces as a supremely conscientious and capable hunter, who tended to shun the extremes of the typical fighter pilot social life, went to bed early and rose early to go on the hunt. In over 800 operational missions he engaged in air combat more than 600 times and there were many days in which he scored multiple victories. It is perhaps reasonable to speculate that, had he not been put out of action for that nine-month period with a broken back, together with his lengthy hospitalization after the loss of his thumb, he would have finished the war as the highest scoring Top Gun in history. As it was, he remains the all-time number three in that category with 275 confirmed victories.

At the end of the war Gunther Rall held the rank of major and the position of *Kommodore* of JG-300, a fighter squadron based near Salzburg. At that point, JG-300 was really a squadron in name only. The German Air Force had disintegrated. For the surviving pilots there were few airworthy planes, few useable facilities, very little aviation fuel and almost no supplies or spare parts.

With the arrival of the U.S. Army in central Germany, Rall disbanded the squadron. He and some of his fellow pilots joined the masses of former combatants on the march across the countryside in an effort to get home to their families. Within a few days he was collected with many others and was brought back to Salzburg, a prisoner of war. He was soon transferred to a large POW camp near Heidelberg, where conditions were extremely poor. But within days the camp commandant ordered a roll call for all *Luftwaffe* officers, at which certain among them were singled out. The Americans it seems were interested in any former *Luftwaffe* officers who had experience flying the Messerschmitt Me-262 jet fighter. After some interrogation, the small group of German fighter aces was given fifteen minutes to gather their belongings and were then taken to England, to a special camp at Bovingdon, near Hemel Hempstead, where interrogation about the Me-262 continued under the British. Then Rall was moved again, to an enormous POW internment camp across the Channel near Cherbourg, followed shortly by a return to England, this time in company with the renowned Stuka pilot Hans-Ulrich Rudel. The pair were taken to RAF Tangmere, a famous fighter station on the south coast near Chichester. At Tangmere Rall spent two weeks responding to a range of technical questions about the 262 and there he met RAF ace Robert Stanford-Tuck. Rall and Tuck would ultimately become life-long friends. After a fortnight at Tangmere, Rall was returned to the POW camp at

Cherbourg. There, after 5½ years of combat, with all the attendent psychological and physical strain, he was in relatively poor condition. In a conversation with the camp surgeon, Rall explained his medical past including his broken back and paralysis and said that he would like to return home to the care of his doctor wife. To his amazement, the surgeon granted his request and released him. "All I had to do was ask!"

Rall had wisely moved his wife away from Vienna before the Russians had arrived. The couple were reunited and moved to Recklingen near the university town of Tübingen. In the course of their wartime marriage Hertha had lost four babies through miscarriage as a result of her proximity to bombing raids. Gunther later said that they had to rebuild their lives together 'from abosulute zero'. In the process he was to discover a problem that many returning German servicemen would face after the war, especially the better known, highly decorated ones.

On attempting to enrol at the university where he planned to study medicine he was told that he could not study there because he was a militarist. He then tried repeatedly to become employed and was always met with the same rejection and 'militarist' label. Once he tried to get work in a textile mill and was told: "No job for you – you are an ex-officer." He recalled:

A regular officer was never allowed to join a political party in pre-war Germany. It was absolutely prohibited to us. So, we were actually the clean ones yet they blamed US. We were just soldiers. This was a matter of internal German policy which was completely wrong. The arrangement forbidding us to join political parties went back to the old Weimar democracy. Some officers were honorary members of the National Socialist Party, but this had nothing to do with the regular joining and serving of the party, which was prohibited. I never was in a political party because I was a regular officer. I was not permitted to join, even if I had wished to do so.

Finally, the Ralls moved to Stuttgart where Gunther went looking for employment with the huge Siemens organization. Siemens was then being run by old German military officers who had served in the First World War and were not in sympathy with the country's unfair post-war policy regarding ex-military personnel. Siemens' management believed that such job applicants did not deserve to be denied simply for having done their duty as soldiers and Gunther Rall was made a representative for the firm in southern Germany, a position he held until 1953. During the preceding years he had maintained his interest in and enthusiasm for aviation and in 1956 he returned to the German Air Force to become instrumental in its development as an eventual part of the NATO defence establishment.

Initially, Rall was retrained at Landsberg on the Lockheed T-33 jet by

American instructors. Then came a period of gunnery training on the Republic F-84 Thunderjet at Luke Air Force Base, Arizona, followed in 1958 by an assignment to the Inspector for Fighter-Bombers. After that posting he was checked out in the Lockheed F-104 Starfighter and was soon appointed to set up a German Air Force Project Staff for the F-104, a role he maintained for 5 years. Then, after attending a 6-month course at the NATO Defense College in Paris, he was made *Kommodore* of the F-104 / F-84 fighter wing at Memmingen. After serving at Wahn Air Base near Cologne as Inspector of Combat Flying Units, he was promoted to the rank of Major General in November 1967 and later became a military attaché to NATO, a position he held until October 1975.

With financial assistance from the Bavarian state government, 28-year-old Willy Messerschmitt was able to establish a company, Messerschmitt Flugzeugbau GMBH, in March 1926. At the time, the government also had a financial interest in another aircraft firm, Bayerische Flugzeugwerke (BFW / Bavarian Aircraft Company) and soon determined that it was impractical to fund both firms. It convinced the two plane makers to merge late in 1927 under the BFW name. Its headquarters and primary manufacturing facility was at Augsburg, Germany.

The new company had an inauspicious beginning. Its first product, an all-metal, single-engine, eight passenger transport aircraft, the M-20, was sold initially to the German state airline, Deutsche Lufthansa (DHL). There were substantial production delays and, during the test phase, the prototype crashed killing its pilot. In the aftermath, a feud developed between Willy Messerschmitt and Erhard Milch, director of procurement for DHL. There were additional crashes in the test programme and Milch cancelled the DHL order. When Adolf Hitler became German Chancellor in 1932 he appointed Milch to be Secretary of State for Aviation and there seemed little liklihood of BFW receiving any meaningful contract work from the new Nazi government. In the depths of the world-wide economic depression, BFW went bankrupt. To rescue the firm, Willy Messerschmitt solicited contracts for a commercial transport from Rumania and this resulted in Milch accusing the BFW management of treason, which led to a Gestapo investigation. But Messerschmitt won the day. There followed, however, a string of misfortunes which continued until the development of the Bf-108A, a two-seat, low-wing, dual-controlled monoplane with flush-rivetting and retractable landing gear. It was called Taifun (Typhoon) and was evolved into the Bf-108B, which would perform well and gave Messerschmitt and his colleagues confidence to compete in the design of an entirely new fighter for the German Air Force which, since the accession to power by Hitler was being openly developed and expanded. The new machine was required to be a monoplane armed with at least two 7.9mm machine-guns and powered by the new liquid-cooled, inverted V-12 engine under joint development by Junkers and Daimler-Benz. The competition to build the new fighter included the Arado, Focke-Wulf, and Heinkel firms. Erhard Milch, in his continuing hatred of Messerschmitt, attempted to block the BFW firm from participating, but Hermann Goering, the Reich Minister for Aviation, intervened on Messerschmitt's behalf and BFW ultimately was awarded the contract. Its entry, designated Bf-109V1, was put through its preliminary flight tests in September 1935. *Luftwaffe* test pilots at Rechlin then began flying the plane and had a number of complaints about it including the tiny, cramped, enclosed cockpit; the narrow, rather suspect-looking main landing gear, the high wing-loading and the restricted forward view on take-off caused by the extremely steep ground angle. These were genuine concerns, disadvantages that would detract from the positive side of the plane throughout its career as a fighter.

The Bf-109 was fast for its time, quite agile and capable in combat. Even General Ernst Udet, the famed First World War German flying ace who had been among the most vocal critics of the early 109, came to appreciate its capabilities and promise, later becoming one of its greatest advocates.

In the competition, the Focke-Wulf and Arado entries had shown insufficient performance and exhibited several mechanical failures in the early testing, and the Heinkel entry was not the equal of the BFW plane. One factor contributing to the Messerschmitt entry's eventual win was a series of German intelligence reports that the British were, in fact, developing a new fighter that was similar in some key ways to the Bf-109 . . . the Spitfire.

With the decision by the Nazi government in 1936 to aid Generalissimo Francisco Franco's nationalist forces in the Spanish Civil War, came an opportunity for the German Air Force to experience and evaluate its new Bf-109 fighter in actual combat. Three pre-production 109s were brought to Seville in December 1936 to be operated in the conflict by members of the German Condor Legion 'volunteer' group. Despite the usual 'bugs' encountered in early service operation, the *Luftwaffe* was pleased with the performance of the plane and enthusiastic about the prospects for its development. The lessons learned in Spain provided BFW with the knowledge and impetus needed to produce the Bf-109B which entered production early in 1937. As soon as these aircraft arrived in Spain to resume Condor combat, the Germans learned that their B or Bertha model was at a distinct disadvantage against its principal opponent, the Soviet Polikarpov-I-16 at lower altitudes, and quickly moved the struggle to higher altitudes where the German fighter gained the upper hand.

The performance of the Bf-109B in Spain soon led to replacing its two-blade, fixed-pitch wooden propeller with an American Hamilton Standard two-blade, variable-pitch metal propeller built in Germany under licence by the firm VDM. Now the *Luftwaffe* couldn't get enough of the little fighters and BFW raced to expand its Augsburg factories while at the same time licensing Fiesler to build the plane at its Kassel plant. A string of improvements followed, including more efficient Jumo engines, fuel injection, a two-stage supercharger for better high-altitude performance, and a 20mm cannon which, while improving the plane's firepower, brought with it an overheating problem. By March 1938 the first C models, called Clara by *Luftwaffe* pilots, were coming off the assembly line at Augsburg and were sent immediately to Spain. While the newer Jumo engines were an improvement over their predecessors, they were not able to give the little fighter the 300+ mph performance needed by the *Luftwaffe* and wanted by the plane's designer, Willy Messerschmitt. What they craved was the as yet unavailable Daimler-Benz DB-601 engine, an automatically supercharged powerplant that would give the desired performance while operating efficiently through negative G combat manoeuvres, but one which was still suffering the teething problems of most complex mechanical wonders. So, as a kind of interim measure, BFW elected to employ two variants of the Jumo 210 engine in the next Bf-109 mark, the D or Dora. And in Spain, Condor Legion pilots Adolf Galland, Werner Mölders and others showed the Dora to be a significantly better fighter than its ancestors. It was then that Mölders was instrumental in devising the all-important 'finger-four' or '*Schwarm*' formation, a brilliant, flexible tactic that would give the Germans a considerable air combat advantage over the pilots of the Royal Air Force in the early days of the Battle of Britain. Mölders was able to make 14 kills in the air war over Spain, as the highest scoring ace of the conflict.

The performance of the 109 in the Spanish war brought Willy Messerschmitt to international prominence, so much so that the Reichs Luftsfahrt Ministerium (RLM), the German Air Ministry, urged BFW to take advantage of this and promote further international recognition for itself through a name change. Aircraft then in current production by the firm would retain the designation Bf, but all new aircraft from the firm would be designated Me for Messerschmitt. The move undoubtedly provided a major coup for the Nazi *propagandameister* Josef Göbbels.

Development continued at Augsburg and in 1939 the first E or Emil models were being delivered to the *Luftwaffe*. These were the first examples of the 109 that began to show the sort of capability the plane's proponents had envisioned. Fitted with a DB-601A-1 engine, a three-bladed variable-pitch propeller, and twin radiators mounted under the wings, the Emil was substantially faster, if slightly less agile, than earlier 109 marks. It was one of the most effective and most feared fighters of the time. It was equipped with four 7.9mm machine-guns (two in the cowling and two in the wings). Some of the new Emils went to Spain early in 1939, but by then the war was nearly over and they saw little action. In their earlier participation, roughly 200 *Luftwaffe* men of the Condor Legion gained the knowledge from their combat exposure to prepare them as seasoned fighter pilots for the aerial warfare to come.

Production of the E model continued at an increased rate and was shifted to a plant at Regensburg to make room for assembly of the Bf-110 twin-engine fighter, and additional production capacity for the 109 was organized as other aircraft manufacturers were brought into the programme. The September 1939 German invasion of Poland saw the utilization of a combined force of more than 200 Bf-109Ds and Es, of which 67 were lost mainly to ground fire. And in an early clash of the *Luftwaffe* fighters and the Royal Air Force, a force of Wellington bombers attacking a target at Wilhelmshaven in daylight on 18 December 1939, was intercepted by 109s which easily downed twelve of the British bombers and damaged three more. In the action the Germans lost two fighters and after it the British were forced to rethink their tactics.

The RAF was clearly worried about the 109 and desperately needed to understand its capabilities and its weaknesses to be able to cope with it in battle. The British had a break in November when a *Luftwaffe* pilot mistakenly landed his Bf-109E on the French side of the Franco-German border. The plane was brought to England where it was flight-tested and put through mock dogfights with British fighters, thus providing the RAF with considerable knowledge about the enemy aircraft. It learned that the little German fighter was superior to its mainstay Hawker Hurricane in virtually all respects and superior in most ways to the much vaunted Spitfire Mk 1 as equipped with a two-bladed propeller. A Spitfire Mk 1 with a three-bladed Rotol propeller, however, was the better mount at high altitude.

The best of the Emils was said to be the Bf-109E-4 which featured a strengthened canopy, armour plate in the seat and above the pilot's head, and two wing-mounted MG-FF/M 20mm cannon. The 'softened' recoil action of these cannon allowed them to fire a powerful, high-explosive 'mine' shell and to utilize a higher rate of fire. These Emils were the aerial spearhead of the Germans' *Blitzkrieg* (lightning war) into the Low Countries and France in spring 1940. In the campaign they realized that the *Luftwaffe* needed an effective fighter-bomber, a *Jagdbomber* or Jabo and several Bf-109s and Bf-110s were fitted with centreline experimental bomb racks. In attacks on Allied shipping in the English Channel, the Jabo proved successful and the *Luftwaffe* began organizing Jabo squadrons of Bf-109s.

The fundamental design of the 109 was flawed, however, in the sense that it possessed only very short range, much like the aeroplane that was soon to become its main opponent, the Supermarine Spitfire. But the Spitfire of 1940 was essentially a defensive fighter, designed primarily to fight its battles over England and the Channel and then quickly return to its nearby base to be refuelled and rearmed for the next round. And in the skies above Dunkirk in May of that year, the *Luftwaffe*'s Bf-109 pilots learned that the Spitfire, in the hands of some very keen and able RAF fliers, was indeed a formidable opponent.

With the coming of the summer months and the start of what would become known as the Battle of Britain, the unusually long and hot sunny days seemed to favour the *Luftwaffe* as it mounted raid after raid across the Channel. At first its air crews concentrated on shipping moving constantly through the waterway separating France from England, but then its attention was focused on the vital British radar chain system along England's south and east coasts. Throughout that summer, until early September, the Bf-109 fighter force of the *Luftwaffe* achieved considerable success. It was essentially free to range as it saw fit, engaging with the fighters of the RAF in the frequent *Luftwaffe* raids against Britain, and putting into practice the tactics that had been developed for it in Spain by Werner Mölders, while the British fighter pilots were still compelled to fly in their standard traditional, obsolete formations which put them at a terrible disadvantage to the German pilots. In those days responsibility for shepherding the German bombers on their raids fell to the crews of the twin-engine Bf-110 fighters. It was a task they were ill-equipped to handle and they suffered greatly under the guns of the Spitfires and Hurricanes. By September the failure of the Bf-110s as proper escorts forced the *Luftwaffe* on to the defensive for the first time and it had no choice but to replace the 110s with 109s, theoretically improving the lot of the German bombers, but at the same time emasculating the Bf-109 fighter pilots by placing them at a distinct disadvantage to their British adversaries. Ordered to stick with their bombers, they could no longer range freely to find and fight the enemy and, due to their extremely short range, could not afford more than 10 or 15 minutes over England to meet and deal with the RAF Normally the Bf-109 pilot then had to race back to his field in France to refuel. If he got it wrong or tried to stretch his fuel a bit too far, he paid the penalty of having to bale out or ditch in the Channel.

When the Germans failed in their effort to bomb the British radar facilities out of existence, they inexplicably switched targets again, apparently in the belief that it was more important to destroy the fighter capability of the RAF by bombing its bases near the south coast. Had they persisted in that campaign they might have actually gained the air superiority and, possibly, the air supremacy they required successfully to launch their invasion of England, Operation Sea Lion. Once again they were unsuccessful, failing to knock out the primary R.A.F. fighter stations permanently, and the *Luftwaffe* was again ordered to change targets. Now it would be the cities of Britain that would bare the brunt of the German attacks in the worst nights and days of the Blitz.

By 31 October, the generally accepted last day of the Battle of Britain, the Germans had lost 610 Bf-109s, 235 Bf-110s, and 937 bombers. The RAF losses amounted to 403 Spitfires, 631 Hurricanes, and 115 Blenheims. With most of the fighting taking place in the air over England and the Channel, downed British pilots who survived were generally back in action within a day or two, whereas the surviving downed German pilots and bomber crew members mostly ended up as prisoners of war. As for the fighter aircraft involved, the Bf-109 certainly proved a brilliant and worthy opponent for the Spitfire which, it must be said, entered the aerial ring armed with mere rifle-calibre machine-guns against the German plane with its impressive cannon hitting power. Numbers aside, most historians agree that Britain won the battle by preventing the Germans from achieving the air supremacy they needed to invade England successfully. As the first nation to square off against Hitler and make him back down, it must be acknowledged that in that campaign Britain handed Germany and her air force their first defeat in the war. However, the *Luftwaffe* came away from the experience with renewed enthusiasm for its principal fighter and went on to develop it into additional variants for specialized roles. There was a reconnaissance version which had no guns and featured a camera in the rear of the fuselage. And, in a move that might have provided a great advantage to the Bf-109 pilots during the Battle of Britain, the long-range Bf-109E-7 was produced with the capability of carrying either an eighty-gallon centre-line fuel drop tank or, as a Jabo, a 550-lb bomb. In North Africa, modified Bf-109Es were fitted with engine sand filters and a desert survival kit for the pilot which contained among other items, food and water, a light-weight carbine rifle, and signal equipment. These planes proved highly successful in their encounters with Kittyhawks and Hurricanes of the Royal Air Force, shooting them down in substantial numbers. An uprated variant of the long-range version soon appeared utilizing a DB-601E engine rated at 1,350 hp for take-off and this was followed by the Bf-109E-9, a long-range reconnaissance variant equipped with a fuselage camera and two 7.9mm machine-guns in the engine cowling. Of the more than 4,000 Bf-109 Emils built, these late variants accounted for only a small portion.

The now considerable experience with the Bf-109E guided Willy Messerschmitt in the continuing evolution of his basic design through important modifications which resulted in the faster, more effective F, G and K marks. With the availability of ever more powerful engines the aeroplane began to look different as well as perform better. The improvements required an elongated cowling and an enlarged prop spinner, resulting in an overall 'cigar-like' profile that it would retain for the balance of production.

Its pilots referred to the F model of the 109 as the 'Friedrich'. A series of crashes occurring through a mysterious loss of control in early examples of the F was traced to one of the recent design modifications – the removal of the bracing struts under the horizontal stabilizer. The problem was soon corrected and many would consider the 390 mph Friedrich the best of the Bf-109 line and on a par with the excellent Spitfire Mk V. What the best of the Bf-109 aces liked most about the F in combat was its armament – initially two MG-17 7.9mm machine-guns in the cowling and one MG-FF/M 20mm *Motorkanone* (cannon) which was engine-mounted, giving them terrific hitting power. On the subsequent F-2 model, the MG-FF was replaced with the MG-151/15, a 15mm electrically operated cannon which featured a faster rate of fire, higher muzzle velocity and a 200-round belt feed instead of a drum. The F-2 aeroplane was built as a standard fighter and in special high-altitude, Jabo and tropicalized variants.

The Nazi campaign against Russia began on 22 June 1941 and the Bf-109 led as the primary *Luftwaffe* fighter. It was augmented in the air by a large number of Emils operating in the Jabo role. On that first day of the campaign, the 109s accounted for over 300 Russian aircraft shot down and a further 1,000 destroyed on the ground. It was in this Eastern Front campaign that the highest achieving *Luftwaffe* fighter aces, Erich Hartmann, Gunther Rall, Gerhard Barkhorn and others, quickly began to build their kill scores. By early 1942, when Messerschmitt was producing the Bf-109F-4 – certainly one of the best of the marks – many of the *Luftwaffe* fighter pilots were taking the new machine into combat, grateful for its powerful DB-601E engine, its 150-round 20mm cannon, its better cockpit armour and its improved self-sealing fuel tanks.

The development by Daimler-Benz of the DB-605, a still more powerful aero engine for the next 109 mark, the G or Gustav, was made possible by the employment of bored-out cylinders and higher compression generating 1,450 hp for take-off, and some of the new G models incorporated cockpit pressurization. But by 1942 the Bf-109, even with all of its development and evolution over the years, was showing its age. Much of the design and technology that had made it special had gradually become obsolete and it was gradually being superceded in the fighter squadrons of the German Air Force by the more sophisticated Focke-Wulf 190, a BMW-powered radial engine fighter masterpiece with greater speed, range and altitude capabilities than the 109. With superb manoeuvrability, 1,700 hp and 418 mph, it was unmatched by its early opposition and had only one significant problem: there were never enough of them. The Germans were rather slow in producing the 190 and, even more importantly, in the development and production of their promising jet fighter, the Me-262. Bureaucratic and technical considerations were behind the delays in getting the jet into the air, into production and into the hands of the pilots who would have had a vital advantage over the best the Allies could put up against it had the *Luftwaffe* been able to equip its squadrons with great numbers of the new and phenomenal fighter.

From March 1942 when Bf-109Gs began arriving at *Luftwaffe* squadrons it was clear that this latest model of the mainstay fighter would have to serve as a stopgap until the Fw-190 could be supplied in sufficient numbers to take over as the lead fighter. So dependent were the units on the G model that despite many wartime manufacturing problems and delays the maker still managed to produce and deliver upwards of 24,000 of the type, with a record 14,000 being produced in 1944 alone. Focke-Wulf, in fact, was never able to produce their exceptional fighter in the quantities required to relieve the 109s in the principal role. Across the

Channel meanwhile, the workers at Vickers-Supermarine were bringing their marvellous Spitfire along through improved mark after mark, refining it with more horsepower, better armament and armour, and with the debut of the Mk IX, surpassing the performance and capability of the Bf-109G. This conclusion was amply shown in many subsequent combats between the two adversaries as well as in mock dogfights between a 109G that had mistakenly landed at RAF Manston in Kent, and Mk IX and Mk XIV Spitfires as well as a North American P-51C Mustang. All of these Allied fighters were demonstrated to have a wide range of advantages over the Messerschmitt plane.

As the war dragged on and Nazi fortunes gradually waned, the *Luftwaffe* was forced to shift its main fighter utilization to the defence of the homeland against the massive, ever-increasing combined British and American bombing campaign. The heavy bomber numerical strength of both Allied air forces was growing impressively. In 1944 both were able to mount consistent attacks of 500 to 1,000 bombers, inflicting unprecedented destruction on German targets including the vitally important aircraft industry. To counter the Allied raiders, Messerschmitt focused on certain special modifications for the Bf-109G. Many of the later Gs were now being built as 'bomber destroyers' by increasing the armament through the addition of an MG-15 20mm cannon in a gondola fitted under each wing (later replaced by 30mm cannon), for a total of five guns on the aircraft. The change adversely affected the handling characteristics of the plane as the greater weight caused instability and a poorer roll rate; this in the G model, already notorious among its pilots for being excessively heavy on the controls, 'a handful' for the best of them and 'downright dangerous' for the less experienced ones. The German pilots called the variant 'gunboats.' Additionally, Gustavs were employed in dropping fragmentation bombs with delayed fuses in an attempt to break up the Allied formations, albeit with little success.

In a further bid to disrupt the enemy bombers attacking Germany, another version of the Bf-109G was developed to be a 'formation breaker.' The cannon gondola were replaced by launch tube clusters which fired 8.2-inch rockets which, in practice rarely hit the enemy aircraft, but did occasionally cause the B-17s and B-24s to scatter briefly. By night, a small number of Bf-109Gs called 'Wilde Saus' operated at altitudes above the attacking RAF bomber force, relying on the lights of the target cities below, and the fires started by the bombing, to illuminate and silhouette the enemy bombers and making it possible for the 109s to bounce them.

Other design modifications to the Gustav line included an improved radio for longer range communication, a taller rudder for better handling, and a new 'Galland' canopy hood that was bulged for greater visibility.

Among the later G variants were models fitted with the Daimler-Benz DB-605AS and AM engines with much improved supercharging. The final Bf-109 mark was the K for Konrad. It featured virtually all the design improvements made up to its October 1944 initial delivery date as well as cockpit pressurization and the latest DB engine with two-stage supercharger, giving it a top speed of 450 mph.

At the end of the war in May 1945, nearly 34,000 Bf-109s had been built. The aeroplane had participated in all the important campaigns, but by the last months of the Allied combined bombing offensive, the *Luftwaffe* could field fewer than 800 of the fighters to go up against the enemy, when it was able to fuel and arm them, and muster the pilots to man them. In one final desperate action, on 7 April, a unit of stripped-down 109s took off with the express intent of ramming aircraft in the U.S.A.A.F. bomber stream. In the attack they destroyed eight of the American bombers.

The late Ray and Mark Hanna of the Old Flying Machine Company at Duxford Airfield near Cambridge, England, have long been known in the aviation community and the wider world as being among the finest all-round pilots ever to fly the aeroplanes of World War Two. Tragically, Mark died after a flying accident at Sabadell, near Barcelona, Spain in September 1999. He was 40. The aeroplane he was flying was a Hispano Buchon, a Spanish-built version of the WWII Bf-109 fighter. He was one of the world's most experienced display pilots of historic military aircraft and was Managing Director and co-founder of the Old Flying Machine Company, a firm which preserves and maintains rare vintage aircraft in airworthy condition. Mark was an ex-RAF fast jet pilot. He had flown more than 4,000 hours, 2,300 of them on historic aircraft. In a bizarre twist of fate, Mark had written about his impressions of the Bf-109 after flying it numerous times.

> To my eye, the aircraft looks dangerous, both to the enemy and to its own pilots. The aircraft's difficult reputation is well known and right from the outset you are aware that it is an aeroplane that needs to be treated with a great deal of respect. Talk to people about the 109 and all you hear about is how you are going to wrap it up on take-off or landing! As you walk up to the 109 one is at first struck by the small size of the aircraft, particularly if parked next to a contemporary American fighter. Closer examination reveals a crazy-looking knocked-knee undercarriage, a very heavily framed, sideways-opening canopy with almost no forward view in the three-point attitude, a long rear fuselage and tiny tail surfaces. A walk-round reveals ingenius split radiator flaps which double as an extension to the landing flaps, ailerons with a lot of movement and rather odd-looking external mass balances. Also, independently operating leading edge slats. These devices should glide open and shut on the ground with DB pressure of a single finger. Other unusual features include the horizontal stabilizer doubling as the elevator trimmer and the complete absence of a rudder trim

system. Overall the finish is a strange mix of the innovative and archaic.

Climbing on board you have to be careful not to stand on the radiator flap, then lower yourself gently downwards and forwards, taking your weight by holding onto the windscreen. Once in you are aware that you are almost lying down in the aeroplane, the position reminiscent of a racing car. The cockpit is very narrow and if you have broad shoulders (don't all fighter pilots?), it is a tight squeeze. Once strapped in, itself a knuckle-wrapping affair, you can take stock. First impressions are of simplicity and straight forwardness.

From left to right, the collocated elevator trim and flap trim wheels fall easily to hand. You need several turns to get the flaps fully down to 40° and the idea is that you can crank both together. In practice this is a little difficult and I tend to operate the services separately. Coming forward we see the tailwheel locking lever. This either allows the tailwheel to castor or locks it dead ahead. Next is the throttle quadrant, consisting of the propeller lever, and a huge throttle handle. Forward and down, on the floor is an enormous and very efffective ki-gass primer and a T-shaped handle. Directly above this and in line with the canopy seal is the yellow and black hood jettison lever. Pulling this releases two very strong springs in the rear part of the canopy, causing the rear section to come loose and therefore the whole main part of the hood becomes unhinged and can be pushed clear away into the airflow. Looking directly forwards we have clustered together the standard instrument panel with vertical select magnetos on the left, starter and booster coil slightly right of centre, and engine instruments all grouped together on the right hand side. Our aeroplane has a mixture of British, Spanish and German instruments in this area.

The centre console under the main instrument panel consists of a 720 channel radio, E2B compass and a large placard courtesy of the Civil Aviation Authority warning of the dire consequences if you land in a crosswind equal to or greater than 10 knots, or trim the aircraft at speeds in excess of 250 knots. Just to the left of the centre console, close to your left knee, is the undercarriage up/down selector and the mechanical and electrical undercarriage position indicator. On this aeroplane, this is a rotary selector with a neutral position. Select the undercarriage up or down, then activate a hydraulic button on the front of the control column. This gives 750 psi to the system instantly. Immediately beneath the undercarriage selector is the control for the Radiator flaps. These are also hydraulically controlled with an open/close and neutral position, and activated by the trigger on the stick at 375 psi. If you leave the radiator flap control in anything other than neutral and then try to activate the undercarriage you will not have enough pressure to enable the gear to travel.

[The] right hand side of the cockpit sees the electrical switches, battery master boost pumps, pitot heat and a self-contained pre-oil system, and that's it! There is no rudder trim, or rudder pedal adjust; also the seat can only be adjusted pre-flight and has the choice of only three settings. If you are any bigger than 6 feet tall, it's all starting to get a bit confined. Once you are strapped in and comfortable, close the canopy to check the seating position. Normally, if you haven't flown the 109 before, you get a clout on the head as you swing the heavy lid over and down. Nobody sits that low in a fighter!

It's getting dangerously close to going flying now. OK, open the hood again (in case we catch fire and have to get out in a hurry). To start, power ON, boost pumps ON. Three good shots on the very stiff primer. Set the throttle about ½ inch open. "CLEAR PROP". Push the start button, a few blades and boost coil and mags together. It's a good starter and with a brief snort of flame the 109 fires up immediately. Checking oil pressure is rising right away. Idle initially at 700 rpm, then gently up to 1,000 to warm up. Less than 1,000 rpm and the whole aeroplane starts to rock from side to side on the gear with some sort of harmonic. This is a most unusual sensation and is quite good fun! One is immediately aware after start that the aeroplane is 'Rattley': engine, canopy, reduction gear all provide little vibrations and shakes transmitted directly to the pilot.

Close the rad flaps with the selector and activate the hydraulic trigger. Check the 375 psi and that they close together. Reopen them now to delay the coolant temperature rise. The 109 needs a lot of power to get moving so you need to allow the engine to warm a little before you pile the power onto it. Power up to 1,800 rpm and suddenly we're rolling. Power back . . . to turn, stick forward against the instrument panel to lighten the tail. A blast of throttle and a jab of brakes. Do this in a Spitfire and you are on your nose! The 109, however, is very tail-heavy and is reluctant to turn. You can very easily lock up a wheel. If you do not use the above technique you will charge off across the airfield in a straight line! Forward view can only be described as appalling, and due to the tail/brake arrangement this makes weaving more difficult than on other similar types. I prefer to taxi with the hood open to help this a little. By the time we are at the end of the strip the aircraft is already starting to get hot. So, quickly on with the run-up. Hood closed again with a satisfying thud. I'm sitting as high as I can and my head is touching the canopy. I am not wearing goggles as they scratch and catch the hood if they are up on your head. A large bonedome is out of the question and, in my opinion, is a flight safety hazard in this aircraft. Hood positively locked . . . and push up on it to check. Oil temperature is 30°, coolant temperature is greater than or at 60°. Brakes hard on (there is no parking brake), stick back and power gently up to 0 boost (30") and

2,300 rpm. Exercise the prop at least twice, rpm falling back to 1,800 each time, keep an eye on the oil pressure. The noise and vibration levels have now increased dramatically. Power back down to 1,800 rpm and check the mags. Insignificant drop on each side. We must hurry as the coolant temperature is at 98°C and going UP. We have to get rolling to get some cooling air through the radiators. Pre-take-off checks . . . elevator trim set to +1°, no rudder trim, throttle friction light. This is vital as I'm going to need to use my left hand for various services immediately after take-off. Mixture is automatic, pitch fully fine . . . fuel-I know we're full (85 gallons); the gauge is unserviceable again so I'm limited to 1 hour and 15 minutes cruise, or 1 hour if any high power work is involved. Fuel/Oil cock is ON, pressure is good, primer is done up. Flaps, crank down to 20° for take-off. Rad flaps checked at full open; if we take off with them closed we will certainly boil the engine and guarantee to crack the head. Gyro is set to Duxford's runway. Instruments, temps and pressures all in the green for take-off. Radiator is now 102°. Oxygen we don't have, hood rechecked down and locked, harness tight and secure, hydraulics select down in the gear and pressurize the system check 750 psi. Controls full and free, tailwheel locked. Got to go – 105°. There's no time to hang around and worry about the take-off. Here we go . . . power gently up and keep it coming smoothly up to +8 (46") . . . it's very noisy! Keep the tail down initially, keep it straight by feel rather than any positive technique . . . tail coming up now . . . once the rudder's effective. Unconscious corrections to the rudder are happening all the time. It's incredibly entertaining to watch the 109 take off or land. The rudder literally flashes around! The alternative technique (rather tongue in cheek) is Walter Eichorn's, of using full right rudder throughout the take-off roll and varying the swing with the throttle!

The little fighter is now bucketing along, accelerating rapidly. As the tail lifts there is a positive tendency to swing left. This can be checked very easily however, although if you are really aggressive lifting the tail it is difficult to stop and happens very quickly. Now the tail's up and you can see vaguely where you are going. It's a rough, wild, buckety ride on grass and with noise, smoke from the stacks and the aeroplane bouncing around, it's exciting.

Quick glance at the ASI [air speed indicator] – 100 mph, slight check back on the stick and we're flying. Hand off the throttle, rotate the gear selector and activate the hydraulic button. The mechanical indicators motor up very quickly and you feel a clonk, clonk as the gear comes home. Re-elect Neutral on the undercarriage selector. Quick look out at the wings and you see the slats fully out, starting to creep in as the airspeed increases and the angle of attack reduces. 130 mph and an immediate climbing turn up and right onto the downwind leg just in case I need to put the aeroplane down in a hurry. Our company S.O.P. [standard operating procedure] is always to fly an overhead orbit of the field to allow everything to stabilize before setting off. This has saved at least one of our aeroplanes.

Start frantically to crank the flap up – now up the speed increasing through 150, power back to +6 (42") and 2,650 rpm for the climb. Plenty of airflow through the narrow radiators now, so close them and remember to keep a careful eye on the coolant gauge for the next few minutes until the temperature has settled down. With the rad flaps closed, the aircraft accelerates positively. I'm aware as we climb that I'm holding in a little right rudder to keep the tail in the middle, but the foot loads are light, and it's no problem. Level off and power back to +4 (38") and 2,000 rpm. The speed has picked up to the 109 cruise of about 235-240 mph and now the tail is right in the middle and no rudder input is necessary.

Once settled down with adrenalin level back down to just high, we can take stock of our situation. The initial reaction is of delight to be flying a classic aeroplane, and next the realization that this is a real fighter! You feel aggressive flying it. The urge is to go looking for something to bounce and shoot down.

The roll rate is very good and very positive below about 250 mph. With the speed further back the roll rate remains good, particularly with a bit of help from the rudder. Above 250 mph, however, the roll rate starts to heavy up and up to 300 or so, is very similar to a P-51. After that it's all getting pretty solid and you need two hands on the stick for any meaningful roll rates. Another peculiarity is that when you have been in a hard turn with the slats deployed, and then you roll rapidly one way and stop, there is a strange sensation for a second or so of a kind of dead area over the ailerons – almost as if they are not connected! Just when you are starting to get worried they work again!

Pitch is also delightful at 250 mph and below. It feels very positive and the amount of effort on the control column needed to produce the relevant nose movement seems exactly right to me. As C_L max is reached the leading edge slats deploy – together if the ball is in the middle, slightly asymmetrically if you have any slip on. The aircraft delights in being pulled into hard manoeuvring turns at these slower speeds. As the slats pop out you feel a slight 'notching' on the stick and you can pull more until the whole airframe is buffeting quite hard. A little more and you will drop a wing, but you have to be crass to do it unintentionally. Pitch tends to be heavy up above 250 mph but it is still easily manageable up to 300 mph and the aircraft is perfectly happy carrying out low-level looping manoeuvres from 300 mph and below. Above 300 mph one peculiarity is a slight nose-down trim change as you accelerate. This means that running in for an airshow above 300 mph the aeroplane has a slight tucking-in sensation – a sort of desire to get down to ground level! This is easily held on the stick or can be trimmed out but is slightly surprising initially. Manoeuvring above 300, two hands can be required for more aggressive performance. Either that or get on the trimmer to help you. Despite this heavying up it is still quite easy to get at 5Gs at these speeds.

The rudder is effective and of medium feel up to 300. It becomes heavier above this speed but regardless, the lack of rudder trim is not a problem for the type of operations we carry out with the aeroplane. Initial acceleration is rapid, particularly with nose down, up to about 320 mph. After that the 109 starts to become a little reluctant and you have to be fairly determined to get over 350-360 mph.

So how does the aeroplane compare with other contemporary fighters? First, let me say that all my comments are based on operation below 10,000 feet and at power settings not exceeding +12 (54") and 2,700 rpm. I like it as an aeroplane, and with familiarity I think it will give most of the Allied fighters I have flown a hard time, particularly in a close, hard-turning slow-speed dogfight. It will definitely out-manoeuvre a P-51 in this type of flight, the roll rate and slow speed characteristics being much better. The Spitfire, on the other hand, is more of a problem for the 109 and I feel it is a superior close-in fighter. Having said that, the aircraft are sufficiently closely matched that pilot ability would probably be the deciding factor. At higher speeds the P-51 is definitely superior, and, provided the Mustang kept his energy up and refused to dogfight, he would be relatively safe against the 109. Other factors affecting the 109 as a combat plane include the small, cramped cockpit. This is quite a tiring working environment, although the view out (in flight) is better than you might expect; the profusion of canopy struts is not particularly a problem. In addition to the above, the small cockpit makes you feel more a part of the aeroplane and the overall smaller dimensions make you more difficult to spot. There's no doubt that when you are flying the 109 and you look out and see the crosses on the wings you feel aggressive; if you are in an Allied fighter it is very intimidating to see this dangerous little aeroplane turning in on you!

Returning to the circuit it is almost essential to join for a run and break. Over the field break from 50 feet, up and over 4Gs onto the downwind leg. Speed at 150 or less, gear select to DOWN and activate the button and feel the gear come down asymmetrically. Check the mechanical indicators (ignore the electric position indicators), pitch fully fine, fuel – both boost pumps ON. If you have less than ¼ fuel and the rear pump is not on, the engine may stop in the three-point attitude. Rad flaps to FULL OPEN and wing flaps to 10° to 15°. As the wing passes the threshold downwind take all the power off and roll into the finals turn, cranking the flap like mad as you go. The important thing is to set up a highish rate of descent and a curved approach. The aircraft is reluctant to lose speed around finals so, ideally, you should initiate the turn quite slow at about 100–105. Slats normally deploy half way round finals but you, the pilot, are not aware they have come out. The ideal is to keep turning with the speed slowly bleeding, and roll out at about 10 feet at the right speed and just starting to transition to the three-point attitude. The last speed I usually see is just about 90; I'm normally too busy to look after that.

The 109 is one of the most controllable aircraft that I have flown at slow speed around finals and, provided you don't get too slow, is one of the easiest to three-point. It just feels right! The only problem is getting it too slow. If this happens you end up with a very high sink rate very quickly and absolutely no ability to check or flare to round out. It falls out of your hands.

Once down on three points the aircraft tends to stay down, but this is when you have to be careful. The forward view has gone to hell and you cannot afford to let any sort of swing develop. The problem is that the initial detection is more difficult. The aeroplane is completely unpredictable and can diverge in either direction. There never seems to be any pattern to this. Sometimes the most immaculate three-pointer will turn into a potential disaster half way through the landing roll. Other times a ropey landing will roll straight as an arrow.

When we first started flying the 109 both my father and I did a lot of practice circuits on the grass before trying a paved strip. Operating off grass is preferred. Although it is a much smoother ride on the hard, directionally the aircraft is definitely more sensitive. Without doubt you cannot afford to relax until you are positively stationary. I would never make a rolling exit from a runway in the 109. It is just as likely to wrap itself up at 25 as it is at 80 mph. Another problem is that you have to go easy on the brakes. Hammer them too early in the landing roll and they will have faded to nothing just when you need them! The final word of advice is always three-point the aircraft and if the wind is such that it makes a three-pointer inadvisable, it's simple; the aeroplane stays in the hangar.

Having said all this, I like the aeroplane very much, and I think I can understand why many of the *Luftwaffe* aces had such a high regard and preference for it.

CHAPTER FOUR

Erich Hartmann

Up till the end of March I was not convinced that Hitler was resolved upon mortal war with Russia, nor how near it was. Our Intelligence reports revealed in much detail the extensive German troop movements towards and into the Balkan States which had marked the first three months of 1941. Our agents could move with a good deal of freedom in these quasi-neutral countries, and were able to keep us accurately posted about the heavy German forces gathering by rail and road to the south-east. But none of these necessarily involved the invasion of Russia, and all were readily explainable by German interests and policy in Rumania and Bulgaria, by her designs on Greece and arrangements with Yugoslavia and Hungary. Our information about the immense movement taking place through Germany towards the main Russian front, stretching from Rumania to the Baltic, was far more difficult to acquire. That Germany should at this stage, and before clearing the Balkan scene, open another major war with Russia seemed to me too good to be true.

We did not know the tenor of the conversations of November, 1940, between Molotov, Hitler, and Ribbontrop at Berlin, nor of the negotiations and proposed pacts which had followed them. There was no sign of lessening German strength opposite us across the Channel. The German air raids on Britain continued with intensity. The manner in which the German troop concentrations in Rumania and Bulgaria had been glossed over and apparently accepted by the Soviet Government, the evidence we had of large and invaluable supplies being sent to Germany from Russia, the obvious community of interest between the two countries in overrunning and dividing the British Empire in the East, all made it seem more likely that Hitler and Stalin would make a bargain at our expense rather than a war upon each other. This bargain we now know was within wide limits of Stalin's aim.

These impressions were shared by our Joint Intelligence

1. *Reichsmarshall* Hermann Goering in France during the Battle of Britain, July, 1940.

2. Hermann Goering, Commander in Chief of the *Luftwaffe*, and his staff look out over the English Channel at Dover.

3. *Luftwaffe* chief Hermann Goering with his pet lion at Carinhall during the Second World War.

4. *Reichsmarshall* Goering gazing through his binoculars at Dover across the English Channel in the summer of 1940.

5. Hermann Goering at
Carinhall in 1941.

6. Adolf Galland, left, Hermann Goering, centre, and, next to him Werner Mölders, in
France during the Battle of Britain, summer 1940.

7. Field Marshall Hugo Sperrle commanded the Condor Legion in Spain during the Spanish Civil War and, during the Battle of Britain, commanded Luftflotte 3 based in France.

8. Gunther Rall flew with III/JG-52 from a base near Calais during the Battle of Britain, but spent much of the war on the Eastern Front and amassed a victory total of 275 enemy aircraft downed.

9. Colonel Werner Mölders accounted for 5 aerial victories in the Battle of Britain and became the first pilot in history to score 100 victories. He was killed on November 22, 1941, in the crash of a Heinkel He-11 bomber in which he was a passenger.

10. German Junkers Ju-88 bombers returning to their French base after a raid on England in the Battle of Britain.

11. The navigator and pilot of a Heinkel He-111 bomber on a mission in the Battle of Britain period.

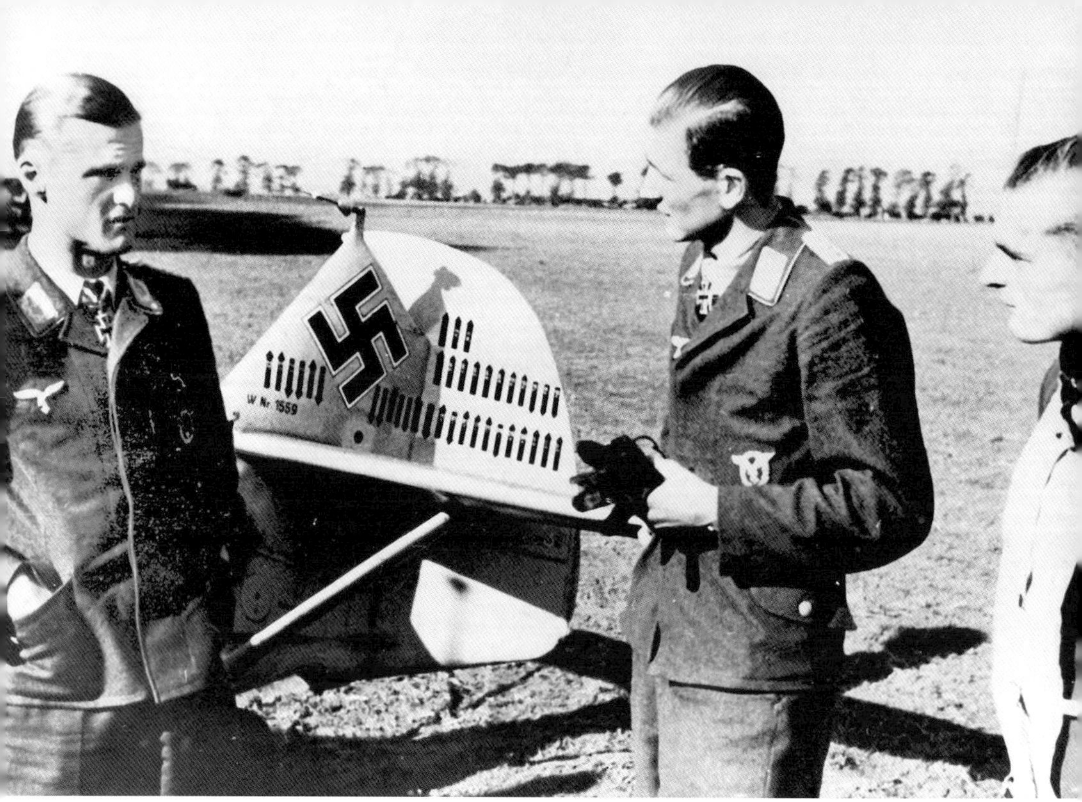

12. *Luftwaffe* fighter pilots in World War Two. The man on the left is believed to be Gunther Lützow.

13. A German airman captured after he baled out over England during the Battle of Britain.

Adolf Galland was *Luftwaffe* General of the Fighter Arm with the rank of Lieutenant-General and was one of the brightest officers of the German Air Force in the Second World War.

15. Colonel-General Hans Jeschonnek was continually made a scapegoat by *Luftwaffe* chief Hermann Goering for the failures of the *Luftwaffe*. Following a major Allied bombing attack on the German secret weapons facility at Peenemunde in August 1943, Jeschonnek committed suicide.

Adolf Galland with ground personnel by his Bf-109 in France during the Battle of Britain.

17. Adolf Galland exits his Bf-109 fighter after a Battle of Britain sortie.

18. Adolf Galland in the cockpit of his Bf-109 fighter at a French field in the Battle of Britain period.

19. Adolf Galland in the cockpit of his Bf-109 fighter at a French field in the Battle of Britain period.

20. Adolf Galland during the filming of the motion picture The Battle of Britain, on location in England during 1968.

21. A view of the Bf-109 cockpit.

22. *Luftwaffe* General Albert Kesselring during the Battle of Britain.

23. General Albert Kesselring, with Werner Mölders in the background.

24. A prominent member of the opposition, Colonel Francis Gabreski, 56th Fighter Group, 8 U.S.A.A.F.

5. Arthur "Bomber" Harris, commander-in-chief, RAF Bomber Command.

26. James H. Doolittle, foreground, commanded the Eighth U.S.A.A.F. from High Wycombe, UK.

27. The fighter pilots of RAF Fighter Command were sometimes referred to as 'the Brylcreem Boys.'

28. A *Luftwaffe* He-111 bomber over central London in September 1940.

29. A Heinkel He-111 bomber during the Battle of Britain.

30. A cockpit view of a Junkers Ju-87 Stuka dive-bomber in flight during the Battle of Britain.

31. A Messerschmitt Bf-109 which probably ran short of fuel on returning from a mission to England and made a forced landing on a French beach.

32. Members of a *Luftwaffe* fighter squadron between sorties on their French airfield.

33. Londoners
sheltering in the
Underground
subway system
during the Blitz,
1940.

34. Devastated London during the Blitz in 1940, with a Christopher Wren church in the background.

35. The broken remains of several Me-262 jet fighters in a bombed-damaged assembly facility.

36. Messerschmitt Bf-109s escorting German bombers during the Battle of Britain.

37. Women assembling de Havilland Mosquito fighter-bombers in the Second World War.

38. A Consolidated B-24 Liberator bomber attacking a German target in the Second World War.

39 A Vickers-Supermarine Spitfire fighter.

40. A Lancaster heavy bomber, N for Nan, being serviced on its hardstand in England.

41. An Avro Lancaster heavy bomber used in RAF night raids over Germany in WWII.

42. A Boeing B-17F bomber on its English hardstand before a raid on Germany.

43 New Boeing B-17Gs in England during the Second World War.

44. A B-17 Flying Fortress bomber attacking Marienburg, Germany, in the Second World War.

45. A Handley-Page Halifax bomber and crew during the Second World War.

46. A North American P-51D Mustang long-range escort fighter at its Leiston, England base.

47. Mustang pilot Major Pierce McKennon of the 4th Fighter Group based at Debden, England.

48. An RAF Bomber Command Short Stirling heavy bomber being fuelled for a raid on Germany.

49. Republic P-47D Thunderbolt fighters.

50. Eric Hartmann, left, with General Josef Kammhuber in the post-war German Air Force.

51. Eric Hartmann in the cockpit of his Bf-109, Karaya One, with his crew chief, Heinz Mertens.

52. Eric Hartmann and his Messerschmitt Bf-109 on the Eastern Front in the Second World War.

53. Major-General Johannes Steinhoff was Chief-of-Staff of the post-war German Air Force.

Committee. On 7 April they stated that there were a number of reports circulating in Europe of a German plan to attack Russia. Although Germany, they said, had considerable forces available in the East, and expected to fight Russia some time or other, it was unlikely that she would choose to make another major war front yet. Her main object in 1941 would, according to them, remain the defeat of the United Kingdom. As late as 23 May this committee from the three services reported that rumours of impending attack on Russia had died down, and that there were reports that a new agreement between the two countries was impending. This they considered likely, since the German economy would require strengthening to meet the needs of a long war. The necessary assistance could be obtained by Germany from Russia either by force or agreement. They thought the latter would be the German choice, although a threat of force would help to bring it about. This threat was now building up. There was plenty of evidence of the construction of roads and railway sidings in German Poland, of the preparation of aerodromes and of large-scale troop concentrations, including troops and air units from the Balkans.

– from The Second World War, The Grand Alliance
by Winston S. Churchill

On 22 June 1941, at 3:15 a.m., the Nazi Government of Germany invaded Communist Russia with the most powerful army the world had ever seen. The Germans rolled across the long Soviet border, between the Arctic Ocean and the Black Sea, with more than 250 divisions. Operation Barbarossa called for the conquest of Russia through the destruction of the Soviet Army. To accomplish this task the Germans massed three million men and all the required machines, armour and matériel on a front that stretched across East Prussia and Poland. These massive forces were joined in the north by allied troops of Finland and in the south by forces from Rumania and Hungary. And in the lead of the assault were the fighters, destroyers and Stukas of the German Air Force.

Until it collapsed, the Nazi-Soviet Pact had operated as both parties wanted. The German dictator had launched his successful blitzkrieg actions into Poland, the Low Countries and France without having to watch his back for possible Soviet intervention. Josef Stalin, meanwhile, had been given free rein to gobble up most of eight Eastern European countries. But with the planned invasion of England stuck in neutral, and the overpowering need of Hitler to crush the Russians and grab their living space and resources, it was inevitable that he would end that peculiar relationship with Stalin. As the time approached for the German invasion to begin, Hitler gathered his top aides and told them "When Barbarossa commences, the world will hold its breath and make no comment."

Interestingly, of Hitler's entire High Command, only *Reichsmarshall*

Hermann Goering stood up to the Führer in vehement objection to the planned German invasion of Russia. Goering knew that his air force had been stretched almost beyond its capacity by the campaign in the west and the Battle of Britain, and was in dire need of rest, resupply and refitting. It was in no condition to carry a heavy role in a major new war in the east. But Hitler had no time for Goering's concerns. His primary objective was the defeat of Russia. Nothing and no one was going to stand in his way.

In its first important assignment of the Russian campaign, the *Luftwaffe* fighter force set out to destroy as much of the Soviet Air Force on the ground as possible, while downing nearly every enemy aircraft that it encountered in the air with unparalleled ruthlessness and efficiency. They destroyed the Russian planes by the hundreds. With these successes, the *Luftwaffe* provided the German Army with the ability once again to operate in a blitzkrieg mode without significant resistance from Soviet aircraft. Thus, the Russian Army was forced into a full-scale retreat.

Adolf Galland has referred to Erich Hartmann as 'the leading fighter pilot of all time', not just for having achieved the world combat record of 352 confirmed victories, but for the uniquely effective tactics that this modest man developed and the inspiring example he became as a soldier and then as a prisoner of the Soviets for more than ten years after the end of the war. Hartmann was born on 19 April, 1922, at Weissach, Württemberg to Elisabeth and Dr. Alfred Hartmann. When Erich was three his parents decided, on the strong recommendation of Dr Hartmann's cousin, the German consul in Shanghai, to leave the food shortages, galloping inflation, economic and political turmoil of post-World War One Germany, for the comparative prosperity and opportunity of China. The adventurous senior Hartmann looked forward to practicing medicine in the foreign land and arranged to send for his family after going on alone to see what awaited them in China. There, he was delighted to be well treated and greatly appreciated by his new Chinese friends and patients. They made him feel welcome where he settled, some 600 miles up the Yangtze River in Changsha. He brought his young family over from Germany and built a new home for them all on a lovely little island he had bought in the middle of the river. It was a wonderful and unspoiled place for Erich to play and grow. But this idyllic life was short-lived as within a few years anti-colonialist feelings and civil unrest began in China. As the situation steadily worsened in the late 1920s, it became clear to the doctor that it was no longer safe for Frau Hartmann, Erich and his younger brother Alfred to remain in the country and he sent them back to Germany on the Trans-Siberian Railway. It was a horrendous journey lasting several weeks. On their return, Frau Hartmann and the boys settled in Weil im Schönbuch, not far from Stuttgart. They had been there six months when Dr Hartmann wrote to tell her that conditions in China had stabilized and it was now quite safe for her to return to him with the boys. She, however, preferred to raise the boys in Germany and persuaded her husband to return to set up a new practice there in Weil.

Elisabeth Hartmann, like her husband, was adventurous and had a keen interest in aviation and flying. Young Erich was developing a similar interest and was not discouraged by his mother when he attempted to build and fly an obviously unairworthy glider. His mother, meanwhile, decided to join a local flying club at the Böblingen aerodrome a few miles from Weil. She soon became a very good pilot and quickly earned her private flying licence. Within a year the Hartmanns acquired a part interest in a light plane and the family was able to enjoy flying with regularity in a time when few people had ever been near an aeroplane. In 1932, however, the economy was collapsing and the Hartmann's had no alternative but to sell the plane.

The following year the Nazis came to power in Germany and, in an effort to pave the way for a new German Air Force, began encouraging the formation of glider clubs. Erich's mother established such a club at Weil im Schönbuch in 1936 and took the boy to glider meets at the field each weekend. His younger brother Alfred remembered Erich being an excellent and gifted pilot with natural ability. By age fourteen, Erich was licensed and an instructor in the Glider Group of the Hitler Youth. He recalled that flying came naturally to him because he had seen his mother, his brother and many friends fly and he had flown so much himself that getting into an aeroplane was as comfortable as getting into a car. Of the two boys, Erich was the most accomplished in sports, with excellent coordination and considerable ability in athletics, swimming, diving, skiing and gymnastics. He was also a natural leader and a believer in fair play. He believed too, in meeting life's challenges directly and without hesitation, an essential quality in a successful fighter pilot. He was well-liked by most who met him and was open, honest and tolerant. He was courteous and respectful to elders and invariably looked for the positive aspects in life. Erich was only an average student in school, but he was highly competitive and devoted most of his spare time and energy to sport and flying.

At school he met and fell instantly in love with a girl named Ursula Paetsch, whom he called 'Usch' [pronounced Oosh]. It was 1939. Erich was seventeen and the world was about to change dramatically. The pair were all but inseperable until he graduated from the Korntal Hochschule shortly after his eighteenth birthday, in April 1940. The Second World War was under way and, knowing that he would soon have to serve in the military he decided to go for the air force. With his substantial experience in flying both gliders and powered aircraft, he felt more than ready. He read in the daily newspapers of the exploits of fighter pilots such as Johannes Steinhoff and Werner Mölders who had already become famous aces, and he longed to join their company and share their success. Dr Hartmann opposed the war and believed that Germany would lose, and both Erich's parents had mixed feelings about his plans, but believed that the decision was his. Usch shared their feelings and hated the prospect of being separated from Erich, but she, too, accepted his decision.

By mid-October 1940 the Battle of Britain was virtually over and Erich Hartmann was reporting to German Air Force Military Training Regiment 10 at Neukuhren, near Königsburg, determined to become a military flyer. His activities there included theory of flight, aircraft and engine design and construction, aviation history, aeronautical engineering, aerodynamics, and meteorology. He moved on to flying training at Berlin-Gatow airfield in March 1941 where he studied hard and did well, being highly motivated to succeed. His first flight with an instructor took place on 5 March, and on the 24th he was ready to solo. His many hours of prior flying experience had prepared him well and he completed his basic flight training in October and transitioned smoothly into advanced pilot training which he completed on 31 January, 1942, when he was posted to the fighter pilot school at Zerbst/Anhalt, near Magdeburg. He had already learned to fly seventeen different types of powered aircraft, but it was here that he would first encounter the Bf-109, the fighter in which he would excel for the remainder of the war. At the fighter base Erich was taught much of what the hot little 109 could do in the air, information and techniques that would serve him well in many air combat engagements. He learned quickly and became proficient in the excellent fighter plane. He then went on to learn about aerial gunnery in June 1942, becoming an expert in all aspects of the skill, even at a long distance from his target, though that would not play much of a part in his future combats. Late in the month, he went aloft to do his first aerial shooting at a drogue target sleeve. Of the alloted fifty rounds in his 7.62mm machine-guns, he managed to hit the sleeve twenty-four times, an impressive beginning. He clearly had promise.

Having graduated from fighter pilot training and commissioned a Second Lieutenant on 31 March, 1942, Erich took an opportunity during his gunnery training to fly over to Zerbst and let off a bit of steam by doing some aerobatics over the airfield. He later paid for the unsanctioned display when he was confined to his room for a week and had $^2/_3$ of his pay forfeited for three months. He had always been a free spirit and still chafed at routine military discipline. Uniformity and conformity were not in his nature. Of the incident he recalled:

That week confined in my room actually saved my life. I had been scheduled to go up on a gunnery flight the afternoon that I was confined. My roommate took the flight instead of me, in an aircraft I had been scheduled to fly. Shortly after he took off, while on the way to the gunnery range, he developed engine trouble and had to crash-land near the Hindenburg-Kattowitz railroad. He was killed in the crash.

In its most polite form, the military acronym SNAFU stands for Situation Normal All Fouled Up. It is a condition common in armies, navies and air forces the world over. Erich Hartmann and three other young *Luftwaffe* Second Lieutenants arrived at Krakau, south of Warsaw on their way to their first combat posting as fighter pilots, JG-52 on the Eastern Front. The commanding officer at the Krakau *Luftwaffe* supply base could find no records assigning replacement Bf-109 aircraft for the men to deliver to JG-52 at its Maykop base in the Caucasus. What he did have on offer were a number of Ju-87 Stuka dive-bombers that he needed to ferry down to Mariupol, a short distance from Maykop. Though none of the four men had ever flown a Stuka, they agreed to take the planes to the base in their transit to Maykop and soon were sitting in the cockpits of the odd-looking bent-wing aircraft, looking over the instrumentation and other panel detail. After starting the engine and doing the run-up and other checks, Hartmann eased the ungainly plane out of its dispersal and off in the direction of the runway. On approaching the take-off end of the runway he spotted a controller's wooden hut and toed the left brake to steer the aircraft around the hut. The brake failed to respond so he then tromped on both brakes to bring the Stuka to a halt, but still to no avail. In the next seconds the controller fled and an instant later the plane ripped into the hut, destroying it and the controller's logbooks.

Of the other three new pilots, one had taken off only to develop engine trouble almost immediately. He struggled to bring the unfamiliar aircraft around for an emergency landing, which he managed reasonably well, but in the rollout he applied a little too much pressure on the brakes and the Stuka went over onto its nose. The furious base commander surveyed the damage and told the young pilots that their services in the ferrying role would no longer be required and they would be travelling to Maykop by Ju-52 transport, with another *Luftwaffe* pilot doing the flying.

During the flight to his new base, Erich learned that significant air combat action was under way as much as 750 miles into Soviet territory. On landing at Maykop, the four young pilots were met by the adjutant of JG-52 who took them to meet their new commanding officer, Colonel Dieter Hrabak. The impression Hrabak made on the new men, was somewhat startling. His uniform was unpressed and showed oil stains on the trousers, his boots were muddy and he presented quite a contrast to his trim and neatly dressed adjutant. But he greeted and quickly briefed the new pilots in such a way that they came away convinced of his competence and professionalism. At that point Hrabak had achieved more than sixty confirmed victories and wore the Knight's Cross of the Iron Cross. And he gave them something serious to think about:

> Up to now, all your training has emphasized controlling your aircraft
> on operations, that is, making your muscles obey your will in flying
> your aircraft. To survive in Russia and be successful fighter pilots you

must now develop your thinking. You must act aggressively always, of course, or you will not be successful, but the aggressive spirit must be tempered with cunning, judgement and intelligent thinking. Fly with your head and not your muscles.

In the Russian campaign, Hitler was 'flying' with his muscles rather than his head, relying entirely on another *blitzkrieg* attack of short duration to bring him victory in six to eight weeks. He intended to occupy Moscow within two months. Still lacking a strategic bomber, however, and not by any means restored to full strength after its Battle of Britain losses, his air force could not deliver the sort of destruction needed to subdue a country of Russia's size and diversity in any reasonable time frame. The heavily armed and armoured *blitzkrieg* had to succeed. The Führer was betting the whole war on a single roll of the dice.

With virtually no reserves, a shortage of the kind of air power required, and some of the most punishing winter days and nights on record in the offing, it would prove to be among the worst and most costly adventure of any armed force in history. Under-strength and near exhaustion, the German Air Force was assigned to lead the army advance on Moscow. Starting Operation Barbarossa later than originally planned, neither the army nor the air force went into it with winterized equipment or proper winter clothing for their personnel who would all suffer terribly in the savage Soviet cold. Their Russian enemy, by contrast, was appropriately equipped and well trained for combat in the conditions. The paralyzing winter cold ground the German offensive to a dead stop, giving the Russians additional time to regroup, rearm and get ready for the fight of their lives.

In the beginning of the campaign the weather was not yet the enemy it would become, and the Germans made considerable progress in their lightning run towards the Russian capital, capturing enemy troops by the hundreds of thousands along with their armour and equipment in great quantities. They also dealt a heavy blow to the Soviet Air Force, destroying much of it in the first weeks. The bulk of this destruction, however, was aircraft, not pilots or air crew, or aircraft production facilities. The Russians quickly relocated entire factories for the production of vital armaments and war matériel well to the east of the battle fronts. They were then producing fighter planes at the rate of three to one over German fighter production, and they were receiving more than 500 supplemental fighter aircraft through British and American Lend-Lease agreements. It must be remembered, too, that all the Russian fighter production output, as well as the Lend-Lease aircraft, were allocated for Eastern Front operations, while Germany's total aircraft production had to be apportioned among the operations on the Channel Front, the Mediterraniean, North Africa, and the Eastern Front, as well as the German nightfighter force. By late 1944, the Soviet aircraft plants had built nearly 100,000 combat planes and they had been provided with 14,700 aircraft by their Allied partners. The majority of these Lend-Lease aircraft were fighters, Bell P-39 Airacobras and P-63 Kingcobras, Curtiss P-40 Tomahawks, Hawker Hurricanes, Supermarine Spitfires, and a small number of Republic P-47 Thunderbolts and North American P-51 Mustangs. Most of these aircraft were inferior technologically to their German opponents, the Messerschmitt Bf-109 and the Focke-Wulf Fw-190, and most of the Russian pilots were not as well trained or proficient as their German counterparts. Without a long-range, four-engined heavy bomber, the Germans could not reach the Russian arms factories to put them out of production. The massive output of these factories, coupled with the kind of weather the Germans would soon face, ultimately cost Hitler his predicted victory.

Of the Lend-Lease aircraft, Erich Hartmann said:

The Airacobra and the Kingcobra were valuable to the Russians in my opinion not because of their flying performance, which was inferior both to Russian-designed fighters and to the Me-109. They were markedly superior, however, in weapons and the weapons system. They had a big edge over contemporary Russian aircraft in this respect. The gunsight on Russian fighters at this time was often only a circle on the windshield. I mean a hand-painted circle on the windshield.

Then came the Airacobra, Kingcobra, Tomahawk, and Hurricane, and all had gunsights of modern Western design. From this time on, the Russians began to shoot the same way we did. In the earlier days, incredible as it may seem, there was no reason to feel fear if the Russian fighter was behind you. With their hand-painted 'gunsights' they couldn't pull lead properly or hit you – other than by luck. But after the lend-lease aircraft came in and the Russians got on to the gunsights, it was very different – especially from longer distances.

Before becoming a renowned *Luftwaffe* fighter leader and high-scoring ace, Adolf Galland flew close-support missions and essentially wrote the book on such operations for the German Air Force (GAF). On the employment of German bombers in the Russian campaign, Galland recalled:

The German Air Force was not used as an air force, but as advanced artillery. This was not the correct way to use bombers, dropping bombs on the enemy's front line. That is the job of the artillery. The air force must attack where the enemy's nerves meet. The *Luftwaffe* misused the bombers because the army wanted to see the immediate visual results in support of its operations. The bombers should have been attacking airfields, railroads and bridges behind the lines. But you don't see the real results from such attacks immediately. The effects come later, in days or weeks. This was not satisfying to the German Army.

The *Luftwaffe* taught the army to use aviation in direct support, which is correct in certain circumstances, but it was not taught as a universal principle. The *Luftwaffe* was wasted in continuing close-support operations. This approach resulted in the air force leading the army instead of just supporting it. The army was then forced to advance and occupy the zone attacked by the close air support, so often in Russia it was the *Luftwaffe* and not the army that started an offensive in a given area. Often Hitler gave the orders to Goering or Jeschonnek, and they would pass the orders on to von Richthofen or another commander to move the army ahead. The army commanders would often object, saying 'We do not have sufficient forces, or artillery, or transport.' When this got back to Hitler he would simply say to the *Luftwaffe*, 'Move the army ahead.'

Inspired by Colonel Hrabak, Erich Hartmann looked forward to his assignment with his new unit, III/JG-52, as he boarded the Ju-52 transport on 10 October, 1942, that would fly him to the group's airfield at Soldatskaya, north of the Caucasus mountains near the Terek River. At the unit headquarters he and the other new pilots met their group commander, Major von Bonin, a hardened veteran fighter pilot of the Spanish Civil War Condor Legion days, when he had shot down four aircraft. He had downed nine more while with JG-26 during the Battle of Britain and, to date, forty more on the Eastern Front. An old man of thirty-two, von Bonin impressed the young men he welcomed to Soldatskaya:

Only aerial victories count here, not rank or other trivia. On the ground, we have military discipline, but in the air each element is always led by the pilot with the most aerial victories and the greatest combat skill and experience. If I fly with a sergeant who has more victories than I, then he leads the element. This eliminates all question between pilots as to who is to lead. There is never any dispute, because only victories count.

In the air, in battle, you'll say things you'll never say on the ground – especially to a superior officer. Under the strain and tension of combat this is unavoidable. Everything that passes in the way of comments – even abuse – in the air, is forgotten the moment you land.

You young second lieutenants will mostly be flying with sergeants. They'll be your leaders in the air. Never let me hear that you didn't follow their orders in the air because of rank.

Soon Erich met Sergeant Eduard 'Paule' Rossmann. He would fly as Rossmann's wingman. The sergeant was jovial, somewhat melodramatic and equipped with a good sense of humour; not a typical fighter pilot in many ways, but he would prove to be the best mentor Erich could have possibly had. With a record of more than eighty aerial victories to that point, Rossmann was highly regarded for his skills by the other officers of III/JG-52. Erich was also favourably impressed by Heinz Mertens, the man who was to be his ground crew chief from when they first met until the end of the war.

The day came for Erich's first combat mission with his new unit. It was 14 October 1942. Flying two Bf-109 G-4 'Gustavs', he and Rossmann were assigned to make a fighter sweep between Digora and Groznyy and had just become airborne when they were ordered by radio to attack seven Russian fighters and three Il-2 Stormovik dive-bombers that had been observed strafing roads near Prokhladnyy. Hartmann and Rossmann were flying at an altitude of 12,000 feet, following the Terek River towards Prokhladnyy. After about 15 minutes the sergeant sighted the enemy aircraft and called for Erich to close in on him as they attacked. They had dived more than 5,000 feet and levelled off before Erich finally spotted two of the dark green-painted Russian planes about 1,000 yards ahead and slightly higher than he and Rossmann. Erich anticipated making his first kill. With his throttle wide open he overtook Rossmann and quickly closed to within 300 yards of the enemy aircraft. He immediately began firing and was dismayed at how far to the left of the target his tracers appeared. Now the enemy plane was filling his windscreen rapidly and a mid-air collision was barely avoided when Erich managed to pull up and away at the last possible second. With no time to think about his miraculous escape, he found himself in the middle of a swarm of Russian aircraft, all of them jockeying for firing position behind him. He'd lost sight of Rossmann and could think of nothing but eluding his pursuers. Spotting a cloud layer above, he whipped the 109 over and climbed for the cloud that he hoped would offer both sanctuary and a chance to collect his thoughts. He was soon in clear blue sky and the R/T crackled with Rossman's voice: "Don't sweat it. I watched your tail. I've lost you now that you've climbed through the clouds. Come down below the layer so I can pick you up again." Descending from the cloud, Erich panicked when he noticed another aircraft chasing him. At full throttle he headed down to tree-top level. Rossmann's voice continued to break the silence but the transmission was garbled and Erich could not understand what his leader was saying. To make himself a smaller target, he crouched down behind his cockpit armour against the imminent arrival of enemy shells and bullets. Within a few minutes he somehow eluded the pursuing plane as Rossmann's garbled comments persisted over the R/T. At that point the red fuel warning light flashed on his panel, indicating that only 5 minutes of fuel remained.

It seemed seconds rather than minutes. His powerful Daimler-Benz engine began to cough and then it quit. At a height of just 1,000 feet he was coming down rapidly towards a road crowded with military vehicles. There was no time to do anything but guide the falling fighter into a reasonably flat belly-landing alongside the road. The slithering Messerschmitt threw up a massive dust cloud in its wake. In seconds German soldiers rescued Hartmann and within minutes a staff car was carrying him back to his base at nearby Soldatskaya where there awaited a savage reprimand, first from Major von Bonin and then Sergeant Rossmann.

The sergeant powered through a catalogue of Erich's errors and indiscretions in this his first combat experience: leaving his leader without permission, flying into and interfering with his leader's firing position, disappearing through the cloud layer, mistaking his leader's aircraft for that of an enemy pilot (the plane that had been chasing Erich as he emerged from the cloud layer was Rossmann), failing to obey his leader's orders to rejoin, losing his orientation and position, and, not least in importance, destroying his own aircraft without even having damaged an enemy aircraft. The mortified Hartmann was then punished by von Bonin who sentenced him to three days working on the ground with the fitters and armourers for his many breaches of aerial discipline. Not a good start for the future ace of all aces.

With time, many opportunities came for Erich to fly with and learn from the wily Rossmann. In the mould of Dieter Hrabak, Paule Rossmann flew with his head rather than his muscles. He flew with a religious dedication to the surprise attack and he invariably approached encounters with the enemy by briefly assessing the possibility for such an attack and only proceeding with the action if the element of surprise was available to him. To Erich, Rossmann's method was impressive, not only for the aerial success it achieved, but for the safety factor it provided. The sergeant gained his victories without taking hits himself. And flying with Rossmann gradually developed in Erich the ability to spot enemy aircraft at great distances, assess the situation, and operate as a leader/wingman team, efficiently and safely. He noted that, as new pilots arrived at Soldatskaya to replace dead, wounded and captured fliers, few of the older hands showed much willingness to nurture and ease the transition of the new men through the hard-learned methods and practices of the group. He would always be grateful to Rossmann for the marvellous mentoring the sergeant had given him. He firmly believed that he owed his life and much of his considerable combat success to Paule Rossmann, whose patience and wise counsel had, from that first mission experience, prepared him to meet the demands of the long war ahead. As he advanced in rank and responsibility within the unit, Erich took it upon himself to pass on as much knowlege as he could to new men on the squadron, in appreciation of all that Rossmann had given him:

> I made it a rule of my life to do this after my experience with Rossmann. I was a young boy, blind like a kitten. Suppose they had started me off with a tough and ruthless leader – we had plenty of

them. I was rigid with fear of what might happen to me as it was, even with Rossmann's reassuring presence. He not only brought me through this critical period, but he taught me the basic technique of the surprise attack, without which I am convinced I would have become just another dogfighter, assuming that I didn't get the thing that I sat on shot off first.

Then came the day of Erich Hartmann's first aerial victory, 5 November 1942. On this day he would fly with the group commander's adjutant, a First Lieutenant Treppe. They were operating in a four-plane *schwarm* near Digora around midday and it was Erich who first sighted the eighteen Il-2 Stormoviks with their escort of ten Lagg-3 fighters. Having been the first man to spot the enemy aircraft, he was ordered by Treppe to lead the German attack. The 109s split into two two-ship elements which then dived separately on the unsuspecting Russians that were busily attacking German transport targets. Down near ground level the Germans ripped into the Stormoviks and Erich watched as his machine-gun bullets and cannon shells hit and bounced off the armour of the enemy dive-bombers. Erich had heard the stories of how well-protected the Stormovik was and how difficult they were to bring down. He also knew that they had a vulnerability, a weak spot on their undersides and he decided to exploit it.

Going around in a second pass on the enemy planes, Erich manoeuvred his Messerschmitt as low as he dared in an effort to get even lower than the Stormovik he was after. When he judged that he was about 200 feet behind and slightly below the target aircraft, he fired and watched with some satisfaction as a long tail of thick black smoke erupted from the oil cooler of the Stormovik, followed almost immediately by flame which soon enveloped the sturdy Russian craft. Erich followed it as the Russian slowly drifted out of its formation in a shallow descent. Then a small explosion occurred under the wing of the Stormovik. Bits flew off, some of them blasting back into the path of Erich's machine, which lurched briefly and began pouring smoke from under the cowling, some seeping into his cockpit. Again, he would have to belly-land and he got ready by turning off his fuel master switch and ignition. He set the crippled plane down successfully and stepped out. As he left the plane he glanced up in time to see the demise of his Il-2 a little over a mile away. Lieutenant Treppe had witnessed Erich's first kill and now circled overhead to satisfy himself that Hartmann was all right. Erich had come down well behind German lines and was once again delivered from his situation back to his base by nearby German infantrymen. Over the next few weeks he contemplated this mission and critiqued his own performance. He was learning fast and on the way he made up his mind that no enemy pilot was going to shoot down his friend and guide, Paule Rossmann, while he was around to protect him. Rossmann had shown Erich that there could be success in surprise attacks and in sharpshooting from a distance without exposure to the hazards of conventional aerial dogfighting. Now he would spend some time flying in company with a few of the unit's best dogfighters, to help round out his education.

Most of the other successful aces of III/JG-52 were conventional dogfighters and Erich soon became familiar with their techniques and the ways in which they differed from Rossmann's. He had great faith in Rossmann's methods but would learn a number of useful tricks from the other veterans as well. One of these men was Alfred Grislawski, a miner's son and a Knight's Cross winner who would survive the war with 133 victories and the addition of the Oak Leaves to his Knight's cross. It was Grislawski who had told Erich of the vulnerability of the oil cooler under the Il-2 Stormovik. As a wingman in this period, Erich was far too busy shooing enemy planes away from his leaders to get many opportunities of his own for air combat. In the air it was Grislawski's way to tease and cajole Erich, and frequently curse him in order to mould the sort of fighter wingman Grislawski wanted. He indulged in taunts and threats and even referred to Erich as a 'baby-face' in front of other pilots, which led to Erich being called 'Bubi', 'boy.' In assigning Erich to Grislawski, Major von Bonin had arranged for just the kind of harsh disciplinarian that he believed Erich needed, and in time Erich would agree that the major's decision was correct. The nickname stuck and thereafter he was known as Erich 'Bubi' Hartmann. Gradually – through observation and experience – he was coming to believe that the best method for success as a fighter pilot might be a combination of the Rossmann surprise tactic and point blank shooting from very close in to the enemy aircraft.

It was not until 27 February, 1943, that Erich achieved his second aerial victory, an event which roughly coincided with the arrival on the squadron of Walter Krupinski, the new unit commander at their recently occupied base, Taman Kuban. Erich had first seen Krupinski the day he and the other three new pilots had arrived at Maykop en route to their initial posting. Krupinski had been airborne that day, engaged in a dogfight and then shot down, apparently by flak. He had crash-landed on the airfield not far from where Erich was standing and had emerged miraculously from the inferno of his wrecked Messerschmitt fighter, smiling and only slightly injured. Now, at Taman Kuban, he wasted no time after introducing himself to the unit pilots, commandeered an armed and serviced Bf-109 and took off. Airborne, he found and engaged an enemy aircraft and was promptly shot down. Undaunted, he returned to the field, took off again in another fighter, located a flight of enemy planes, shot down two of them and returned triumphantly to Taman, where the other pilots, including Erich, were most impressed by his performance.

Walter Krupinski was a complex officer, commissioned late in 1941, a former wingman of the renowned Johannes 'Macky' Steinhoff, and a well-known ace in his own right with more than seventy victories to his credit. He was a rather odd combination of playboy and tough, deadly-serious air fighter who would survive the war with a score of 197 kills after serving with Adolf Galland's elite jet fighter squadron, JV-44. Before joining Erich's unit, he had experienced more than his fair share of crash-landings, bale-outs and minor wounds. It was with some trepidation that Erich Hartmann introduced himself to Krupinski as the latter's new wingman. Krupinski asked Erich how long he had been with the outfit and who he had been flying with. Satisfied, he told Erich that he thought they would get along all right. In the beginning it was a somewhat difficult relationship, but they soon adjusted to each other and became an effective team against the enemy. Krupinski constantly urged Erich to get in closer to his target and the closer he got, the more effective his shooting became. He found that the majority of the enemy aircraft he targetted at close range exploded under the weight of his strikes. He soon perfected his own four-part approach to air fighting: See, Decide, Attack, and Depart. By that he meant: Spot the enemy aircraft, determine whether a surprise attack is possible in the situation, make the attack and then break away immediately after it. Do not get into a turning dogfight with an enemy who knows you are there. Throughout his long series of missions, he tried never to deviate from this tactic.

Socially, Erich and Krupinski got along well and partied together wherever they were. Erich recalled: 'From Krupinski I eagerly learned many bad things'.

While flying with Walter Krupinski, Erich won the Iron Cross 2nd Class after shooting down his fifth enemy aircraft. He came away from their operations together with the view that survival was the most important consideration and never to lose a wingman. In the entire course of his long, distinguished aerial career, Erich lost just one wingman, a former bomber pilot who had been sent to fly fighters near the end of the war. Erich believed that the man, Major Günther Capito, had been shot down (he survived) simply through lack of experience in fighters. Capito had long been badgering Erich for a chance to fly as his wingman and Erich had always discouraged him in the belief that Capito was insufficiently trained on fighters and was not yet up to the challenge and demands of the job. But Capito continued to pester Erich for the opportunity and he relented, briefing Capito on the vital need to stay in close to him through the extreme turns of air combat. They took off and after a bit were bounced by two elements of Russian Airacobras. Erich:

I let the Russian fighters close in to firing range, calling to Capito to stay close to me. It was just the kind of situation concerning which I had briefed him earlier. When the Russians fired, I broke into them horizontally in a very steep turn, but Capito could not stay with me. He made a standard-rate bomber turn. After a 180° turn he and the attacking Airacobras were opposite me. I called to him to turn hard opposite, so that I could sandwich the Red fighters, but in his second standard-rate bomber turn he got hit. I saw the whole thing and ordered him to dive and bale out immediately. To my intense relief I saw him leave the aircraft and his parachute blossom, but was brassed off at his inability to follow instructions. I got behind the Airacobra, closed right in, and after a short burst the enemy fighter went down and crashed with a tremendous explosion about 2 miles from Capito's touchdown point by parachute and about a mile from our base. I was happy to get this Airacobra down, but I was mad at myself for not harkening to my intuition not to fly with Günther Capito.

On landing, Erich took a car and went out to collect Capito. They then drove on to the crash site of the Airacobra. On impact with the ground the Russian pilot, a Captain, had been thrown from the plane and killed. In more than 1,400 air combat missions, this was the only one in which a wingman of Erich Hartmann met misfortune. Capito was shaken and humbled by the experience. Only later that evening, when the other pilot's of the squadron threw the traditional 'birthday party', held when one of their number survived being shot down, did he start to recover from the events of the day.

Von Bonin was replaced as Group Commander by Günther Rall, who would finish the war as the third highest scoring ace in history with 275 confirmed victories. Rall promoted Hartmann to commander of the 9th Squadron in August 1943. By July Erich was excelling himself, his score well into double figures. On one occasion he downed four Lagg-5s and three Stormoviks, for a total of seven victories in a single day. Always keeping what he had learned from Rossmann in mind, he was still reluctant to get in too close in his attacks. He realized, though, that the closer he forced himself to go before firing, the greater his success. By 3 August his victory total reached 50. He was still 'Bubi' to the other pilots, but now he was also a mature fighter leader.

On 17 August Hartmann's score reached 80 victories, tying that of Baron Manfred von Richthofen of First World War fame. His combat days with multiple victories had become relatively commonplace and by the end of September his score had passed that of the late Werner Mölders: 115, and he achieved his 150th victory on 29 October. For that feat he received the award of the Knight's Cross of the Iron Cross. In the air his callsign had become Karaya One (Sweetheart One) and the business-like profile of his Bf-109 fighter was adorned with a large, red heart which had an arrow through it and the name Usch painted on it.

A great part of any fighter pilot's success must be credited to his ground crew chief, the man who keeps his aircraft in perfect running order. In Heinz 'Bimmel' Mertens, Erich knew that he had a mechanic and friend whose devotion and amazing skill were unparalleled.

My closest relationship was with Heinz Mertens, my crew chief. You rely upon your wingman to cover you in the air, and your team mates in aerial battle, but the man who keeps your machine flying and safe is the most important man you know. We became best of friends, and none of my success would have been possible if not for Mertens.

19 August. The Russians were on the move and making substantial progress towards the area where Erich was based. In the morning hours a response was being activated by Colonel Dieter Hrabak, Commodore of JG-52. Hrabak briefed Erich on the enemy action. The Russians had broken through German lines and were on the verge of surrounding a large contingent of the German Army. He ordered that Erich take his squadron up on the first mission of the day, to clear the air of enemy fighter-bombers and protect the German's Stuka dive-bombers in the area. Should the enemy aircraft fail to appear, Erich and his pilots were to strafe the Russian infantrymen. Erich briefed his men and they were off. A Lieutenant Puls was flying as his wingman and the other six pilots of his unit were all seasoned and confident airmen. Erich knew that in them he had a formidable force.

Approaching the battle area, the German pilots scanned the sky and sighted roughly forty Stormoviks bombing the German infantry. Additionally, there were about forty Russian fighters, Yak-9s and Lagg-5s, flying protective cover for the dive-bombers. Erich led his pilots down, knifing through the enemy fighters, shooting as they went. The 109s emerged from the Russian fighter mass unscathed and began manoeuvring to attack the Stormoviks. Erich selected one and approached it from directly behind and beneath the Russian, not shooting until the enemy plane completely filled his windscreen when he was about 75 yards from the Russian. Then, firing a single short burst, he was gratified to see the dive-bomber explode, its left wing separating from the fuselage. Erich did not pause to relish the moment, but banked away sharply to get on the tail of another Il-2. He quickly closed on the second plane, whose pilot was busy strafing German ground troops. At a distance of 50 yards, gunfire burst from Karaya One and the Russian machine flashed into flame. Erich pulled up and over his victim and was startled by a rapid series of bangs from his own aircraft. A large piece of his engine cowling flew off and a plume of smoke appeared, some of it entering the cockpit. He still had control of the Messerschmitt, but realized that the plane was finished as he coaxed it through a hard turn to the west. He spotted a large field of sunflowers and nursed the little fighter into it as gently as he could. When Karaya One had slithered to a stop among the tall flower stalks, he felt sure he was behind German lines and paid little attention to the truck approaching his wrecked plane. He concentrated on removing the clock from his instrument panel, for clocks were in short supply and, like pilots, needed to be rescued.

As the truck stopped near the site of his belly-landing, Erich realized that it was a captured German vehicle in the hands of two Russian soldiers.

There was no chance for escape for him and he decided to feign injury from the crash-landing. The Russians got down from their truck and walked over to the Messerschmitt. Erich groaned and yelled in pain as the pair tried to lift him from the cockpit. They seemed to believe that he was genuinely injured and carefully eased him out of the plane. He then collapsed on the ground and they retrieved a canvas sheet from the truck and used it as a stretcher to move Erich into the truck bed. They drove him back to their headquarters and brought a doctor to attend to him. Erich even managed to convince the doctor that he was injured. In a few hours the two soldiers reappeared and carried him back to the truck to take him further behind the Russian lines. As they drove they heard the sound of approaching Stuka dive-bombers which passed low overhead. One of the soldiers was driving while the other guarded Erich on the bed of the vehicle. When the Stukas came over the soldier guarding their captive was briefly distracted by the planes and Erich took advantage of the opportunity to attack the guard, taking him by surprise. Erich leapt from the truck into the field of six-foot tall sunflowers. As he ran he heard shots, and bullets spattered through nearby plants. The two soldiers were in pursuit but soon lost track of him. Erich continued to run for several minutes, putting as much distance between himself and his captors as he could. He came to a pleasant little valley filled with wild flowers, trees and a meandering stream. He estimated that he was still on the Russian side of the front lines, but relatively close to the nearest German troops. From his hiding place he could see a number of Russian soldiers and peasants, and decided to lie low for rest of the day and wait for the cover of darkness before resuming his trek. He slept until dusk.

Hartmann's crew chief, Bimmel Mertens, was greatly upset about his pilot's failure to return from the mission and remained out on the flight line long after he knew that Karaya One's fuel would have been exhausted. Erich's wingman, Lieutenant Puls, had seen his leader go down, trailing smoke, but in the mêlée with the eighty Russian planes, none of the other German pilots could confirm Erich's loss. Hours later, with still no word about Erich, Mertens decided to act on his own. He grabbed a rifle and a water canteen and told his comrades that he was going out to find his pilot and bring him in. When questioned about the wisdom of such an action, Mertens said that he spoke Russian and was sure he would receive help from the peasants near the front lines.

As darkness fell, Erich began walking in the direction of the German lines, moving slowly and cautiously through another field of giant sunflowers. At one point he heard the sounds of an enemy reconnaissance patrol moving through the field and decided to follow them, at a safe distance, hoping they were heading towards the front. After a while, Erich heard a staccatto rattle of automatic weapons fire from the direction of the patrol ahead. As he approached, he came across the bodies of the patrol soldiers and knew that German infantry had to be very near. Erich guessed that it must be around midnight. He continued walking westward for another two hours and began to hear distant sounds of artillery fire. Then, a challenging command: "Halten!" followed instantly by the crack of a rifle shot and a bullet tearing into his trouser leg but, luckily, missing his leg. He shouted to whoever had fired at him, and then cursed the man, yelling that he was a German pilot and not to shoot, for Christ's sake. "I'm a German pilot who has been shot down. I've been walking for hours from behind the Russian lines. For God's sake, let me come through." The German sentry prodded Erich in the back with his rifle muzzle until they reached a foxhole occupied by the commanding officer of the little unit, a second lieutenant who interrogated him. Unfortunately, the Russian guards had taken everything from his pockets leaving him without any identification. All he could do was provide the officer with his name, rank and the approximate location where he had been shot down the previous morning. He asked the lieutenant to telephone his wing headquarters to confirm his identity, but the officer had no phone. He gave Erich a little food and allowed him to sleep in a foxhole. At first light, a young corporal escorted Erich to a head-quarters company where they were able to contact Colonel Hrabak at Kuteynikovo, the JG-52 base. Hrabak confirmed Erich's identity and the infantry lieutenant had him driven back to base where he heard, to his distress, that Bimmel Mertens, his loyal crew chief, had gone out searching for him, risking his own life. The next day Mertens returned, exhausted and dejected – until Erich appeared. Years later Mertens recalled that it was the happiest moment of his life, seeing that his pilot was safe and well.

The winter of 1943-44 in that part of Russia was as brutal as any in living memory. The brutality would have come as no surprise to the soldiers of the Red Army, who were properly dressed and equipped for it, both physically and psychologically, but for their invading enemy it was savage and demanding beyond anything they had ever known. Inadequately clothed German troops suffered and died in many thousands from the weather alone, while many more thousands lost ears, fingers, toes and limbs to the effects of frostbite. Tanks, trucks, and all types of powered vehicles became unserviceable as their oil and lubricants congealed in the extreme cold; while others became bogged down and virtually immoveable in thigh-high mud. The German airmen, whose living conditions were only slightly better than those of the infantrymen, found that equipment problems frequently kept them grounded. They, and their crew chiefs, were amazed when day after sub-zero day, dozens of Russian fighter planes overflew the German airfields, on mornings when no Bf-109 or Ju-87 could even be started. It was only when a captured Russian pilot was brought to Erich's squadron that the Germans overcame their troubles. The pilot was proud to cooperate with his captors by teaching them how the Russians coped with stubborn aero engines in -40° temperatures. He asked for a small amount of gasoline in a filler can and carried it over to a nearby Bf-109 fighter and shocked the watching JG-52 personnel as he poured the gasoline into the plane's oil sump. The Germans were certain that the plane would explode when the engine start-up was attempted. A nervous German pilot sat in the cockpit as mechanics hand-cranked the motor and the gasoline mixed with the congealed oil. The Russian called for ignition and the powerful Daimler-Benz engine roared into life quite normally. Through an interpreter the Russian airman said that the 'frozen' oil prevented the aero engines from starting, but the gasoline liquefied the oil and, after engine start-up, evaporated in the warm-up. He further explained that, for safety, it would be necessary to change the engine oil more frequently when employing the gasoline-in-sub-zero starting procedure.

Later, another captured Russian airman offered his own advice on starting aero engines in those conditions. Placing a shallow spare-parts tray on the ground under the opened engine compartment of a 109, he then filled the tray with gasoline, dropped a lighted match onto the tray and jumped back as the gasoline ignited. The flames from the tray continued warming the engine area for nearly ten minutes. Again, the sceptical German fliers and ground crew worried that the fire would ruin the electrical system of the fighter, but when the flames finally died out the Russian prisoner told them to start the engine. It started immediately and ran smoothly. The prisoner then went on to explain how to keep the guns of the 109 functioning properly in the dreadful temperatures. He ignored the recommendation of the *Luftwaffe* armament manual that the guns should be carefully greased and lubricated, pointing out the congealed grease on a machine-gun that had been removed from one of the aircraft. He then placed the entire gun in a tank of boiling water. The hot water flushed the grease and oil from the weapon. It was then tested and functioned perfectly.

By the autumn of 1943, many Russian Air Force pilots had become familiar with a particular Bf-109. They recognized it as the mount of an especially accomplished killer whom they referred to as 'the Black Devil of the South'. Erich Hartmann had had the nose of Karaya One painted with a pattern of pointed black tulip petals running back from the propeller spinner and around the circumference of the engine cowling. The Russians did not know the identity of the pilot, but most of them knew to avoid combat with him, if possible. A legend was building around the spectre of this Messerschmitt and soon they had placed a 10,000 ruble bounty on the Black Devil. But fear of encountering the Devil overcame the financial inducement for most Russian pilots and Erich found that he was having less contact with enemy aircraft. They were clearly avoiding him and his downing of enemy planes was decreasing markedly. So, he decided that anonymity in the air was the better course and had Bimmel Mertens repaint Karaya One to look like all the other Bf-109s of the unit. The effect of the change was dramatic. In the sixty days before the end of February 1944, he achieved more than 50 aerial victories, running his score to over 150 in the more than 500 sorties he had flown since joining JG-52.

JG-52 was the highest-scoring Fighter Wing in the German Air Force, credited with more than 10,000 aerial victories in 4 years of the war. The nature of the Wing and its competitive environment made it a breeding ground for fighter aces including the three highest-achieving aces of Germany, the war, and all time, Erich Hartmann with 352 victories, Gerhard Barkhorn with 301, and Günther Rall with 275. Others among the high-scoring pilots of the Wing are Wilhelm Batz with 237, Hermann Graf with 212, Helmut Lipfert with 203, Walter Krupinski with 196, Johannes Steinhoff with 176 and Heinz Schmidt with 173. Together, the spectacular total of enemy aircraft destroyed by just these nine pilots was 2,025.

The scores of enemy aircraft downed by pilots of the *Luftwaffe* in World War Two will seem to be greatly exaggerated to those not familiar with the differences in the confirmation and crediting procedures of the various air forces in that conflict. Authors Trevor J. Constable and Colonel Raymond F. Toliver, in the research for their book *Horrido!* devoted years to determining the thoroughness and accuracy of the German system, its mechanics and how it compared with that of the Americans and the British. For years after the war British and American historians were sceptical about the scores credited by the Germans to the fighter pilots of the *Luftwaffe*, suspicious of so many extraordinarily high scores. The efforts of Constable and Toliver in examining German official documents, records, procedures, logbooks, and wing histories, and interviewing German aces, have clearly established for many, if not most historians, the credibility of the German victory claims system and shown it to be considerably more rigid, precise and valid than either the British or American systems.

In the British and American approach to victory scoring, partial credit was often given for the destruction of an enemy plane if more than one pilot was believed to have shared in the downing. Under the German system, if more than one pilot was involved in such an action, the pilots had to decide between themselves which of them deserved the kill credit. In an impasse, the credit for the kill was awarded to the pilot's unit, with no individual pilot credited. Without a witness, a victory claim by a *Luftwaffe* fighter pilot could not be confirmed. The final destruction or explosion of an enemy aircraft in the air, or the bale-out of the pilot, had to be observed either on gun-camera film or by at least one other human witness. The witness could be the German pilot's wingman, a squadron mate, or a ground observer of the encounter. There were no exceptions to this rule, up to and including the credits of the General of the Fighter Arm, Adolf Galland. Authors Constable and Toliver obtained a copy of one of Galland's own combat reports of a downing claim which ends with Galland's statement: 'I resign the confirmation of this victory for lack of a witness.' The German system of accreditation was impartial and inflexible.

It was also linked directly to a points system relating to the award of the highest German military decorations, a system with no British or American counterpart. The German points system was only in effect on the Western Front and applied only to decoration awards and not to the accreditation of pilot claims. Points were awarded as follows: single-engined plane destroyed = 1 point, twin-engined plane destroyed = 2 points, three-engined plane destroyed = 3 points, four-engined plane destroyed = 3 points, twin-engined plane damaged = 1 point, three or four-engined plane damaged = 2 points, final destruction of a damaged twin-engined plane = ½ point, final destruction of a damaged four-engined plane = 1 point. Toliver and Constable:

> This point-decoration system was used only on the Western Front, because the Germans believed it was easier to shoot down Russian fighters and bombers on the Eastern Front than to down Mustangs, Thunderbolts, and Mosquitos in the West. They considered the mighty Allied bomber streams, with their lethal volumes of protective fire and hordes of accompanying fighters, to be a far tougher proposition than Soviet air power. Although the point-decoration system for the Russian front was therefore not in effect, the kill-confirmation rules were the same. Late in the war, there were pilots on the Russian front with over 100 confirmed victories who had still to receive the Knight's Cross awarded for 40 points won in the West.

JG-52 is often referred to by historians and others as an 'elite Fighter Wing', for the quality of its pilots, for its achievement as the highest scoring and most successful fighter unit of the *Luftwaffe*, and not least, for the quality of its leadership during the war years, from the inspiration of Dietrich Hrabak and Hubertus von Bonin, to the dynamism and directness of Gunther Rall and Johannes Steinhoff.

The name of Dietrich Hrabak ranks 44th in the listing of the world's fighter aces, but in the view of those who knew and flew with him during the war, he ranks far higher. Dieter, as he was known by many of his wartime comrades, came from a small village near Leipzig. From his recollections of his teenage years he was fascinated by the exploits of Charles Lindbergh and the great aviators of the time. At age 20 he joined the German Navy and underwent naval officer's training before transferring to the *Luftwaffe* for pilot training in late 1935. At first he seemed less than gifted as an aviator, having wrecked several training planes in the course of his instruction, but he survived the course and qualified as a pilot the following year. His first posting was to a fighter group stationed at Bernburg. Through the assignment he met and became a friend of two outstanding future leaders of the *Luftwaffe*, Adolf Galland and Hannes Trautloft.

Hrabak was then assigned to a new fighter squadron at Bad Eibling which was led by Trautloft. In January 1939 Hrabak was given command of a squadron of mainly Austrian pilots and ground crews and this unit was moved to Upper Silesia in time to participate in the German invasion of Poland. It was not uncommon for a fighter pilot new to combat to be shot down within his first five missions. It was believed by many that, if a man could somehow survive those first five sorties, he would probably last a long time. Dieter was shot down in his first aerial combat, over Poland on 1 September 1939, one of the first German pilots to be downed in the war. He was brought down a total of seven times during the war, each time managing to crash-land his plane safely.

Following the Polish invasion, Squadron Leader Hrabak was assigned to JG-76, initially at Abbeville and then at Orléans, flying army support missions. His first aerial victory came on 13 May 1940, near the Meuse River by Sedan. The unit was protecting German troop movements crossing the river and the Trier-based Hrabak was leading a four-plane *schwarm* when they spotted a French Potez 63 reconnaissance aircraft. He was quickly in position to fire on the enemy plane and was rewarded when the left engine of the Potez began belching black smoke. It bellied-in near some German troops. As his four aircraft re-formed to return to Trier, they were bounced by nine Curtiss P-36 fighters, American aircraft purchased and flown by the French Air Force. All the German pilots had exhausted their ammunition and had no option but to run from the encounter. Hrabak remembered the experience as a good lesson for him and his pilots and vowed, never again, to waste all his bullets and shells on a single target, especially a low-value one.

The French adventure was followed by the Battle of Britain, during which Hrabak added many victories to his total and by the spring of 1941 this stood at 18. He then became a founding member of JG-54 Grunherz, the 'Green Heart' wing, whose Kommodore was Hannes Trautloft. After the Battle of Britain, Hrabak operated in support of the German Army in the invasion of Greece. His group was then sent to East Prussia to get ready for the invasion of Russia. He remained with JG-54 until October 1942 when he was promoted to Kommodore of JG-52, flying in the southern sector of the Russian Front. It was with JG-52 that his strength of character and his influence most affected the young pilots. He told them: 'If you come back from an operation with a kill but without your wingman, you lost your battle'. That message deeply impressed Erich Hartmann who never lost a wingman in his entire career as a fighter pilot.

Such was the level of admiration for Hrabak among the veteran pilots of the wing that when he reached 120 accredited victories, needing only five more to earn the Oak Leaves decoration to his Knight's Cross, his colleagues secretly conspired to fly with him on his next several missions. Their intention was to make absolutely sure that his back was protected while he accrued those five victories. It was, according to Hartmann, the finest tribute that they could pay to the leader they revered. They were honoured to go up and make sure he came back.

After the war Dieter Hrabak, like Gunther Rall, tried to enroll in university in Germany. He intended to study architecture to follow his father in that profession, but like Rall, he was denied admission because he was 'a militarist'. He then went to work for a machinery company where he eventually became sales manager. When organizational work began on the building of a new German Air Force under Chancellor Konrad Adenauer, Hrabak joined Johannes Steinhoff on the project and was one of the first German pilots to enter the jet fighter refresher course in the United States in 1955.

Of the many fine pilots who developed in the environment of JG-52, the man who was Erich Hartmann's closest rival in the German ace race and the second highest-scoring fighter pilot in history, was Gerhard 'Gerd' Barkhorn. Credited with 301 aerial victories, Barkhorn was highly regarded by virtually everyone in the Wing . . . as a father- or brother-figure, as a friend and certainly as one of the greatest fighter pilots ever. Much has been written about various flyers since the First World War who were celebrated as chivalrous 'knights of the air', but that reference is probably most aptly applied to Barkhorn who, in addition to his obvious aerial skills, is remembered by many as generous, honourable, chivalrous and merciful. Fighter pilots are, of course, trained to kill. In most cases, this may not be their primary motivation, but it is necessarily a part of their occupation. Barkhorn was unquestionably an efficient fighter pilot. Constable and Toliver:

> In combat his chivalrous spirit expressed itself frequently in a heroic quality that is often forgotten – mercy. Hartmann and others have told of Barkhorn's efforts, after disabling a Soviet aircraft, to persuade the pilot of the stricken machine to forsake his plane for a parachute, flying alongside his foe and gesturing for him to jump. Gerd Barkhorn never lost his humanity in the bitter Eastern Front struggle. He fought but did not hate. To his comrade Erich Hartmann, he is the most unforgettable character of the war.

For six decades since the end of the Second World War historians have frequently echoed the notion that the Russian pilots opposing the fighter pilots of the *Luftwaffe* were not up to the challenge and their aircraft were inferior to those of the Germans. They rarely mention that some of the Soviet aircraft were equal or superior to the Bf-109; that as the war continued the Russians produced aircraft significantly better than the 109, and relatively little has been written in the West about the prowess and accomplishments of the Red Air Force aces. To understand the achievements of Erich and other aces of JG-52, it is important to consider the nature of their opposition. As in most air forces, the quality of the Russian fighter pilots was mixed. Many of the German pilots who survived the war have expressed the view that, in most cases, the Germans were superior both in pilot skills and aircraft technology. A distinction must be drawn, however, when considering the quality and character of the Russian units known as the Guards Fighter Regiments, which were the elite fighter arm of the Red Air Force. These units fronted the best of the best, the most aggressive, skilled, fearless and formidable fighter pilots the Russians had produced, and they flew some of the finest aircraft in the world at the time. They compared well with the best of the Royal Air Force pilots in the Battle of Britain and, in part, for the same fundamental reason – they were defending their homeland.

While the great majority of Red Air Force fighter pilots were probably not as well trained as the majority of their German opponents, the Russians outproduced the Germans in both trained pilots and aircraft to the extent that they ultimately won the war of attrition. The ranks of the elite pilots of both sides generated many aces of such high calibre that they seemed to be fighting a separate war within a war. The principal Russian ace of the war was Ivan Kozhedub, who finished the war with a victory score of 62. Kozhedub was born in the Ukraine in 1920 and learned to fly after joining one of the plethora of aviation clubs started in Russia during the 1930s. In his flying career with the Guards Regiments, his pattern of successes brought him three gold stars of the Hero of the Soviet Union, the Russian equivalent of the American Congressional Medal of Honor. Arguably, the best known of the Soviet World War Two fighter aces is Alexander 'Sacha' Pokryshkin, also of the Guards Fighter Regiments. The 59 victory ace and Hero of the Soviet Union award holder frequently met the pilots of JG-52 in the skies over the Eastern Front. He proved to be a brilliant aeronautical mechanic and eventually was allowed to transfer to pilot training, initially on gliders. It was October 1937 before he first flew in a powered aircraft. When assigned to his first fighter unit, Pokryshkin found himself ostracized by his fellow pilots because of his background as a mechanic. They looked on him as inferior, but his mechanical and aeronautical knowledge and his exceptional skill as a pilot soon enabled him to surpass the other pilots of the squadron. Like Erich Hartmann, Pokryshkin was also an able tactician. He found inspiration in the writings of the World War One French fighter ace and highest scoring Allied airman of that conflict, René Fonck, who had detailed his beliefs and achievements in his book, *My Air Combats*. In hours of mock combat, Pokryshkin practiced and refined many of Fonck's tactics and techniques, perfecting and adapting them to the many changes in aircraft and fighter combat since the great war. His attention to detail, coupled with his determination to prevail in every aerial encounter, defined him as a superior opponent through most of his career. It was, however, quite different in the beginning.

Pokryshkin had progressed from becoming a skilled pilot to the aerial gunnery phase of his training when he discovered that he was an impossibly poor shot. He could not put bullets into the towed drogue target sleeve and could not understand why. He devoted himself to solving the problem and finally did so, both mathematically and mechanically. The answer for him was the same as that for Erich Hartmann. Extremely close range. A scholar of air fighting, he kept detailed notes and sketches of his combats, recording not only his own manoeuvres but those of his German opponents as well. And he took every opportunity to fly captured enemy planes, writing lengthy opinions about the strengths and deficiencies of the German fighters. Like Hartmann, Pokryshkin believed religiously in the doctrine of sighting the enemy aircraft early, approaching unseen at great speed, waiting until extremely close before firing, and immediately turning away from the action to escape. In another parallel to Hartmann, Pokryshkin felt a heavy responsibility to keep his newer, younger pilots alive by tutoring them and giving them the benefit of his vast knowlege in tactics, manoeuvring and gunnery. Many of them owed their accomplishments and their survival to him.

The pride of the Guards Regiment pilots was sky high and they were delighted to advertise their presence in the air on every occasion. Their planes were brightly painted, with red often dominating, and it was common practice for them to tune in to German radio frequencies on their r/t transmitters to deliver taunts such as: "Beware, all German pilots. The ace Pokryshkin is in the air!"

A friendly rivalry had developed between Erich Hartmann and Gerd Barkhorn in the Eastern Front air war. By 22 August 1944, the victory totals of both men were very close, with Erich having 282. The lead changed hands many times until Barkhorn was seriously wounded in June and spent weeks confined to a hospital bed while Erich continued to increase his score. Barkhorn had been in the lead in their rivalry until his wounds took him out of action and, on 23 August Erich managed to bag eight enemy planes, raising his total to 290 and surpassing Barkhorn for the final time. On recovering, Barkhorn was transferred to Germany for the Defence of the Reich where the nature of the air combat varied considerably from that on the Russian Front and his personal score of victories would slow in pace compared to that of Hartmann. Now, as Erich's victory total closed in on the 300 mark, his fellow pilots of JG-52 were nervous for him but hopeful that the Hartmann luck and skill would hold and he would live to reach and even surpass the 300 score.

The next day, 24 August , Erich flew two missions and achieved the staggering feat of scoring 11 aerial victories, bringing his total to 301. Members of his unit recalled their excitement and elation as their universal question, can Bubi do it?, was answered in the affirmative. The weather had not been promising and remained so until midday when it finally began to clear. There would be no more than a half day of action. Shortly after lunch Erich and his wingman took off and exactly 1 hour later returned. He made pass after pass, waggling his wings each time to indicate the number of kills he had scored during that brief flight. He landed with another new total: 296, and prepared to go up again while his Bf-109 was quickly rearmed and refuelled. Ground crew personnel and other pilots seemed to be willing him on to break the 300 mark that day and he aimed to do just that. Then a second mission was called and Erich climbed aboard the 109, was assisted in the process of buckling in and began his cockpit check. When ready he signalled a mechanic to start the engine. As the starter reached a high rpm the propeller began turning and Erich's engine, along with that of his wingman's, roared into life. Taxiing into the wind, the Messerschmitts were put through a final run-up, creating whirlwinds of dust behind them before they were released and leapt forward. Their tails came off the grass almost immediately and soon they were airborne, climbing swiftly to hunt for the nearby enemy aircraft.

In another hour they were back, approaching the field to land. Those on the ground who had been listening in on the air-to-air conversations were already aware that something special had happened this day. A few of them had been rushing around finishing roughly-fashioned banners of congratulation and scrambling to be ready with glasses and champagne as soon as Karaya One and Erich's wingman rolled into their dispersals. Again the ritual of a separate pass across the field for each kill achieved during the mission. After five passes, Erich pulled around and set his plane up for a soft landing. At the dispersal he seemed in no hurry to depart from Karaya One and lingered an extra moment, running up the engine with his canopy open. His crew chief, Bimmel Mertens, was there as the first man to greet him and shake his hand. And then they were all there, the Group Commander, Willi Batz, Erich's friends and fellow pilots, and finally the Commodore, Dieter Hrabak, who jumped up on the wing of the 109 to congratulate the all-time ace of aces. Photographs were made as Erich was lifted on the shoulders of two ground types, one of them Bimmel Mertens, and carried from the aircraft. Then the champagne toasts began.

Erich Hartmann's 300th aerial victory earned him the award of the Diamonds to his Knight's Cross and he was informed that Adolf Hitler would be presenting him with it in 2 days time at the Wolf's redoubt, Insterburg. Erich knew that only seven *Luftwaffe* day-fighter pilots had been awarded the Diamonds.

The unsuccessful attempt to assassinate Hitler had occured on 20 July and the Führer had acted swiftly to eliminate everyone involved or remotely connected to the plot. The atmosphere surrounding him since the attempt was one of strictest security and extreme precautions, including the absolute prohibition of sidearms in the vicinity of the Nazi leader. While understanding the new regulation, Erich bridled at the idea that loyal officers like himself might be suspect and he struggled to control his rage at the notion. He told a security officer to please tell Hitler that he did not wish to receive the Diamonds if the Führer had no trust in his front-line officers. The shocked officer passed the message on to Hitler's Luftwaffe aide, Colonel von Below, who had on various occasions dealt with what he construed as the eccentricities of young fighter pilots. Von Below came out to speak with Erich: "Hartmann, you can wear your pistol if you insist. Now please come in and get your Diamonds."

When Erich entered the large room he noted the stooped stance of Hitler and that the Führer's right arm was hanging limply at his side. He saw too that he looked exhausted and that his left arm was shaking. After presenting Erich with the award, they went into a dining room and sat down to lunch. It was then that Hitler told Erich that, militarily, the war was lost. He believed, however, that soon the British and Americans would be fighting the Russians as well as the Germans, there being such enormous political differences between the East and West. Hitler then called attention to how unreliable the information provided by his own generals had been and he asked Erich's opinion of the current Anglo-American bombing attacks on Germany. Erich told Hitler that he disagreed with *Reichsmarshall* Goering's order that the fighter pilots of the *Luftwaffe* must fly at any time against the enemy bombers – day, night, no matter what the weather or visibility. "We lose too many pilots unnecessarily by forcing them to take off and land in weather so bad that a crash is a certainty. To convert all pilots to competent instrument flyers would take too long – at least a year. So, I believe that we should save all our efforts for hard flying against the Americans in blue-sky weather – daylight operations. Then I think the bombing could be deterred." Hitler then asked Hartmann if he thought the training of their fighter pilots was insufficient and Erich replied that it was. He said that young pilots were reporting to his squadron in Russia with fewer than 60 hours' total flying time, and only 20 hours of that in the 109, which, in his opinion, accounted for the majority of their Eastern Front fighter losses. Slumped in his chair, the Führer reiterated his view that the war was already lost. He said that people were coming to him every day with ideas for guns, tanks, rockets, submarines, new types of operations and offensives . . . but that they had run out of time. On Erich's return to the squadron he was greeted warmly by his fellow pilots who admired the Diamonds award and celebrated his achievement with an enthusiasm that he did not share. His only interest at that moment was the 10-day leave that went with the award and marrying the girl who waited for him in Weil.

Before the start of his leave, however, Erich was asked to come to Berlin-Gatow airfield to meet with General of the Fighter Arm Adolf Galland. Galland wanted Erich to transfer to the new Messerschmitt Me-262 Test Commando unit which was combining flight testing of the revolutionary twin-jet fighter with limited combat operations. Erich was just the sort of high-achieving pilot that Galland required for the unit, but the transfer was not what Erich wanted. He told Galland that he believed he was of much greater value with his unit in Russia. Galland accepted this and the brief interview was over, but not before he ordered Erich to spend a short time at the *Jagdfliegerheim*, the fighter pilot's home, in Bad Wiessee for a bit of rest and recuperation before returning to the Front. Bad Wiessee would make an ideal honeymoon destination and Erich began to think about their wedding as he rode the train from Berlin to Stuttgart and its Weil suburb.

Erich and Usch had put off marrying because of the war and she was surprised when he got off the train and told her that they were going to be married at once, with no more delays. They talked it over and agreed that she would come to Bad Wiessee for the wedding in 2 days time. She was to arrive on the noon train on Friday, leaving them enough time to take care of last minute details and paperwork before the Saturday wedding. A large wedding reception was planned at the central banquet hall of the Fighter Pilot's Home, and Erich busied himself arranging for the food, champagne, an orchestra for dancing at the reception, and the marriage licence.

As the early morning train bringing Usch from Weil pulled into Munich, the wail of air raid sirens announced an imminent bombing raid by the American Air Force. She ran to the nearest air raid shelter where she had to spend the next 3 hours. Erich, meanwhile, unable to get through to Weil by phone, would spend the rest of the day and much of the evening, meeting all the trains arriving from Stuttgart, none of them carrying his bride. Finally, just after midnight, she arrived on the last train of the day, tired but in good spirits and looking forward to their wedding the next day.

Among the wedding guests were Gerd Barkhorn, Willi Batz and Walter Krupinski. With the ceremony and reception behind them, Erich and Usch enjoyed their honeymoon in the pleasant countryside around Bad Wiessee and put aside all thoughts of the war for a few days. But soon, Erich began feeling guilty about being away from his group at the Front and decided to cut short his time with his new wife to return to JG-52.

On New Year's Eve Erich arrived back in Stuttgart, having been granted a 10-day leave. Usch was pregnant and living with Erich's parents in their Weil home. She wasn't getting much rest as the bombing raids on Stuttgart were frequent, but she and Erich were happily reunited for a short time. Four days later he was ordered back to JG-52 – in Hungary this time, where the Russians were keeping the *Luftwaffe* busy. Within the next days of air combat activity, his score reached 336, well ahead of his nearest rival, Gerd Barkhorn. The action continued into March when Erich received an urgent telegram ordering him to cease operational flying immediately and report directly to Lechfeld for conversion training on the Me-262 turbojet fighter. Thoroughly convinced that Germany had lost the war, and fearing a massive influx of Russian troops and equipment, he decided that it was essential to relocate Usch to somewhere safer than the Stuttgart area – a place out in the countryside. His adjutant, Captain Will Van de Kamp, came to his rescue, offering Usch the use of his family's home at Schongau. After reporting at Lechfeld, Erich borrowed a van and moved Usch and their few belongings to the Van de Kamp home where she was made welcome by the adjutant's wife. Now Erich had some peace of mind about his wife and their unborn child. The rural surroundings of Schongau were quiet and mostly free of the cares of war and so he was relatively relaxed about leaving her this time.

His new home base at Lechfeld was hardly a relaxing venue, however. The highly-touted new German jet fighter that he was learning to fly, was attracting the attentions of American bombers nearly every morning, preventing any flying activity until later in the day, after the bomb craters had been filled in. Even then, flying was usually limited to a few hours, after which yet more formations of U.S. fighter-bombers would arrive to strafe the field. RAF Mosquito fighter-bombers often appeared late in the day to add their bombs to the mix, followed in the evening by further Mosquito attacks. The airfield was in almost constant turmoil, creating a dangerous and difficult learning experience for the students of the Me-262 school.

One of the *Luftwaffe*'s top aces, Lt Col. Heinz 'Pritzl' Baer, was in command of the 262 instruction at Lechfeld. He also commanded the greatest respect from the pilots, being a hero figure, a charming, witty personality, and the holder of a 204-victory record at the time of Erich's arrival on the course. By the war's end he would bring his total to 220, having shot down an additional sixteen British and American aircraft while flying the jet.

Erich enjoyed checking out on the new Me-262, even in the difficult conditions posed by the frequent enemy attacks on the airfield. Being a brilliant flyer, he adapted readily to the new plane. He could not have been surprised when Adolf Galland dropped in at Lechfeld on a brief visit at the end of March for another chat. The former General of the Fighter Arm explained that he was merely a squadron commander now (demoted by Goering) and was in the process of gathering some top fighter pilots together to take the Me-262 into action against the enemy daylight bomber formations. They included Col. Steinhoff, Col. Lutzow, Major Krupinski and Major Hohagen. Galland invited Erich to join the squadron too, but Erich expressed concern about fitting in with such high-ranking super aces and added that he would not wish to fly as someone else's wingman again. He was rescued from the dilemma by another urgent telegram – this one from Hermann Graf, Commodore of JG-52, requesting that he return immediately to the unit, now operating in Czechoslovakia and under heavy enemy pressure. He was being asked to come back in command of 1/JG-52. Erich managed to persuade Gordon Gollob, Galland's replacement as General of the Fighter Arm, to transfer him back to JG-52 on the Eastern Front. Within hours he was on the way back to his old group.

1/JG-52 was now reassigned to emergency oil field protection duty on the Rumanian Front and was operating from a small grass airstrip at Zilistea near Ploesti. On arriving at the makeshift field, the ground crews had only just completed refuelling and arming the unit's Bf-109s when an order to scramble was issued. Erich's wingman on this trip was Carl Junger. The second element was made up of Lt. Puls and Sgt. Wester, completing the *schwarm*. They took off, followed by a second *schwarm*, and were directed to protect other fighters of JG-52 in pursuit of an American bomber stream heading for the Ploesti oil fields. The American bombers were under an intense anti-aircraft barrage in the target area. The bomber stream was several miles long. Erich and his comrades climbed steadily up through 25,000 feet to gain a height advantage over the enemy bombers and he positioned his fighters with the sun at their backs, preparing for a perfect bounce attack. As they eased over into a dive on the B-17s, Erich spotted a flight of four P-51 Mustang fighters 3,000 feet below him. He ordered the other Germans to attack the Mustangs and headed for the fighter in the rear of the flight. At a distance of 100 yards, he fired a short burst and the Mustang began to disintegrate. As it became an orange fire-ball, he was already on the tail of another P-51. There was no explosion this time; his bullets and shells ripped into the hapless victim which slipped into an uncontrollable spin. Erich witnessed two more Mustangs destroyed by his fellow pilots. His ammunition gone, he gathered his charges and headed back to base.

Having tangled with the Mustangs, Erich realized that, in the hands of more competent American pilots, they would have the advantage over him and his 109. The days of relatively easy kills were behind him. This view was confirmed during the next few days when vastly better American fighter opposition appeared with their bombers and provided excellent protection for the heavies. The Mustangs were now showing up in huge numbers and were more than holding their own against the German fighters.

Most of the German pilots expressed their concerns about the Mustang fighter and its ability to shepherd the enemy bombers to any German target and back to their English bases. Erich shared these concerns as he stepped up onto the wing of Karaya One for his fifth mission against the formidable American fighters. The Germans spotted the Americans below them in good visibility conditions, providing top cover for their bombers at 20,000 feet. Erich's planes were flying at 23,000 feet. He was watching four Messerschmitts diving to attack a flight of Mustangs when he was startled by the appearance of several more Mustangs that were diving on the Germans from a much higher altitude. Fortunately for him, the P-51 pilots had not seen Erich and his pilots, who were flying top cover for the attacking 109s. He called a warning over the R/T and dived to chase a P-51 that was blasting bits off a 109. The American never saw Erich's 109 as it closed to within 100 yards. Erich fired and the Mustang exploded. Without pausing, he positioned himself behind another enemy fighter and peppered it with gun and cannon fire, setting it alight. And then the voice of his wingman crackled in his ears, warning him of a Mustang immediately behind him. Erich dived violently to his left to evade the enemy fighter, realizing that he and his comrades were greatly outnumbered by the Mustang force and the only sensible course was to get back to base by the shortest route. He now noted that a string of Mustangs were chasing him and gaining on him. There are times in the air combat arena when ham-fisted flying is called for over elegant manoeuvring. For Erich, this was one of those times and he began wracking the Messerschmitt over into hard left and right turns in an attempt to dodge the tracer fire on either side. Eight unyielding American fighters were tracking him across Rumania and he could feel the heat. He was thoroughly sweat-soaked as the tail-chase progressed and he struggled to stay clear of the closing 0.50 calibre rounds. At one point in the difficult manoeuvring, he found himself lined up for a shot at one of his pursuers only to discover that he was out of ammunition. The determined American pilots were not quite able to overhaul Erich, but they were staying with him and showing no sign of letting up the pressure. He hoped that the flak guns at his field would distract the Americans sufficiently to allow him to escape.

Going through yet another stressful high-G turn, Erich was alerted by the red fuel warning light. He was nearly out of fuel and still too far from his base to risk crash-landing. His only option was to bale out. He prepared to leave Karaya One as quickly as he could, releasing his seat belt and rolling the plane inverted. He used the emergency release to shed the canopy into the slipstream and popped out after it. As he tumbled down, he glimpsed the enemy aircraft above him and groped for his parachute D-ring. The violence of the 'chute deploying was both jarring and re-assuring. As he floated downwards, he looked up at the Mustangs circling above and wondered if any of them would seize this opportunity to machine-gun an enemy pilot in his parachute. One of the P-51s lined up to target Erich but at the last second flashed past him and waved a hand. Again, the Hartmann luck had held.

Landing a few minutes later, Erich was relieved to be picked up within an hour and driven back to his base, but saddened when told that nearly half of his group had been shot down that day. Two of the pilots had been killed and several of them wounded. Clearly, the men of JG-52 had met their match.

Nearly a year had passed since that first week of air combat with the Mustangs. Germany had all but lost the war and her remaining fighting forces were struggling desperately in the final weeks before the un-conditional surrender. Now 1/JG-52 was stationed at Deutsch Brod in Czechoslovakia, contending with a far more powerful American Air Force than it had encountered the previous spring. When the B-17 and B-24 heavy bombers of the U.S.A.A.F. appeared in European skies, they were now accompanied by hundreds of P-51 Mustangs, often 800 or more of the powerful, fast and efficient fighters, providing protective cover for their charges. The Americans had long since learned that the bristling armament carried on their four-engine bombers was, in fact, insufficient for defending themselves against the fighters of the *Luftwaffe*. The losses they had experienced prior to the advent of the Mustang long-range escort fighter were unsustainable. Once the Mustang had become fully operational with the U.S.A.A.F., everything changed and the odds against the Germans increased dramatically. Now, whenever the P-51s appeared, many of them were wholly or partially unpainted, left in a shiny aluminium finish that flashed in the sunshine. This made them easier for the Germans to spot at a great distance, but it also demonstrated the complete confidence that the American Air Force now had in its dominance and superiority in the skies over Europe. These were the final encounters between the pilots of 1/JG-52 and those of the American Mustangs.

On the last day of hostilities in the European conflict, 8 May 1945, Erich Hartmann's final mission of the war was a reconnaissance flight to determine the positions of the advancing Russian Army units relative to the fighter base at Deutsch Brod. He and his wingman took off at 8:30 in the morning and turned towards the east in their climb to 12,000 feet. They immediately spotted a massive smoke plume rising from the town of Brünn which appeared to be either under Russian bombardment or already in Russian control. As they neared the town, they could see eight Soviet YAK-11 fighters circling the smoke cloud. The YAK pilots had not yet seen the two German planes and, incredibly, one of the Russian pilots climbed into a loop over the town, an invitation that Erich could not resist. Karaya One fell on the YAK and blasted it from a distance of 200 feet. The enemy fighter flamed and went down in a tumbling fall and crashing in flames that added to the pall over Brünn. As he was lining up on another of the YAKs, Erich glanced up for an instant and sighted a mass of 12 shiny Mustangs heading into the area from the west. Rather than face the combined aircraft of the Russians and the Americans, he and his wingman took refuge in the cover of the smoke pall. They broke out the other side of the smoke cloud and made for Deutsch Brod at full throttle. On landing there, Erich taxied in to his dispersal. There was no time to dwell on his 352nd victory, which would also be his last. Bimmel Mertens, his crew chief, was up on the wing with the news that the Russians had been shelling the airfield. Mertens was ready to refuel and rearm Karaya One, but both men knew the truth was the plane would never fly again. When he reported to his commander, Lt Col Hermann Graf, he was told that, for them, the war was over. They had an order to surrender which read: 'Graf and Hartmann both fly immediately to Dortmund and surrender to British forces. All other JG-52 personnel will surrender at Deutsch Brod to Soviet forces. From General

Seidemann, Air Fleet Commander'. The two men talked briefly about the fate awaiting the 2,000 women, children and elderly people – the relatives of JG-52 personnel on the base who were trying to flee the approaching Russians – and decided that the general's order would have to be disobeyed. They must do what they could for the refugees. Graf's plan was to try leading the refugees to the American zone where they could surrender to the U.S. Army and that while he prepared them for the march, Erich would see to the destruction of all JG-52 aircraft, ammunition and fuel. Twenty-five Bf-109s, including Karaya One, would be drenched in gasoline and torched. Erich supervised the demolition work and watched as dense black smoke rose from the airfield, before he left with the others. Together with Lt Col Graf and Major Hartmann Grasser, Erich led the column of civilian refugees away from Deutsch Brod.

Late that afternoon the column met a few American tanks which halted when they saw the approaching Germans. Graf introduced himself and Erich to the U.S. Army tank commander, explained what they were trying to do, and surrendered to the nonplussed Yank who reported the encounter by walkie-talkie to his headquarters commander. Truckloads of American troops soon arrived to disarm the Germans and took them into custody. Erich was relieved that, in American hands, the civilians would not be subject to the abuses of the Russian troops whose unsavoury reputation had preceded them. What he was soon to learn was that his captors, the U.S. 90th Infantry Division and 16th Armored Division, were conducting unauthorized advances beyond Pilsen, their eastern-most objective, by agreement with the Soviets who had been selected to liberate Czechoslovakia. As such, the Americans were compelled to hand over all Germans captured east of Pilsen to the Russians, it being a prime aim of the Russians to acquire and punish all professional German officers, soldiers and airmen, who had fought against the Soviet Union. This was in contradiction of the spirit and principles of the Geneva accords on prisoners of war.

Initially, the surrendering German officers, airmen and civilians, were placed in a large open-air compound and the number of prisoners soon grew to more than 50,000 with ages ranging from young children to old people. Living conditions in the compound quickly deteriorated and sympathetic American guards turned a blind eye to the escape of many prisoners, frequently assisting them by providing maps, chocolate and other GI rations. Unfortunately, for the remaining Germans in the compound, their American captivity lasted only about 8 days before they were moved in trucks a few miles to a field where they were turned over to the Russians. The first thing the Russian troops did was to separate the German women and girls from the men. What followed was a brutal and savage orgy of rape and debauchery by Red Army soldiers. When the greatly out-numbered American guards still present tried to intervene, the Russians charged towards them, firing into the air and threatening to kill them all if they interfered. The raping continued through the night. The next day a Russian general arrived in the encampment and immediately ordered the cessation of the brutal behaviour. Later, when a few Russian soldiers violated the order and assaulted a young German girl, she was asked to identify the men from a line-up of soldiers. There were no formalities, no court martial. The guilty parties were immediately hanged in front of all their comrades. The point was made.

The next stop for Erich, Graf, the other German officers and airmen, was Neubistritz, where over a period of three weeks the men were given physical examinations to determine their state of health and their ability to work as forced labourers. Strangely, he and the other Germans were then told by their Russian captors that they were to be taken to Vienna by train and from there they would be released to return to their homes in Germany. The Vienna destination was later changed to Budapest, and it soon became apparent to Erich and some of the others that they were actually heading for Russia. The east-bound train rattled on for two weeks, passing through Kiev, Moscow and Kirov, before emerging into a desolate region of bogs and marshes. There, in the middle of nowhere, the German prisoners were told to hack out crude shelters for themselves from the peat they were ordered to dig from the swamp. After five weeks of the back-breaking work, the Russians transported all the German officers with the rank of major or higher, to a special officers' camp at Gryazovets where conditions were substantially better than in the swamp. The improvement would not last.

The Russians held Erich as their prisoner for more than ten years, during which he experienced a range of deprivations and maltreatment at the hands of the NKVD (Soviet Secret Police) who administered the camps. He was, at one point, shown a list of his fellow German officers who were being accused of 'serious crimes against the Russian people' and he was asked to spy on them and become an informer for the secret police about the wartime 'crimes' of these officers. When he refused to cooperate and become a stukatchka or stool pigeon, he was given ten days' solitary confinement in the camp bunker, a filthy chamber 4 feet wide, 9 feet long and 6 feet high with little light and ventilation. He was given bread and water only and had to sleep on the cold ground.

On another occasion, when met with his continuing resistance to their demands that he work for them, the NKVD official threatened to bring the heads of his wife and baby to him on a tray, saying that they could easily have their East German operatives go right to Stuttgart and spirit his family out of Germany. It was just one of the many ploys they tried on Erich to break him from his steadfast resistance. Unlike the German Gestapo, the NKVD was strictly forbidden by Soviet regulations to use physical torture on their war prisoners, so they relied on other far more insidious methods including starvation and propaganda to break the will of the prisoners. Hartmann:

> The main pressure . . . and the real force in brainwashing is hunger. Starve a man, and in the ensuing egocentric fight of the individual for his own life all else is rapidly obliterated. The unavoidable, self-preservational choice 'him or me?' sunders all bonds of comradeship. Surrounded by a mass of his fellows, yet becomes isolated within the limits of his own shrivelling personality. Helpless and fearful, cut off even from the faintest glimmer of hope, he functions within ever-diminishing boundaries. Ethical connections to his fellow men and to the culture that produced him, all teachings, laws, rules and regulations dissolve under the acid of self-preservation. Thus divested of his resources of resistance, the bereft individual is pitted against a remorseless and inhuman regime. Collapse was virtually unavoidable. This was how the NKVD reached the masses of the prisoners and made them instruments of the Soviet will.

Another technique they employed was the interception of mail to the prisoners. The letters were then destroyed or used for persuasion or blackmail purposes, a tactic in some ways more cruel than beatings. It was not until 8 months after Erich's capture that he was allowed to send a postcard home. His wife received it in January 1946: 'Dear Usch, I can tell you that I am alive. I wish you all a nice Christmas and a good New Year. Fear not for me. For which do I congratulate you, a daughter or a son? All my thoughts are with you. With a lot of kisses, Your Erich'. For 2 years, beginning in 1947, Erich's NKVD interrogators interferred with his in-coming and out-going mail, teasing him with tiny bits of information and withholding the bulk of the communications. They even kept the news of his infant son's death from him.

One thing that worked in Erich's favour in the camps was his ability as a linguist. He spoke good Russian, English and French as well as his native language. The other key factor in his struggle for survival was the abiding faith and devotion that he and his wife shared.

On learning that Erich had flown the Me-262 jet fighter, a secret police interrogator questioned him for hours about the aircraft. The interviewer became increasingly hostile as Erich was unable to provide the sort of detailed information wanted by the NKVD. Erich explained that he had just checked out on the plane and had only flown it about ten times. Perceiving Hartmann as the world's most successful fighter pilot, the interrogator insisted on him providing technical information about the jet that he didn't possess. The interrogator was not particularly knowledgeable in aviation matters and he decided that Erich was not cooperating. Finally, he lost his temper and struck Erich across the face with his walking stick. Until that moment Hartmann had been remarkably restrained and controlled in his behaviour towards his captors, who had, so far, refrained from physical violence. But this was too much to tolerate. He picked up a chair and slammed it down on the head of the Russian who slumped unconscious to the floor. Fully expecting to be beaten or shot, Erich opened the door and summoned a guard. When the interrogator was revived he had Erich sent back to the bunker. Three days later, he was released from the hell-hole and brought to the same room with the same interrogating officer. Amazingly, the Russian seemed in a good humour and offered Erich some food and drink as well as an apology for having struck him with the cane.

The NKVD set out to brand the uncooperative Erich a 'war criminal' and produced elaborate confessions of his 'crimes' which he refused to sign, regardless of the threats and bribes accompanying the papers. Much of the last 9 months of this campaign to break Erich saw him serving long stretches in the confinement bunker. Near the end of this period the 27 year-old fighter ace decided to go on a hunger strike and, if necessary, commit suicide rather than give in. The Russians allowed the strike to go on for 4 days before force-feeding Erich a nauseating mixture of eggs and sugar to keep him alive. They kept him in the bunker for 27 days, while continuing this procedure. At the end of that time, the interrogator taunted Erich with a handful of letters from Usch, offering to let him read them if he would end his hunger strike and sign a confession to having committed war crimes against the Soviets. He summoned what remaining will power he had and again refused to eat or sign the papers. He continued his resistance for two more days before deciding to live for the sake of his wife and child. As a reward for ending the hunger strike Erich was allowed to read the letters from Usch, but having read them he still refused to sign the false confession, telling the interrogator that he had never murdered women and children as the document alleged and that he was not ashamed of having been a soldier for his country.

Pleased with Erich's decision to eat again, the NKVD officers allowed him to regain his health before trying a new tack. This time they told him that the Soviet Union was supporting the development of a new, modern air force for the East German People's Republic, by providing the latest Soviet jet fighters. With Erich's record as a fighter pilot and ace of aces, he would be of great value to the Russians after attending some training in Moscow. He could then decide whether to work as an officer in the East German Air Force or in the political end of the organization. Erich insisted that he first be sent out of prison as a free man home to his family in Germany. "If, after I am home in the West, you make me a normal contract offer – a business deal such as people sign every day all over the world – and I like your offer, then I will come back and work with you in accordance with the contract. But if you try to put me to work under coercion of any kind, then I will resist to my dying gasp." This time, in the view of the interrogator, Erich had gone too far. He told the German that he would never see his family again. Within a few weeks of that conversation, 1,400 German soldiers were repatriated from the camp in a group that did not include Erich. Instead, his name was on a long list of Germans who had been convicted of 'war crimes', by order of the Soviet government. Henceforth they were to be denied the protection of the Geneva Convention and the International Red Cross, and were sentenced to 25 years at hard labour. He and a few other German officers were later taken before a Russian judge in a crude courtroom near the camp. The room held an audience of about fifty Russian civilians. When called to approach the judge, Erich asked why he had been charged with war crimes. Reading from a dossier before him, the judge specified the charges. Erich was accused of participating in illegal, brutal and unprovoked attacks on the Soviet Union and destroying at least 345 expensive Russian aircraft. He was further accused of attacking a bread factory in the central sector of the Russian Front on 23 May 1943, and, finally, of killing 780 civilians, including women and children, in the Russian village of Briansk. Erich defended himself against the charges, accepting only the destruction of the Russian aircraft which, as a German soldier, was only his duty and not a war crime. His defence against the charges was a waste of time and effort. Even the judge conceded as much and urged Erich, once again, to sign the confession prepared for him. Again Erich refused to sign, and this time he asked for a bullet. The furious judge declared: "War criminal! 25 years' hard labour. Take him away."

Erich and the other German prisoners condemned to hard labour were taken by train to a camp called Shakhty where he vowed that he would not be turned into a slave labourer. At Shakhty the prisoners were required to work in coal mines and, in the morning of their first day at the camp, Erich and the others were awakened early to leave for the mine. As the group marched off to work, Erich stayed behind. A guard motioned with his rifle for Erich to move off with the others and Erich responded that he was a German officer and under the rules of the Geneva Convention he was not required to work. He demanded to see the camp commandant who told him that the Geneva Convention did not apply to him. The commandant then had Erich placed in solitary confinement in a small bunker near the guard room by the camp gates. The sergeant of the guard, meanwhile, informed the other German officer prisoners that Erich was being confined in the bunker. Over the next 5 days, the Germans' bitterness over the treatment of Erich, their acknowledged leader, grew to anger and then rage. By the end of the fifth day, as the officers trudged back from the mine, their mood was ugly. The next morning, instead of lining up for the daily march to the mine, they poured from the barracks, overpowered the guards and headed for the office of the commandant. On the way they freed Erich and locked his guard in the bunker.

At the Russian commandant's office, Erich detached himself from the angry crowd of German officers and ordered them not to harm the commandant, his aides or the other guards. Before any of the German prisoners could reach the camp gate and make a dash for freedom, Erich shouted at them to stay put inside the camp confines. He warned that, if they left the camp the Russians would shoot them as escaped fugitives. Much as they longed to be free of Russian captivity, they accepted Erich's order. He then led them to the commandant and demanded that he contact his higher headquarters and inform his superiors about the prisoners' revolt. When a Russian general came on the line, Erich took the phone and identified himself as responsible for the revolt. He described the intolerable conditions in the camp, the food unfit for pigs and the 12-hour workdays underground that were killing the prisoners. He insisted that a government representative from Moscow come and inspect the camp and put their complaints before an international tribunal. Within the hour a large contingent of the Red Army arrived at the camp. Erich confronted them at the wire. Order was slowly restored, the prisoners returned to their barracks and Erich once again sat down with the camp commandant. The Russian informed Erich that all work in the mine was to be suspended for 5 days and that Erich and the other 'ring leaders' of the revolt were to be sent away to another camp, Novocherkassk. At Novocherkassk Erich spent a total of 5 months in the solitary confinement bunker before the camp officials finally agreed to set up a special tribunal for him.

At the trial Erich conducted his own defence, stating that the Soviet government had 'convicted' him of war crimes without any evidence; that they had ignored the provisions of the Geneva Conventions on the treatment of prisoners of war and had sentenced him to a 25 year term as a slave labourer. Ultimately, the court upheld the hard labour sentence. He was then sent on to another prison camp, at Diaterka, in the Ural mountains, where his reputation as a 'revolutionary' preceded him. His new commandant interviewed him and raised the subject of the revolt at the Shakhty camp. Erich explained that the revolt had occurred because he, as a staff officer, had been required to work at hard labour (against the provisions of the Geneva Conventions) and that, when he refused to do so, he was punished in the bunker. The Diaterka commandant agreed that staff officers should not have to work and Erich undertook that there would be no more revolts. But the conditions at Diaterka were appalling. The overcrowding was such that more than 4,000 prisoners were forced to live in barracks built to accommodate 400. The security precautions were so severe that escape was all but impossible.

Erich's release from 10½ years of Russian incarceration finally came about through the efforts of his mother, Elisabeth Hartmann, and the intervention of the newly elected German Chancellor, Konrad Adenauer. Germany was rebuilding rapidly in the 1950s and was already showing signs of the economic miracle it was to achieve in the post-war world. Mrs Hartmann wrote to Adenauer asking for his help to gain the release of her son. In setting out to negotiate a new trade agreement with the Soviets, Dr.

Adenauer insisted that the return of the more than 16,000 German soldiers still held by the Russians as prisoners of war, be a mandatory concession as part of the agreement. The Russians saw their German war prisoners then as an important bargaining chip in the negotiations and, with the agreement came freedom at last. Erich was given a meagre clothing issue and, within a few days, was released and put on a train bound for Germany.

The German Prisoner of War Organization was planning a large reception for him on his return to Stuttgart. When he arrived at the railway station and was greeted by representatives of the organization, he told them that there must be no celebrations or reception as he feared for the continued imprisonment of some of his fellow German POWs by the NKVD. He asked that any such celebrations be deferred until the last German war prisoner was repatriated. He then thanked the members of the committee and left by bus for Weil. As he rode through Stuttgart he marvelled at the changes in fashions, the brightly-coloured clothes, the designs of cars and other ordinary things that had taken place in the decade of his isolation from the western world.

His reunion with Usch was blissful and in the first few days of his return, literally hundreds of relatives and friends came by to welcome him home. His brother Alfred, now a doctor like their father, was shocked at Erich's physical condition. At just over 100 lb, Erich presented an imaciated image of his former athletic build and it would require many weeks of nourishment and exercise to regain his proper weight and condition. During that time he read as much as he could in an attempt to catch up with the altered world of the 1950s. He helped with the housework, the gardening and the shopping and revelled in the simple pleasures of life at home with his wife, free to do as he pleased. But at night, he was bothered by persistent and vivid dreams about being watched, as though he were still in a Russian prison camp – a common reaction among former war prisoners. With time, care and love Erich came through this difficult period and, at the age of 33, prepared to deal with his next challenge – how to earn a living for his wife and himself.

His original plan had been to study medicine and become a doctor like his father, but the war had intervened and now such a programme seemed out of the question. He had no real business experience nor much experience in any area apart from flying, at which he had excelled. It was no surprise, therefore, when, only a few weeks after his repatriation he received a phone call from his old friend, Walter Krupinski who, with Gerd Barkhorn, was about to leave for a jet refresher course in England and wanted Erich to join them. He thanked his old comrade but declined the invitation and asked Krupinski to call on their return and tell him how the course had gone. It seemed that under Chancellor Adenauer, the government was trying to rebuild the German Air Force and was encouraging some of the great wartime aces to join in the effort. Over the next weeks he heard from a number of his old air force comrades, including Barkhorn, Dieter Hrabak, Gunther Rall and Macky Steinhoff, all urging him to think hard about joining them in becoming a part of the new German Air Force which was to join NATO, the North Atlantic Treaty Organization, established following the 1948 Soviet blockade of Berlin. The realization that all he really knew about was fighter piloting worried him and Usch, but wanting his happiness, she left the decision to him. In 1956, he rejoined the service and entered a second military career.

The personnel office of the service proposed, initially, to bring Erich back in with the rank of Captain, even though he had been promoted to Major a few months before being turned over to the Russians. They maintained that, having been a major for only 2 months when the war ended, it was appropriate for him to return as a captain. But influential friends like Gunther Rall took exception to this view and Erich was returned to duty as a major.

Erich went back to flying by re-qualifying for a Light Aeroplane Pilot's Licence in a two-seat Piper Cub, considerably less of an aircraft than the Messerschmitt fighter he had flown during the war, or the jet fighters he would fly in the future. In 1956 he reported to Landsberg air base in Germany for retraining by United States Air Force instructors. There he flew the North American T-6 Texan trainer, known to the British and Canadians as the Harvard, before transitioning to the Lockheed T-33 advanced jet trainer. It was the second jet he had flown and, unlike the twin-engined Me-262 fighter, the T-33 was a two-seat, single-engined jet of proven reliability.

In February 1957 a daughter was born to Usch and Erich and shortly thereafter he was again parted from his little family when the air force sent him to Luke Air Force Base near Phoenix, Arizona, for advanced jet fighter training. He was schooled in bombing, gunnery and strafing in the dry and pleasant flying weather of the American desert. Erich was popular with the American pilots training at Luke. They were greatly impressed by his combat experience and his wartime record of more than 800 aerial engagements in more than 1,400 fighter missions. In time, Erich was able to send for Usch and their baby, to come to Arizona for the duration of his training assignment.

On the completion of his training in the U.S., Major Erich Hartmann returned to Germany where he became commander of the first jet fighter wing of the new German Air Force, JG-71, the Richthofen Wing. Equipped with North American F-86 Sabre jets, the U.S.A.F. stalwart in the Korean War, his challenge was to mould it into an effective operational unit. One of his first actions was to track down an old fellow prisoner from Diaterka, the highly capable Sigi Graf von der Schulenburg, whom he ran to earth in an officer's training school at Hamburg. He arranged for the transfer of Schulenburg to JG-71 as his executive officer. Working together, the pair spent the next weeks consulting with NATO officials, building the new Wing and acquiring the matériel needed for its operation. He was also anticipating the impending acquisition of the highly-regarded Mach-2 Lockheed F-104 air superiority jet, the Starfighter. While training in America, he had begun learning all he could about this new and developing weapon system, visiting an F-104 training squadron at Nellis AFB near Las Vegas on a number of occasions. He was impressed by the overall performance, speed, rate of climb and weapons capability of this 'hot rod of the sky', but had also taken note of the chatter among the off-duty fighter pilots at Nellis when the subject of the plane's serviceability came up. He had questioned them about problems associated with the Starfighter and had been told of engine troubles, problems with nozzles and nose wheels, spare parts shortages, equipment defects, maintenance difficulties and other troubles that plagued the plane's readiness to fly. The aircraft had also accumulated a dark history of accidents in its operational career to date and, believing that the NATO fighter squadrons would soon be equipping with the Starfighter, Erich studied the findings of the accident investigators for the many incidents involving the plane. He saw that the relatively inexperienced pilots of his coming command would need to become seasoned veterans before they could handle the red-hot F-104.

Erich Hartmann was essentially non-political and was determined to remain so after re-entering the military. Unfortunately for him, the German Air Force of the 1950s was heavily politicized, and fiercely independent officers like Erich, who were by nature rather unmilitary in their perspective, were not likely to prosper in the new GAF. He knew what had to be done to work JG-71 up to operational readiness and had little time for fancy, parade-ground traditionalism. He was determined that the sort of destruction suffered by the Soviet Air Force on the ground in June 1941 at the hands of the *Luftwaffe* would never happen to his Wing. His single-minded determination frequently saw him knocking heads with some of his superior officers – powerful but inadequately experienced men who held positions of authority, operated in a climate of fear, and feared officers like Hartmann. They spread the word through the ranks of the GAF that Erich was 'not a good officer'. Never much of a diplomat, Erich could not – would not – employ tact when he thought it might interfere with a more direct presentation of his views on a matter.

One such matter was the coming purchase of the F-104 Starfighter by the German Air Force, an acquisition which Erich questioned. Based on his own study of the plane and its history with the American air force, he felt strongly that the Starfighter might eventually prove a good weapon system for the GAF, but not yet. He believed in the plane, but could not envision it being safely operated by the relatively inexperienced pilots of his new air force. He expressed that view to his old wartime friend, General Josef Kammhuber, now the Inspector of the *Bundesluftwaffe*, the new German Air Force, and briefed the General on his investigation into the problems with the Starfighter. When Kammhuber asked Erich what aircraft he thought the GAF should purchase instead of the F-104, he suggested the North American F-100 Super Sabre or the Convair F-102 Delta Dagger – both of them highly-capable, next-generation fighter-interceptors which, in his opinion, would make ideal transition aircraft for his pilots on their way to becoming ready to handle the Starfighter.

The Lockheed F-104 Starfighter was way ahead of its time when it underwent flight testing and became operational with the U.S. Air Force. In service with various NATO air forces by the late 1950s, it provided them with important tactical and technological advantages over the best operational Soviet fighters of the time. In the first major multinational military aircraft manufacturing enterprise, aeroplane makers of seven NATO nations cooperatively produced a total of 2,780 examples of the F-104 in fighter, interceptor, trainer and reconnaissance variants. Of the total F-104 production run, more than thirty-five per cent were operated by the German Air Force which received 917 of the aircraft including 30 F-104Fs, 96 F-104Gs, 136 TF-104Gs, 255 F/RF-104Gs from the North Group, 210 F-104Gs from the South Group, 88 F-104Gs from the West Group, 50 F/RF-104Gs from the Italian Group, plus 50 replacement F-104Gs. By the mid-1970s, five nuclear-armed fighter-bomber wings, two interceptor wings and two reconnaissance wings of the GAF, as well as two attack wings of the Federal German Navy, were all equipped with the Starfighter.

The concept behind the F-104 came out of conversations with U.S. Air Force pilots who had flown fighter combat missions in the Korean War and concluded that the primary requirements for a new interceptor-fighter were great speed and rate of climb. The Starfighter met those needs becoming the first aircraft capable of climbing faster than the speed of sound. At the sacrifice of range and endurance it could be flown at up to 1,450 mph or Mach 2.2 in level flight.

The Starfighter prototypes first flew in February 1954, with the first actual production aircraft flying in 1956. Before it was delivered, 17 YF-104 aircraft were test-flown and evaluated by the U.S. Aerospace Defense and Tactical Air Commands for nearly two years. The first 153 F-104A aircraft were powered by the General Electric J-79-GE-3B engine and went into service with the 83rd Fighter Interceptor Squadron in 1958 and with the Aerospace Defense Command in Spain. Within a year, however, the plane's limited range, limited capability in poor weather conditions, and high accident rate, caused it to be withdrawn from operational service.

Some of the early aircraft then went to Jordan and Pakistan as part of the Military Assistance Plan. Others were reassigned to units of the U.S.

Air National Guard which operated them until 1966. With America's involvement in the Vietnam War, one squadron of F-104s was sent to that country to deal with the threat posed by the new Soviet MiG-21 fighter. After more than a year on station there, the vaunted MiG jet finally began to appear, but very little actual combat occured between the two types.

A decision by the NATO organization in 1955 to adopt one common aircraft type that would function in the strike, interceptor and reconnaissance roles had led to bids being requested for an appropriate design from the plane makers Convair, Grumman, Saab, Northrup, Dassault and Lockheed. This resulted in a final competition between the entries of Lockheed and Dassault, the Starfighter and Mirage III, respectively. The West German Defence Minister, Franz-Josef Strauss, then selected the Starfighter and West Germany became the largest and most important market for the plane.

The first German Starfighters were Lockheed-built two-seat trainers used in America for the training of German instructor pilots. These aircraft were then turned over to the GAF *Waffenschule* 10 in Germany where they were put to work in the conversion training of pilots for JBG-31 in July 1960. JBG-31, 'Boelcke', was the first German operational unit (a fighter-bomber squadron) to be equipped with the Starfighter, becoming fully operational with the plane in 1963. The other GAF fighter-bomber squadrons to receive the F-104G were JBG-32 at Lechfeld, JBG-33 at Buchel, JBG-34 at Memmingen and JBG-36 at Rheine-Hopsten. F-104Gs went to fighter squadrons JG-71 at Wittmundhafen and JG-74 at Neuburg. The reconnaissance squadrons AKG-51 at Ingoldstadt/Manching and AKG-52 at Leck also were equipped with F-104Gs, while West German Navy squadrons MGF-1 at Schleswig and MGF-2 at Eggebeck received F-104Gs for use as armed reconnaissance and anti-shipping strike aircraft.

As F-104 aircraft began coming off production assembly lines and being delivered to NATO purchasers in large numbers, with the German Air Force principal among them, a huge pilot training prorgramme had to be implemented rapidly. The programme was severely hampered by the frequently poor weather over Northern Europe, which radically limited the training hours. The American and German air forces then set up a standard pilot training programme at Luke AFB in Arizona where the weather was nearly always good and the practice areas immense. The training aircraft were F-104Gs belonging to the GAF. Final flight operational training in the European environment was conducted at *Waffenschule* 10.

Starfighter pilots referred to the plane as 'unforgiving'. With a requirement to achieve high thrust with low drag, the aeroplane amounted to a long, bullet-shaped fuselage of narrow diameter and minimal air resistance, containing a single engine of great power output. The wings were extremely short and stubby, just 7½ feet long and provided very little lift. As such, they were positioned well aft near the tailplane so as to gain an overall lift effect through the combination of the wings and the horizontal tail surfaces. To counter the negative effect on vertical movement caused by the adjacency of the wings and the tailplane, the aircraft was provided with a rather large, moveable horizontal tail-surface to be operated like a large single flap. But solutions sometimes lead to other problems and, in this case, the aircraft became more prone to roll than aircraft having more conventional designs. To counter this tendency Lockheed machined the leading edges of the Starfighter wing to a knife-edge, further reducing air resistance. They also lowered the downward angle of the wing to an anhedral of 10 degrees, both measures helping to overcome the roll tendency. Still, many pilots found it difficult to keep the aeroplane level and upright in normal flight.

In the time that the German Air Force operated the Starfighter, 270 of the aircraft were lost in accidents with 110 pilots killed. The aeroplane developed a poor reputation in GAF service and the German press referred to it derogatorily as the 'widowmaker' and 'flying coffin'. With the beginning of operational flying in 1961, only two crashes occurred involving F-104s, but then the accident rate began to climb, with seven in 1962, 12 in 1964 and 28 in 1965. By the summer of 1965 German Starfighters had suffered 61 crashes with 35 pilots killed. The rate of Starfighter attrition in the GAF was, in fact, not that much greater than that of the same type with other air forces, including those of Canada and the United States. The Royal Canadian Air Force actually lost more than fifty per cent of its 200 CF-104s to flying accidents. The German press, however, caused much of the public to believe that there was something intrinsically wrong with the Starfighter and that it was too difficult and demanding an aircraft for the inexperienced young GAF pilots. In the furore over the high accident rate, critics of the West German government in Bonn criticised the Starfighter programme as having been politcally motivated, and called for its immediate cancellation.

The Starfighter was a well-designed high-speed interceptor that was pressed into additional roles for which it was not as well suited. It was designed to achieve high speed and remain in the air almost entirely through the forward thrust of its engine, actually becoming more stable in level flight as its speed increased. Its tiny wing provided very little stable glide capability should it lose power or suffer an engine flame-out. It demanded precise, sensitive control and was not an appropriate aircraft for an average or inexperienced pilot. While it is true that the plane had its share of technical problems, some of them contributing to the accidents suffered by the units operating it, it seems that many, if not the majority, of the German Air Force Starfighter crashes were attributable to the danger involved in high-speed, low-altitude missions flown in the often bad weather of Northern Europe.

Other factors undoubtedly contributing to the F-104 loss rate were the reduced number of flying hours that GAF pilots accrued in the plane compared with the pilots of other NATO air forces, and the high rate of maintenance required per flying hour for the Starfighter, which was being performed by GAF ground personnel who may have been too hastily trained. Additionally, the transition from training flying in the near-perfect conditions of the American south-west to the far-from-perfect north European weather may well have affected the crash rate. All things considered, it seems probable that human error played a prime role in the majority of the Starfighter accidents.

'It sounded like dinosaurs calling their mates' was what people used to say. And it was what I heard when I saw a 104 for the first time in the circuit of Luke Air Force Base, Arizona in 1957.

Oberst a.D. Gerd Gloystein, *Memories*

Polished beauties, neatly lined up. It's not detrimental that she has no waist (aerodynamics of the time did not include that). Like a spear her pitot tube stretches far forward, her body smooth and shapely, the leading edges of her short wings razor-sharp. The high tail commands respect and the big jet exhaust symbolizes harnessed power. We saw our so-called Gustav [the F-104G of the German Air Force] as a genial composition, a vision far ahead of its time, an exceptional merger of power, grace, and beauty.

I am about to fly it. The many switches, handles, instruments and lights are no longer threatening. The cockpit has lost its strangeness. The engine is running. I have completed the final technical checks and have been cleared for take-off. I confess that I have not been on easy terms with the lady. The canopy closed, I taxi onto the runway and step on the brakes. The enormous outside noise is but a hush inside. When accelerating the engine, the 104 tilts sideways a bit, with the nose dropping low and the fuselage trembling impatiently. Off the brakes – into the first reheat increment. The afterburner lights. Throttle forward through the second, third, and into the fourth increment: full power. The speed is increasing impressively; 170 knots. Stick aft a bit. The nose rises skyward and she lifts off at 185 knots into the cool morning. The wheels are still rumbling. Undercarriage 'up' quickly and, a moment later, reheat 'off'. Retard the take-off flaps. I'm flying the 104.

My breathing decelerates and the field of vision improves. Reaching the operating speed and altitude, I retard the throttle. At 400 knots, she floats through the air as steady as a board. In the next twenty years of flying the 104, I find that she 'feels' the same no matter what speed is attained. Only violent turbulence disturbs her steadyness. In the 1970s we flew very fast and very low over the Arizona

desert and even at 831 knots indicated she barely shook.
Generalmajor a.D. Peter Vogler, *Offener Brief an die F-104*

On the 17th of July 1973, we took off from Luke in Arizona on a mission called 'Basic Fighter Manoeuvres', or: aerial combat with an originally standard set-up. I was flying a two-seater (TF-104G) with my good friend 'Yogi' Soeldner in the rear seat. It was one of the typical Arizona July days with a 100°F+ ground temperature as we climbed at 10.35 a.m.

The flight was 'normal' until, during an engagement, our adversary achieved a superior position and I decided to evade with a 'separation'. In the Starfighter this was done by entering a steep downward spiral and then pushing forward to 'zero g' while accelerating with full afterburner power. Mach 1+ was quickly achieved and we reached 840 knots while descending through 13,000 feet. At 8,500 feet and 829 knots indicated airspeed, I began my recovery from the dive by pulling into a 6g upward spiral. To my surprise the stick would not move. I asked Yogi if he was holding it and then saw his arms resting on the canopy sills. Quickly glancing at the 'emergency panel', I saw only red and yellow illuminated labels as almost all the systems were 'off.' I retarded the throttle to idle and extended the air brakes in a single move – it felt like running into a wall – but the pitch of the aircraft didn't change. I tried the electric trim. Very slowly, the nose began to come up. I mentioned the possibility of ejecting to Yogi and he replied, 'Hell no, not at this speed'. We approached 4,000 feet with upward trim and the brown desert floor was coming at us at frightening rate. My adrenaline level was rising recipriocally to our diminishing height. At 2,000 feet, we saw a big hill rising in front of us. With some right aileron trim we barely avoided the hill's peak and finally began to climb. We must have blown up a tremendous cloud of desert dust. As we climbed, the stick was still rigid. Steering with trim, I climbed to 16,000 feet and contacted our auxiliary airfield for an emergency landing. Everything was set up. I entered the emergency circuit at 16,000 feet when suddenly the stick began to move. I had normal control response again.

'Downgrading' the emergency, I left the pattern and called Luke tower for a long, straight-in final approach. All went well, allowing us time to calm down. As our friends at the emergency field had reported our predicament to Luke Approach, we were greeted after landing by the big 'welcome party' – fire service, base commander, flight surgeon, and the chaplain. The debrief was done with Lockheed's chief technian, Dan McEvoy, 'Mister 104.' It was to no avail as maintenance 'could not duplicate the situation.' That evening, Yogi and I celebrated our very special 'birthday' at the stag bar of the Luke Officers Mess with our bosses and friends.

Some days later, McEvoy told us that the same type of incident had just occurred over water in Taiwan, where they found that, during zero-g conditions, gas bubbles had formed, blocking the hydraulic pipes. We also learned of a few fatal related incidents, with 'causes not determined.'

Oberst a.D. Gerd Gloystein, *Memories*

The Starfighter cockpit fits like it was tailor-made. She reacts to control pressures like a pure-bred race horse: delicately, eagerly, immediately, and with buzzing nerves. Her rolls are as fast as a thought; she'll roll twice in a second. Her trim can be accurately adjusted, her reaction to throttle movement is instantaneous, her flight position balanced and stable. I learned to cherish all of these characteristics when I had to find my airdrome in the worst of weather.

Her performance was then unequalled and would be respectable even today, more than 50 years after her 'birth.' She attained twice the speed of sound in little more than 5 minutes from jump start, flew nearly Mach 1.3 at ground level and climbed to 43,000 feet in a bit more than 2 minutes. The F-104 convincingly proved the tremendous leap forward of western aircraft design.

The Starfighter was a strict mistress. She forgave negligence and cockiness only within narrow limits. She taught us flexible thinking, quickness in decision-making, independence, and both pride and modesty.

Of course, the F-104 was not a flying toy, but a highly effective weapons system for her time. Originally designed as a light day interceptor, she had to fulfil all tactical flying tasks in the *Luftwaffe*. That made her heavier and more complex, yet did not detract from her uniqueness. With the F-104 we won coveted trophies in serious competitions with top experts of friendly air forces and with her we proved the new *Luftwaffe* a match for the demands of the modern age.

The F-104 was manual terrain following by radar in bad weather, efficient (analogue) computers for all her weapons, an inertial navigation system independent of ground stations, a very dependable engine with a previously-unequalled thrust-to-weight ratio, material processing of the highest precision and quality (the 3.9 inch-thick wing roots could take aircraft loads of 8+ g), an infra-red missile-and-gun sight, maintenance-friendly placement of sub-systems, and modular construction reducing the changing of unserviceable parts to a single move. In many ways she was a pioneer, a trail-blazer for today's German Air Force.

Generalmajor a.D. Peter Vogler, *Offener Brief an die F-104*

It was a day like nearly every other day. The sun was shining and the Phoenix Valley air was dry and warm. The old parking area of the former 'Kraut Field' looked as it always had, except for a new reviewing stand on the south side. Three *Luftwaffe* generals and a German admiral had been invited. Many famous officers were present who had led the German F-104 Training Squadron or had supported our training since 1967. Members of the German 'Cactus Starfighter Squadron filled the other seats. The speeches were delivered in the desert wind and, with barely visible smoke trails, eight Starfighters led by Lt. Col. 'Heini' Thüringer, Officer Commanding 1st GAF Training Squadron/USA, appeared in the distance. There were tears in the eyes of young and old pilots in the reviewing stand as the planes flew by. It was the end of an era. The F-104s landed and in the afternoon there was a reception. Our affair with the Starfighter was over.

The *Luftwaffe* phased out its last operational F-104G, from *Jagdbombergeschwader* 34 '*Allgäu*' in Memmingen, Bavaria, in 1987. The last aircraft was withdrawn from service at the *Wehrtechnische Dienststelle* 61 (Technical Trials Unit) in Ingolstadt in 1991.

Oberst a.D. Gerd Gloystein, *Memories*

General Kammhuber listened intently to Erich Hartmann's advice and recommendation to defer purchase of the Starfighter for the German Air Force until its new pilots were up to the challenge of the new plane. Finally he responded, cautioning Erich never to talk about the subject to anyone else. He said that the GAF was happy to buy the F-104 and that it was a political decision. However, word of Erich's private views about the Starfighter gradually spread through the higher circles of the air force, reinforcing the opinion of many that he was not a good officer.

With the subsequent pattern of German Starfighter crashes and pilot losses, the accuracy of Erich's opinion was confirmed. The tragic operational losses continued and mounted until mid-1966 when the GAF chief, General Wernher Panitzki, who had replaced Kammhuber, was himself replaced after criticizing the German F-104 programme as politically motivated. Panitzki's successor was the famous World War Two fighter ace, *Lieutenant General* Johannes Steinhoff, who had flown and led the Messerschmitt Me-262 jets in the final months of the war. The brilliant Steinhoff was a gifted organizer and, on acceding to the inspectorship of the German Air Force, insisted on being given appropriate authority with the job, which led to his resolving the critical German Starfighter situation. Initially, Steinhoff had not favoured the acquisition of the Starfighter for the GAF. When the purchase went ahead he had proposed improvements to the ejection system of the plane, improvements which had not been implemented by the German Defence Ministry. Now, as head of the air force Steinhoff ordered a review of the Starfighter ejection system in order to improve his pilots' chances of survival. The F-104G had originally been fitted with a Lockheed ejection seat which was found to have a destabilizing effect after ejection. Steinhoff had the seat replaced with the Martin-Baker GQ7 zero-zero seat which, in combination with significantly revised training techniques and procedures, immediately lowered the loss rate of his Starfighter pilots. F-104 accidents and crashes, however, did continue at the rate of about ten a year until the early 1980s when the German Starfighter force had been largely replaced by McDonnell-Douglas F-4 Phantoms and later by Panavia Tornados. JBG-34 flew the last operational F-104G Starfighters of the German Air Force, retiring them in 1987.

While occupied with the effort to develop JG-71, Erich Hartmann neglected the annual re-validation of his pilot's licence. The oversight caught the attention of one of Erich's politically zealous detractors in the GAF, who forced the matter to the point of a legal proceeding. The military judges absolved Erich in the case, but the affair resulted in further defamation of his character, fuelling the persistent view of many in the service that Erich was simply not a good officer. The negative opinion finally led to his being relieved of his JG-71 command and transferred to a desk job at a staff headquarters near Cologne. He lived in near-obscurity for several years, his service to his country largely unappreciated. In 1968, thanks to the recommendation of his wartime friend, *General* Gunther Rall, Erich was finally promoted to the rank of full *Colonel*. He retired from active service with the German Air Force in September 1970. He died in September 1993.

Johannes Steinhoff

April 1945. The Second World War in Europe was almost over. With the presence of several hundred Mustang, Lightning and Thunderbolt escort fighters shepherding the massive American bomber formations by day in the skies over Germany, and the equally massive raids by the Lancasters and Halifaxes of the Royal Air Force by night, the Allies had finally achieved air supremacy over the Germans. The monumental errors of Hitler and Goering in their conduct of the air war had contributed as much to the Nazi defeat as the astonishing manufacturing productivity of the Allies in filling those skies with aircraft.

On the 18 April, Colonels Johannes Steinhoff and Franz Lützow visited the operations room of their unit, JV-44. The elite jet fighter squadron, sometimes referred to as 'the Squadron of Experts', had been organized on Hitler's order by the former General of the Fighters, Adolf Galland, to demonstrate the capability of the Messerschmitt Me-262 when pitted against the heavily armed B-17s and B-24s of the American bomber force. The ops room was in Feldkirchen near Riem, their Munich base. Steinhoff and Lützow knew that at around midday they would be taking off to intercept the enemy bombers and, like so many other officers in the squadron, were well aware that the odds were stacked against them. Their only comfort was the thought that, from the following day, they would be protected during their most vulnerable moments of take-off and landing by the Focke-Wulf Fw-190s of Lieutenant Heinz Sachsenberg's *schwarm* – the enemy fighters had become alarmingly effective at destroying the jets near their airfield. The Fw-190s would give the pilots of JV-44 a better chance of survival. Galland, Steinhoff and Lützow boarded a jeep for the ride to the airfield.

From the perimeter track surrounding the field they noted the heavily pock-marked terrain, where the ground crews were constantly at work filling-in craters made during the frequent visits of the Allied fighter-bombers. In a scene reminiscent of English airfields during the Battle of Britain, German pilots were sprawled in deck chairs on the grass near their dispersed jets, reading and sipping coffee in the cold morning air, recuperating from the drinking of the previous evening.

A field telephone rang and word was spread that the enemy bomber stream was passing over Stuttgart. In the windless late morning air the heavily-loaded jets would require a rather long ground run before lifting off. They would carry full magazines of cannon shells, 24 aerial rockets and full fuel loads making them even more sluggish in the take-off roll than usual. In the mission today, General Galland would lead the first flight and Steinhoff the second. They would be encountering the American bomber force somewhere between Stuttgart and Munich. In anticipation of the engagement, Macky Steinhoff thought about the immense firepower of the enemy bombers, stacked as they always were in their precise combat box formations, designed to present maximum exposure of their 0.50 calibre machine-guns in every direction. He wondered what it would be like if he had to bale out of his jet at 26,000 feet in −50° temperatures. Word was passed around that they would be taking off in 10 minutes. It was time for the ground crewmen to get the jets ready for starting.

Steinhoff turned his attention to the operating procedures of the Me-262, reminding himself that he must hold the aircraft still until the twin turbine engines were running at full revs. Another phone call and a shout that the huge force of enemy bombers was heading for Regensburg, and Galland yelled, "Let's go!"

Steinhoff did a very quick ground inspection of the jet, tugging on the rockets and pulling one of the slotted leading-edge flaps out from the wing. He climbed up on the wing and settled into the tiny cockpit, patting the aluminium skin of the machine just below the canopy. He had been flying this particular plane since the unit was organized at Brandenburg. He squirmed on his parachute in the seat shell trying to find the most comfortable sitting position and making sure that the seat height was properly adjusted with the gunsight exactly at his eye level. Attaching and adjusting his waist and shoulder belts to a comfortably tight fit, he then fitted his helmet and oxygen mask, checking the oxygen flow meter and his other instruments. He tested the free movement of the aileron and rudder controls, set the altimeter and turned on his radio. Galland then signalled a circular wave to indicate that it was time to start engines. Small auxiliary starter motors whined and the turbojets began to spool into operation. The pilots checked temperatures and pressures before closing their cockpit canopies. Galland rolled slowly out of his dispersal area, his turbine engines screaming, and the other jets of his flight followed him onto the airfield. The air stank of kerosene.

As Galland and the other two jets of his flight lifted off, Macky Steinhoff led his flight into their take-off roll. The three Messerschmitt fighters rocked and bumped across the grass field, gathering momentum. The unevenness of the grass surface, punctuated by the roughly filled shallow bomb craters, made the take-off roll a jarring and unnerving experience.

Steinhoff saw the three aircraft of the general's flight depart and their undercarriages retract. His own aircraft suddenly lurched to the right, causing him to react with rudder input to correct the movement. The jet entered into a skid and, as it did so, one of his turbine engines burst into flame. He had passed the point at which he would have been able to stop the plane. The jet was less than 200 yards from the perimeter track embankment and moving fast. His only option was to try to take off. He pulled back hard on the stick, but the heavily-loaded fighter lacked sufficient speed and lift for flight.

The landing gear of the 262 smashed into the embankment. The jet became briefly airborne as though it had tripped . . . and then it was down hard, disintegrating around Steinhoff. Bits of the plane were flying off and the remains of the cockpit, where he sat, were spinning slowly, engulfed in fire.

Johannes Steinhoff came from Bottendorf, Thuringia, in central Germany. He was born on 15 September 1913, the son of an agricultural mill worker. He had two brothers, Wolf, who became a doctor, Bernd, an engineer who eventually moved to Columbus, Ohio, and two sisters, one of whom died. He was well-educated and studied languages including French, English, Latin and Greek. He credited his excellent English in part to his many conversations with captured Allied aviators during the war.

He had planned to become a teacher, but in 1930s Germany he was unable to find a job so he enlisted in the German Navy for officer training and there he met and became a friend of Dieter Hrabak, also destined to be a legendary *Luftwaffe* ace. Both men served in the Navy for one year before becoming naval aviation cadets and later transferring to the burgeoning German Air Force. In flight training, Steinhoff and Hrabak met other young airmen who would one day form the elite corps of the *Luftwaffe* fighter arm, including Adolf Galland, Hannes Trautloft and Günther Lützow.

Steinhoff served from first to last in the Second World War. He fought in the Polish Campaign in 1939, in the Battle of France and the Battle of Britain in 1940, in North Africa, Sicily, the Russian Campaign and finally in the West again during the defence of the Reich. His tally of 176 aerial victories was credited in 993 sorties. He was shot down 12 times and wounded once. Against the expectations of his doctors, he survived a horrifying crash and hideously disfiguring burns and after the war rose to the rank of Inspector of the German Air Force, its chief. In the new GAF he insisted on being combat-qualified on all current jet aircraft and in his long and illustrious career flew more than one hundred different types of aircraft, from biplanes to the most high-performance jet fighters.

A high-achiever in and out of combat, Macky Steinhoff had benefitted enormously from both his naval and *Luftwaffe* officer training, emerging as an officer and a gentleman possessed of the finest qualities – decency, fairness, chivalry and honour. His personal code was exemplified by an event that occurred late in 1943 during the Italian Campaign. In an encounter with a P-38 Lightning, he shot down the American and, on landing, located the pilot who was unhurt, brought him back to the German airfield, shared food and drink with the man and then offered to put him up for the night in his own tent. According to legend, some of Kommodore Steinhoff's men urged him to tie the American up with rope and attach a string from him to Steinhoff's toe. Instead, Steinhoff asked the Yank to give his word as an officer that he would not run away during the night, and the American agreed. The two pilots who, a few hours before, had been trying to knock each other out of the sky then settled down to share the victor's tent, entirely on the basis of the traditional military prisoner's parole. Having drunk a lot of alcohol, the two shared breakfast the next morning with cups of strong black coffee. The American pilot asked the Kommodore if he could stick around their base for a while as he doubted that his prisoner of war camp would be providing Schnaps and such good coffee.

Lieutenant General Steinhoff's own summation of the European air war, from his perspective follows:

> 'The 15 September 1940 was the day of our victory.' These words of Churchill, spoken after the breakdown of Germany, might be hard to understand at the first appraisal by many people, but for us fliers who had a part on that important 15 September it contains a great truth.
>
> Throughout that long, hot summer during the so-called 'Battle of Britain' we flew over the island and in the fight for air superiority had used up the best part of our fighters, and even more so our bombers. For a month it seemed as though our objective, air superiority, had been reached. We flew with the assurance of owning the airspace from Calais to London. But this enormous exertion led to the almost complete expenditure of our physical and moral reserves. The fact remains that by the end of July the English fighter force was sharply reduced.
>
> But then, the situation changed. Literally out of the blue sky came the surprise, and we found ourselves saying, 'They are here again!' They hadn't slept on that island. No, exactly the opposite.
>
> On the 15 September we escorted a bomber formation to an attack on the southern railroad terminals of London. At the same time, for demonstration purposes, everything that we had in the way of bombers and fighters was thrown into the air. Then our formation, after assembling, began the flight to England. At that time we had no idea that three years later the 'other side' would show us the practical application of the theories of the great air tactician Douhet – pioneer

of air power. General Douhet's demand for a 'strong formation of flying fortresses' was demonstrated for us by the Allies, with terrible consequences for Germany.

While flying over the Straits of Dover we saw an unusually large number of Spitfires (the best English fighter) high above us. They were shadowing us at what was for us an unreachable height. The sky was streaked with a great number of white contrails. Suddenly we understood! The English had started their counterattack. When we reached our target, we knew it would all go wrong, for the number of our 'silent companions' became uncontrollably large.

On the way back we had to leave the bombers behind. We did it with the feeling that everything would have to take its course now. The fighters' fuel was almost used up. For an hour we had flown without orientation and there was the danger that we, the entire fighter force, would not reach the French coast. We might run out of fuel and crash in the Channel.

On the evening of that day, the English radio reported the downing of 99 German bombers. That was the average they took for the defeat they suffered in the air battle over the German 'Bucht' in December 1939. This crushing result of irresponsible conduct of an aerial war had a devastating effect on us pilots. But it is doubtful if it had the same effect on Hitler and Goering. The 15 September should have caused Hitler to begin planning defensively, at least in the air.

The English had ingeniously found a way to defend their island. Every pilot, except a small group of night flyers and bomber pilots who were the nucleus of the coming night-bomber fleet, was retrained as a fighter pilot. It made no difference if he was a liaison plane pilot, a bomber or fighter-bomber pilot, he was retrained. Industry was instructed to concentrate on fighters. And in this way it was possible to seal the gap – and more! In one stroke, the lost air superiority was regained, and henceforth we did not own the airspace from Calais to London.

The Decline of the Fighters

Like a red threat, a series of bad decisions and compromises weaves its way through every action in the planning and production of the German aircraft industry. The leaders would not admit that 'the stongest air force in the world', after such an auspicious beginning, had now lost the lead. The subsequent mass victories on the Russian Front contributed to the delusions of the leaders, as it did to the units active there with such success. Hitler seemed determined to remain oblivious to the air struggle on the Channel coast, where the three and then two wings left there were fighting a hard and eventually hope-less battle.

Then it seemed for a time as if Hitler had seen the need for planning new fighter wings. It gave us renewed hope at the front. But if fighter production was given top industrial priority today, then it was usual that tomorrow this programme would be cut or changed. Not only we flyers at the front, but also the economic planners could not understand this catastrophic lack of planning and foresight. Eventually they just resigned themselves and carried out orders. Often on their own initiative, they tried to prevent the worst.

Then came the inevitable. It happened sooner than expected, and was disastrously underestimated. The first formation of four-engined American bombers flew over the Channel coast – an ominous development which Goering made into a bagatelle! The advent of the four-engined 'heavies' hit the German fighters a devastating blow, and unsettled the fighter leaders.

The time of mass attacks and saturation bombings began. This decisive weapon within the space of a year reduced us fighters to the role of a fire department in perpetual action from one call to the next. Ultimately the big bombers raced through all Europe, including Hitler's fortress, to the total exhaustion of men and machines.

Churchill said in 1944: 'Hitler did make Europe into a fortress, but he forgot the roof.'

In the spring of 1943 a rumour ran like wildfire through the front. Industry was reported to have developed an all-new aircraft. This machine did not propel itself with the old method of piston engine driving a propeller, but used the air compressed by turbines to fly. It had reached speeds never previously attained.

The rumour proved to be the truth. The chief pilot of the Messerschmitt works had made the first flights in this machine, and soon afterward the General of the Fighter Arm, Galland, tried it and enthusiastically talked of the fighter of the future. Endless technical problems had to be solved before production could commence and the machine find its way to combat. But before this stage could begin, the means for further production had to be authorized. And that needed the approval of Hitler!

Neither the builder, Professor Messerschmitt, nor the leaders of the *Luftwaffe* had for even one second thought that this new aircraft would be anything but a fighter plane. The later misuse of this Me-262 type, which we knew for short as 'Turbo,' proved incredible. It was used for everything except as a fighter. The situation demonstrated how little Hitler and Goering understood the possibilities. It also shows how, in the last three years of the war, with Hitler's blind hitting-out, even the best thoughts and ideas had to be lost.

In the autumn of 1943, at the air base at Insterburg in East Prussia there was one of those displays of new weapons so beloved by Army and industry notables. Among the new weapons was the Me-262.

After an impressive flying display, we flyers, defence-production leaders, members of the General Staff, escort officers, and engineers thoughtfully admired the machine and waited for the all-highest verdict.

After Hitler asked Messerschmitt about the flying performance, range, and fuel consumption, he further inquired if the aircraft could carry bombs. When this was reluctantly admitted, Hitler turned to the *Luftwaffe* leaders with a dramatic gesture. "This is the bomber with which I will fight off the invasion – this is my revenge bomber. Of course, none of you thought of that".

With these words all Galland's hopes were destroyed. Hitler's edict meant forgetting the idea that fighters could once again play the role of strong defenders. The bomber pilots were now in the foreground, as were the bombers in 1940, except that now all possibility of their conducting effective attacks against England had vanished. The *Luftwaffe* went into a deep sleep after the end of the Battle of Britain – a sleep out of which it was now cruelly awakened.

The Great Tug O'War

Thus the bomber wings sat at home and waited for the birth of the new bomber Hitler had promised them. But the bomber did not come.

After the Insterburg display a tug o' war began over the Me-262 which was disgraceful not only for the leaders, but also for the combat pilots. Bitter fights and rancour existed between bomber pilots and fighter pilots to get the awaited, longed-for new type. In the meantime, Galland, as Udet before him, tirelessly tried to convince Goering that the morale of the fighter pilots alone was not enough in the aerial battle to stop the attacks of the four-engined heavy bombers. He asked for a better aircraft – demanded the 'Turbo'.

Squadron of Experts

In the last months of the war our dream of forming a team of fighter aces was realized. There is no connection now to HQ. Berlin has enough to do with itself and so has Goering. Word gets around that we need 'great guns.' Those who do not volunteer we retrieve from rest homes and hospitals, where most of the people wait for the war's end. 'Galland' and the miracle word 'Turbo' galvanize every pilot. Once again air superiority – The Great Aviation – will be experienced.

There are no dreams of great victory or turning the tide, as some fools may believe, but it is an opportunity to show once more what flying experience and technical superiority are able to do. This prospect lures even men who, from the flight surgeon's standpoint, are everything else but able to fly.

Those officers who came to visit us during those last days at Riem, whether they came from HQ or elsewhere, were dazzled by the array of high war decorations accumulated in one spot. The Knight's Cross was almost our squadron badge. The unique composition of the outfit also evoked surprise: One General (a General as a squadron leader is certainly unique); two Colonels; one Lieutenant Colonel; three Majors; two Captains; eight Lieutenants; combined with a similar number of noncommissioned officers, these were our pilots.

There was Colonel Günther Lützow, exiled until now from Germany because of his courageous opposition to Goering. Major Heinz Baer came to us, a brilliant sharpshooter and outstanding fighter. And Gerd Barkhorn, who had 301 kills to his account on the Eastern Front. With Barkhorn came Hohagen, Schnell, and Krupinski, whom we enticed to come from the hospitals. All were in the war from the first day. All were at least once wounded, some many times. All had high decorations.

Each one of them wanted to know once more the feel of air superiority after years of flying under oppressing circumstances. They wanted this experience even if they had to pay for it with their lives. Such was the spirit of the 'Squadron of Experts.'

With nervous activity, preparations go forward for the mission. Our actions are ruled by urgency. The Americans are fighting near Crailsheim, but there is no clear battle line. Everything is in flux.

The evening after arrival in Riem we discussed the mission against the four-engined bomber stream. The jet fighters which remain in Brandenburg have already had this experience. Under the leadership of Weissenberger this squadron was successful – indicating the damage that could be done with a planned mission at the right time.

However, Galland said: 'Let the Mustangs and Thunderbolts go by, don't tangle with them even if they are right in front of your gunsight. I want to know what chance we have against the Flying Fortress, which brings death to thousands of helpless people on the ground.'

The next morning from the 10 available jets, three are ready for operations. With those three, I am supposed to fly the first mission. With me goes Fährmann, my wingman for 2 years, a very elegant, natural pilot who is able to follow instinctively all my decisions. Also with me is a third man, Krupinski, who has been wounded five times and burnt severely. With enviable nonchalance he climbs again and again into the cockpit.

'Lightnings coming across the Alps,' blares the radio.

Mustang invasion starts and Operations reports, 'Many Mustangs are coming from the west.'

Galland: 'This looks like a fighter invasion, but I think the four-engined bombers will follow.'

Nuremberg reports: 'Bombs dropped by two-engined airplanes. Keep your nerve, they are coming for certain.'

By noon the situation is clear: 'Long-range bomber formation near Frankfurt flying east.'

Now they are there. An hour later Galland orders Steinhoff: 'Take off!'

The first formation is reported directly north of Munich and between Munich and the Danube. Then Fährmann reports a large formation at nine o'clock. There the stream straggles between 6,000 and 8,000 metres. While we are flying over the first bombers we cannot see the end of the formation. At the tip, the Liberators are flying, a bomber of older type somewhat more vulnerable than the Forts and therefore flying ahead of the formation. Then come the B-17s, for which we have some respect from experience.

At the end of the formation I make a large, wide turn which carries me up to 9,000 metres altitude and brings me to the head of the bomber formation. I call 'get ready,' then we dive for the attack on the last small formation. The airspeed indicator shows 900 km per hour when I recognize the little dots ahead of me moving at an incredible speed.

A short burst from my four cannons, fired at the left airplane, and then I have to jerk my stick back to avoid a collision. Looking back, I see black smoke and flames leaping out of the bomber's engines.

At the same time, the airplane in the centre is burning. That's the one Fährmann attacked. Approach and kill! It is all over in seconds. Krupinski, our third man, works alone and in his own particular way. He picks a Boeing. Mustangs and Thunderbolts which are above the formation in the correct attack position prepare to dive on us from all directions. It is a grotesque picture. They look like balloons standing still in the air, since we have a speed margin of at least 400–500 km per hour. Literally we ride through the bombers. Still I do not know how many kills we had – the ride was too fast. Then my guns jam while Fährmann kills another bomber. While in a chandelle he radios, 'My right engine is dead.'

Fährmann slows down more and more and there is a new emergency call: 'My left engine is also dying.' With that, he is chased by a lot of Thunderbolts. When I turn around to help him, my right turbine stops. Now I have to think of myself, and I take off heading for Munich. I report to Operations on the way, telling them of my condition. Back comes the ominous reply: 'If possible, do not land in Riem. The field is under surveillance by Mustangs.'

I still have enough fuel, and therefore I would like to convince myself that the situation is really precarious. Then I see the polished wings of four Mustangs as they fly across the field in absolutely perfect formation.

I cannot miss this chance, even with one engine dead. None of the Mustang pilots sees me coming. Only one of my 30mm cannons is operational, but it goes through the wing of the Mustang like a buzz saw. The other three Mustangs drop their tanks and disappear.

After I land, Fährmann calls the base and reports that he parachuted into the Danube. Krupinski is already home and says jauntily, 'That was a lot of fun. Why don't we refuel and go again? We could still catch them.'

The Proof

During the middle of April we finally receive additional weapons for our jets. This looks promising. Under each of the wings, 24 rockets can be mounted. The trajectory of these rockets is practically straight up to a distance of 1,200 metres, and during this distance their velocity rises to 15 x 30 metres. According to our estimates one could not miss if all rockets were fired simultaneously into a bomber formation.

Only a few aircraft can be fitted with this equipment. The rockets are manufactured in northern Germany while the factory for the launchers is in Czechoslovakia. There is no possibility of proper logistic support. During the night a transport plane brings ammunition from the Baltic coast, but there is only one such flight before the airfield in the north is in enemy hands.

During the first trial to fire the rockets into a close formation, Galland demonstrates that at Germany's dying gasp we finally have the means to destroy the bomber formations, which up to this point seemed to be untouchable.

The rockets roar among the bombers like a shotgun into a flock of ducks. Two of the bombers move close to each other and then fuselage hits fuselage. Both dive together into the ground. The bomber formation is in a state of confusion and as two more rockets burst two other Flying Fortresses are destroyed.

We work day and night to patch up our wounded jets. We also receive hits, but we don't lose one pilot. We do not have spare parts, and during the night the familiar drone of the well-feared Mosquitos can be heard circling our airfield.

We fight to see who will be permitted to fly next. The few airplanes we have are not able to stand the continuous use, and if we have six jets flying we are very proud. Near Nuremberg, near Augsberg, above the Danube and the Alps we shoot the Flying Fortresses from the sky.

Maybe there are only two or three during each mission, but we know before we take off that we will not return without a kill.

The supply problem is suddenly solved. In mid-April we receive jets from all quarters as presents. The reconnaissance squadrons, bomber squadrons, and the fighter-bombers park their airplanes next to ours. 'Here's a present for you', they say, 'you can use it.'

If only the Americans did not make our lives so miserable. It is a perpetual race between the bomb shelter and the airplane. The harassment is nerve-wracking. You always hope you will have sufficient time for an undetected take-off. You are not safe until the airspeed indicator shows 500 km per hour.

Four Me-262s land. They are special machines, fitted with a 5cm cannon. This is one of Hitler's ideas. There were many fights regarding the merits of this cannon and its role in air defence, but we prove in the meantime that this weapon's time has passed.

Soon we have 70 jets on our airfield. Only a month ago we had to beg for one on our knees. We reflect bitterly on these events.

JUNE 1943. SICILY. HEADQUARTERS, 77TH FIGHTER WING

Steinhoff:

We, the HQ officers, lived and ate in a small inconspicuous villa. It stood in a vineyard, its front colour-washed in pink. This was the domain of Corporal Rieber, my batman, mess cook, and orderly – in short, my maid-of-all-work. He was a glass-blower by trade and there was not a man in the whole group whose weight or chest measurement exceeded his. For this reason he needed neither name nor rank and everyone addressed him simply as 'Tubby.'

In the half-light their faces showed up like flat, bluish green disks. How tired and worn out everyone was! Two months had now passed since the hurried evacuation of North Africa. At this particular moment the wan faces revealed what no one wanted to admit: We've been beaten. All of them – Bernhard excepted – had reached Sicily at the eleventh hour, mentally and physically exhausted. And there was little hope that circumstances would change.

It had been more like a hasty retreat than a move. The group's Messerschmitts landed at Trapani on 8 May; they were riddled with bullets and had not been serviced for days. Inside the fuselage of each aircraft knelt a mechanic, peering over the pilot's shoulder, a position he had reached with some difficulty by squeezing through the wireless hatch. Without a parachute and with no hope of escaping from his prison in an emergency, he was at the mercy of his fate and his pilot's skill.

The deck chairs were set out in a semicircle under the olive trees beside the hut. There we sat down and told each other what had happened to us since our last meeting. Fighter pilots at readiness, deprived of these items of furniture, would be altogether inconceivable. How many hours had I spent in a deck chair since the outbreak of war? It had started in the west during the 'sitzkrieg' against France when we would occasionally chase away a reconnaissance aircraft – a harmless occupation compared with what we were doing now. But since that time we had been in an almost constant state of readiness, either 'cockpit readiness,' sitting in our aircraft, or else in deck chairs close by our machines. A day seems very long when it is spent in waiting, with nothing to occupy one's imagination except the war in the air.

The general has been asking vainly and all too long for more fighter groups. But they can't just be produced from thin air. Ever since it's been appreciated that these four-engined bombers are in fact real fortresses that can only be taken on individually, some ludicrous proposals have been put forward about how to deal with them. You'll soon be getting some rockets from the army – they call them *Nebelwerfer*. They're large-calibre missiles and one of them is mounted beneath each wing. They're fired so that they explode in the middle of the bombers and cause them to scatter. Once flushed from their defensive hedgehog the Fortresses can be destroyed without difficulty. Others are trying to drop large bombs above the formations in such a way that they explode at the same height as the enemy. Here the intention is to destroy the whole formation in one go, or at least to make it disperse. But it's extraordinarily difficult to position yourself correctly above the Fortresses. Your altitude must be calculated with absolute accuracy since the bomb has a time fuse and is quite ineffective if it goes off at the wrong height.

I fixed my gaze through the front windscreen, keeping the illuminated reflector sight on the aircraft at the centre of the formation. 'You have to aim at the Fortresse's glass cockpit...' Exactly when I opened fire I do not know – the moment to do so must have been conveyed automatically to my thumb on the stick. In that last brief phase of the attack it was all suddenly like the sequence of a familiar exercise. I pulled my 'Me' up to the same height as the bombers as though I had done it a hundred times before. My task was to spray the gleaming cockpit with a hail of shot. In a curving trajectory the incendiary tracer streaked away from the machine guns towards the giant bomber, crossing the blue smears of smoke tracer. The luminous cross-wires of my sights shoot to the 'pop-pop-pop' of the cannons. The flashing panels of glass were plainly visible, and then I had to wrench the machine upwards, the 'g' force pressing me hard down into my seat. The impetus from this burst of speed took me high above the bombers. My mouth felt as though it had dried up and my saliva tasted bitter. The cockpit was full of the smell of cordite. As I banked I noticed that I was on my own; the HQ flight had broken. Looking back I saw a column of white water rising as high as a house at the point where the bomber had crashed.

We can't go on like this. The answer to the heavies is the massed attack. So long as we commit ourselves in penny packets and try to fight off every intruder, we'll never be successful. It's time you learned how to tackle the bombers, how to approach them in tight formation and attack them head-on. You're hesitating and you're failing to get close enough . . .'   –Adolf Galland

To the Fighter Leader, Sicily. During the defensive action against the bombing attack on the Straights of Messina the fighter element failed in its task. One pilot from each of the fighter wings taking part will be tried by court martial for cowardice in the face of the enemy.

(signed) Goering, *Reichsmarshall*

I almost regretted now having gone for the group in North Africa when the general had given me the choice between a command in the Reich and one in the south. I had arrived on a short home leave from my fighter wing in the Crimea, having flown to Berlin in a Storch. The General of Fighters [Galland] was expecting me. When he greeted me his mood was sombre. At first he had wanted to know how things were going with our fighter defence in the east but I soon realized that his immediate preoccupation lay elsewhere. Almost at once he came around to the subject of the Flying Fortresses, telling me about their first attacks on the Channel coast and their apparent invulnerability which had so surprised the German fighter pilots. He had warned the *Reichsmarshall* and had demanded a build-up of the fighter arm. In the same context he had pointed out that the armament of the Messerschmitt 109 and Focke-Wulf 190 was inadequate and had suggested certain improvements. When he had predicted that one day the Fortresses would be able to fly to Berlin itself the *Reichsmarshall* had brushed the suggestion rudely aside, declaring that he refused to listen to such defeatist tittle-tattle.

'You'll be taking over the 77th Fighter Group in North Africa. The CO's been killed.' Not very encouraging, but in wartime this was the way promotion happened. We all moved up by stepping into dead men's shoes, we no less than those on the other side, those whom at every opportunity we tried to shoot down.

There's no longer any doubt in my mind that the island's being softened up for a landing. Now that Pantelleria has surrendered without a shot being fired, they don't need aircraft carriers any more. Malta and Pantelleria are ideal springboards for their fighters – you might even say they're unsinkable aircraft carriers. The bombers are being flown from further away, from Tunis, Bizerta, and Tripoli.

–Adolf Galland

You criticize the higher command and the *Reichsmarshall* and you know as well as I that there are omissions which can now never be made good. You describe the higher and middle echelons of the command as distant and inhuman and maintain that they don't understand 'your,' or rather 'our,' war. But where is the experience of modern aerial warfare to come from if higher commanders refuse to serve on staffs or on the General Staff? A unit that is led with desperate fanaticism but with failing powers and bad nerves is a badly led unit, Steinhoff. Consider, for a moment what I myself am faced with: I request an immediate build-up of the fighter arm and I have reason to believe that my request will be met, yet at the same time I'm perfectly well aware that the number of properly qualified senior leaders can be counted on the fingers of one hand. A lot of groups and wings today are being led by people who are actually no more than competent squadron commanders. There are those who chase and fight and those who simply blaze away, as you yourself know . . .

–Adolf Galland

Up to now we've failed in our attacks against the Flying Fortresses, the enemy's most effective weapon by far. The *Reichsmarshall* is angry about it and rightly so. You must all concentrate on one thing and one thing only – shooting down bombers. Forget about the fighters. The only thing that counts is the destruction of the bombers and the ten crew that each of them carries.   –Adolf Galland

Traffic with the mainland is vital to our existence whether, in the event of a landing, we manage to hold the island or whether we have to evacuate it. The flow of supplies must not be interrupted. And if we have to evacuate Sicily the ferry traffic must be maintained up to the last minute. At this stage of the war the Straits of Messina are crucial to our fortunes.   –Adolf Galland

Steinhoff:

It was a relief to be in the air again. After the doubts as to whether we would manage to take off unscathed there now followed a short period of carefree flight. We had escaped being bombed on the ground and we had not yet intercepted the enemy in the air. One had only to concentrate on the mechanics of flying, on navigation, and on the interchange of messages with the controller, but these few moments were quickly over and already people's eyes were beginning to search the sky and to watch out for surprise attacks.

Usually the report that someone was turning back came shortly after take-off and before there was any real danger. It was invariably accompanied by an expression of regret; for instance: 'Oh sod it, my engine keeps cutting. I'll have to turn back.' In some cases the regret was perfectly genuine, in others less so, and it needed long experience of command to distinguish between them.

Hurtling head-on towards us at the same height, the elegant fighters went racing through our formation. For a split second I seemed to see – though it may only have been my imagination – the colourful insignia on the Spitfires' fuselages, the pointed wing tips, the bellies milky blue like those of fish.

There was a loud thud against the fuselage and I wrenched my head around. Looking past the armour plate I saw a Spitfire in a steep turn a few yards behind. Smoke from his tracer groped toward me like fingers. My engine stuttered violently. Bullets shattered against the armour plate behind my head with appalling cracks. Immediately the cockpit was filled with the smell of cordite. His shooting was damned good! Almost as though on an exercise I broke out of the circle, half-rolled and went into a vertical dive. Rigid in my seat I felt almost of a piece with my aircraft as I put it through the classic evasive manoeuvre. It spiralled steeply earthwards as though in a vortex. With almost complete detachment my eyes took note of the wildly oscillating instruments, of the failing engine which these gyrations conveyed. The controls were ominously heavy while the fabric-covered ailerons began to balloon, inducing a virtually uncontrollable spin. Escaping coolant had covered the windscreen with a milky, opaque film. I was now in a state of cold, considered purposefulness, as though observing the behaviour of one who has landed himself in a hopeless predicament. Only for a second or two had such thoughts as 'this is it' or 'it's all over' impaired the powerful instinct of self-preservation. At 6,000 feet it became apparent that no one was shooting at me anymore. The windscreen was a little clearer. What I could see lurching toward me must be the slopes of Etna. I switched off because the oil and coolant temperatures had risen dangerously. The propeller windmilled idly in the air stream. My rate of descent was very high indeed. Small details could now be discerned: narrow strips of cultivated land surrounded by vine hedges – not the best of country for a belly-landing. However, I made a successful approach between tall trees towards a long, narrow field that sloped up towards Etna. Only when the tips of my airscrew struck the ground did I notice that the land was strewn everywhere with lumps of rock. But it was too late to do anything about it now. I had tightened my shoulder straps shortly before touching down. Therre was a heavy impact – the hood flew up and away in a high arc while lumps of earth came thudding down on wings, windscreen, and fuselage. I was thrown forward violently but my harness held. The aircraft finally came to a halt with a sudden jerk which tipped it on its propeller boss, nearly causing a somersault. There was one last almighty crash as the fuselage fell back onto the stony ground.

18 April, 1945.
Now I am sitting amid leaping flames. These flames will leave marks on me forever. 'It's happened.' I know only one thing, as I see everything through red glasses, wedged as I am in the jet I wanted so much: 'Get out!' 'Get out!' Then my hands began to work with feverish urgency, yet as fast and as accurately as if they had been pieces of machinery: 'Release waist belt, grasp parachute catch with right hand, turn clockwise, and punch.' Off came the canopy and I was staring out at the field, at the turbine that had been torn off the wing and was bouncing over the soft ground, and at the puddles of fuel spreading over the green grass and bursting into fresh sheets of towering orange flame. Two, three breaths and I was inhaling fire. It felt as if a pair of iron tongs had been clamped round my chest. I don't know how I got out, but I ran away from the airplane blindly, knowing that any moment the ammunition and the rockets would explode. In unbearable agony from burns, the last thing I knew was the explosion.

The rockets began exploding beneath the wings and careering off into the field. Steinhoff had run out along the wing, away from the fire, gasping for air and collapsing onto the ground near the wreck. Forcing himself up again, he staggered a few more yards, unable to see where he was going. The pain set in, the worst of it seemed to come from where his arms had burned between his gloves and the cuffs of his leather flying jacket. A comforting voice told him that he would be taken to a car and driven to a hospital.

October 1944. Steinhoff's unit, Fighter Group 77, was operating from an advance field in Transylvania when an order came through to move immediately to an airfield at Schönwalde where it was to participate in the defence of the Reich. Enemy artillery was increasing in both volume and quantity as the *Luftwaffe* personnel and the local villagers hurriedly prepared to evacuate the area, packing what they could before the artillery shells began falling on the airfield and the homes. Steinhoff was billeted in a forester's house in a wood near the field. The forester's short-haired dachshund had recently given birth to a litter of lively pups and one was offered to Steinhoff as the airmen got ready to leave. He named it Piefke and put the little dog in the small space behind the headrest of his Bf-109 fighter for the short flight to their new airfield.

Just after taking off, the radio crackled with word of an air battle under way near Klausenburg, and Steinhoff decided to fly to their new field via Klausenburg, hoping the battle would still be going on. As the climbing 109s passed through 13,000 feet, Steinhoff realized that he didn't know if Piefke would survive in combat at high altitude. He chose not to continue climbing.

As the six Bf-109s arrived in the Klausenburg area the air battle appeared to have run its course, but one of the pilots sighted a string of Messerschmitts off to their flank, curving around to line up behind Steinhoff's flight. Fährmann, his wingman, yelled into his mike: "The Me's are attacking! Look out, they're Rumanians!" The attacking 109s were E-models, 'Emils', and were wearing the insignia of the Royal Rumanian Air Force. A week ago they had been fighting on the side of the Germans, but now they were enemies. At first, Steinhoff's pilots were confused and reluctant to engage the other 109s, but he led them into a brief and decisive encounter in which he shot down one of the Rumanian fighters. The German pilots pulled up to regroup and continue on to their new base, Steinhoff remembered the little dog behind him. On the ground, poor Piefke trembled as he was lifted from his nook and let down in the grass.

October 1944. Hermann Goering called a meeting of all the unit commanders who could be spared from their duties at the front. The conference was to be at the *Luftwaffe* Imperial Air Defence School at Gatow airfield southwest of Berlin, and he would be speaking to them on the state of the Reich. Every seat was taken as Goering entered the room.

There were no preliminaries. The *Reichsmarshall* began with a salvo aimed directly at his fighter pilots. He said the situation was critical. The German people wanted to know why its fighter pilots were such craven failures. He declared that formation upon formation of Flying Fortresses went about their work of destruction in a clear blue sky – and not a single German fighter to be seen.

> I've spoiled you. I've given you too many decorations. They've made you fat and lazy. All that about the planes you'd shot down was just one big lie. Do you think anybody believes those astronomical figures? A pack of lies, I tell you! We've made the most almighty fools of ourselves in the eyes of the British. You didn't make a fraction of the kills you reported.

Steinhoff became aware of the cables running from the microphones on the speaker's dais into a control room where technicians sat behind sound-proof glass. Goering's tirade was being recorded. He later learned that the recordings were being sent out to all *Luftwaffe* units. The *Reichsmarshall* referred to his fighter pilots as cowards, liars and malingerers, and he continued: "I'm not saying they're all cowards . . . but there's many a sergeant who's an example to his officers".

Lützow then said to Steinhoff: "We've got to do something, Macky. Fatty's got to go".

November 1944. Steinhoff received an order to attend another conference to be chaired by *Reichsmarshall* Goering at Gatow. Also attending would be the most highly-decorated officers of the *Luftwaffe* Bomber, Fighter and Reconnaissance Commands. Representing the fighter pilots were Steinhoff, Lützow and General of the Fighter Arm Adolf Galland. Goering appeared in an uncharacteristically plain light grey uniform, no medals, and red Russian-leather boots. He told the group that he expected them to discuss critically anything about the *Luftwaffe* that, in their view, needed improvement – excepting their commander- in-chief. Off limits, too, was any discussion of the new Me-262 jet and whether it should be used as a fighter or a bomber, having long since decided in favour of his bomber pilots. He stated:

> I want you to help me give the *Luftwaffe* back its reputation. The German people expects that, because we have failed – failed disgracefully. This is the *Luftwaffe*'s darkest hour. The nation cannot understand why it is that the Allied bombers can come waltzing over the Reich as they did on the very day of our party congress and the fighters do not take off – because of fog, or because they are not ready, or because they are indisposed . . .

He then announced that "We are on the threshhold of the battle that will win us the war!" and said he regretted that other commitments prevented him from staying for the discussion, which would be led by the General of the Bomber Pilots. He closed by announcing that the General of the Fighter Pilots had been promoted to *Generalleutnant*: "My dear Galland, I share your delight." To that, Galland whispered to Steinhoff, "Bad sign. That means it won't be long before they sling me out".

Goering left the room and the conversation then turned to conventional situation reports by the various departments, focusing mostly on shortages and stoppages throughout the service. Defence of the Reich was largely ignored, with discussion of the Me-262 having been banned. Instead, the bomber general directed the conversation towards 'retribution' through a new campaign of vengeance bombing against England by a relative handful of Heinkels, four years after the Blitz on Britain, and in a time when the enemy's defences of its cities and ports were all but impenetrable. The fighter leaders in the room were staggered by the bizaare nature of the discussion given that the *Luftwaffe* lacked an effective four-engined strategic bomber and the air force was unable to put up enough fighters to defend the Reich, much less provide adequate escort of a German bomber force on new raids to Britain.

The focus of the meeting shifted to the development and implementation of a new programme to re-indoctrinate the entire *Luftwaffe* with National Socialist ideology and the progress along those lines which had already been made among the bomber pilots. The nonplussed fighter leaders then came to the chilling realization that, after 5 years of all-out war, there was a serious move to purge their air force of all officers and troops 'whose past life and present conduct were not consonant with the National-Socialist type and who did not stand firm on National-Socialist principles'. An editorial committee was then formed and adjourned into a closed session to draw up a new 'profession of faith' in the Führer and Nazi ideals. Just before the peculiar session broke up, Galland passed a note to Steinhoff: 'Under pressure from the Führer the *Reichsmarshall* has given permission for the first jet-fighter group to be set up. Do you want to command it?'

Steinhoff faced the challenge of putting together the new jet-fighter group and training it to fight against the 'viermots', the four-engined bombers of the Americans in the air over Germany. The new unit, Fighter Group 7, was to be comprised of three wings, based at Brandenburg, Parchim and Kaltenkirchen, north of Hamburg. By late November the first Me-262s that had been delivered by rail in sections and then assembled by the new mechanics of the group, were in the air and being used in small element training flights. The intensifying raids of the American bombers by day and the British by night caused Steinhoff and his pilots to billet in quarters well away from the airfields. The continuing air attacks on Berlin and its environs led them to anticipate raids on their airfields, though for the time being, they were untouched. Suprisingly, the many and varied needs of the fledgling jet fighter unit, were met promptly and unquestioningly.

This was a period of relative quiet before the storm. As they pushed and pulled the new organization into shape, Steinhoff and his men found that they could still enjoy the comforts of their officers' mess with good food, ample supplies of wine, brandy and champagne, as well as cigarettes and cigars. Nor did they lack for female companionship; the local girls were happy to be in the company of these heroic young airmen.

But the going was not all smooth. The sophisticated new jet brought with it a number of technical and mechanical problems: glitches with varying degrees of potential hazard demanding many hours of intense effort to locate, resolve and correct. After six weeks of concentrated effort, Steinhoff was able to tell his superiors that his new group was reasonably ready for action. There was, however, little actual combat experience against the viermots among his wing commanders, who were charged with moulding their young pilots into effective fighter pilots. By now, the

American heavy bombers were punishing the cities of Germany every day while facing little interference from the German Air Force, and the bombers of the Royal Air Force were achieving devastating results against their Reich targets every night, also with near impunity. The pilots of Steinhoff's new group eagerly awaited their first opportunity to test the Me-262 against the Allied heavies, convinced that they would be able to turn the enemy raiders back and save what was left of their German homeland. As that time approached, there was still no agreement within the group as to an ideal method of attacking the big bombers in their dangerous box formations. In the Me-262 Steinhoff's men had a potentially important weapon of great speed and enormous firepower of four 3 cm cannon. But the Germans had to be cautious. The 262 had no dive-brakes, thus ruling out high-level attacks and frontal attacks were out of the question, due to the extraordinarily high closing speeds of the jet. They would have to make conventional attacks on the enemy from behind their formations, flying through the defensive fire of the bomber rear gunners, and firing their own cannon at close range.

In late November, Galland asked Steinhoff to meet him at Parchim airfield where one of the group's new wings was being set up. Galland's mood was sombre and he wasted no words as he told Steinhoff how bad things really were for the Germans and that Goering would no longer see or listen to him. From then on, Galland informed Steinhoff that they would be judged by history. Even though they had the means (with the Me-262) to prevent it, Germany's cities were being destroyed. He warned Steinhoff that now they were both on Goering's black list.

Progress in December saw the group's Brandenburg wing brought up to strength with sufficient aircraft assembled and ready in the hangars to make their first strike against the American bombers. But the northern European weather, with heavy low cloud, fog and persistent snow showers, made that initial strike virtually impossible. Galland, meanwhile, continued to build up his fighter reserve, developing a substantial fighter force of both jets and props to employ in great numbers against a large formation of the viermots. The poor weather continued through the month, but an improvement forecast for early January promised the ideal attack opportunity. Galland ordered Steinhoff to the new jet group in western Germany, to position them for a primary attack against the American bomber stream at the first opportunity in January, and Steinhoff left to reconnoitre new airfields in the west for his three wings. He then returned to Brandenburg by train. At the station he phoned the transport pool at his group headquarters and when the sergeant answered, Steinhoff told him to send his car around to pick him up at the station. The embarrassed 'non-com' responded that the NEW commander had taken the car to Berlin. That was how Steinhoff learned that he had been sacked as group commander. Galland had been right. When Steinhoff arrived back at his billet, he was greeted with a simple telex: '*Oberst* Steinhoff, Johannes, to hand over Fighter Group 7 to Major W. with immediate effect. Further duties to be determined in due course. Signed, Head of Personnel'. In January 1945 came the 'revolt of the fighter pilots' referred to in the previous chapter on Adolf Galland. It began when Galland and Steinhoff were sacked within days of each other.

Macky Steinhoff had mixed feelings about his dismissal. It was not so much that he was upset at the break-up of his relationship with the men of his new unit, having been their commander for only 2 months. His anger and resentment passed after a week's leave in Greifswald. He returned to Berlin where he stayed another week in the guest barracks at Gatow, awaiting a new posting. Having heard nothing by early February, he decided to visit Lützow who had been exiled to a command posting in Italy. When the train arrived at Verona just before midnight, Steinhoff was asked by a German military police major for his papers and travel orders. He had no travel orders and asked to speak to the commanding general. When the call was put through, the general asked Steinhoff on whose orders he was travelling. He replied that he had no posting as yet and was visiting his old friend Lützow. The general replied that since Steinhoff had no travel orders he must return to Germany immediately and report to the Head of *Luftwaffe* Personnel. On the return journey, the train came to a halt at four in the afternoon near Erlangen. Steinhoff heard the Merlin engines of American Mustang fighters and shouted for everyone to get out of the train quickly as it was about to be attacked. As he did so, a German military policeman ran down the corridor shouting that no one was to leave the train. Most of the passengers heeded Steinhoff's warning, flattening themselves in the field near the train while the Mustangs attacked the locomotive in their first pass. The terrified passengers made a dash for a nearby copse. The Mustangs had been escorting a large force of American Eighth Air Force bombers on their return to their English bases from an attack in southern Germany. The escort fighters had been released to go hunting for targets of opportunity. The American fighters returned to make a few more passes, strafing the length of the train. In a few minutes the attack was over, leaving wounded and dead lying beside the track. Steinhoff was among the fortunate survivors who were later transferred to another train.

On his arrival at Anhalt Station in Berlin, Steinhoff expected to be hauled up before the Head of Personnel and accused of plotting with Lützow. Instead, he was given a message that he was to phone General Galland immediately. Galland explained that Albert Speer, the Reich Armaments Minister, had told Hitler about the fighter pilots' efforts to achieve vital reforms in the *Luftwaffe*. Hitler summoned Goering and asked him what Galland and the so-called 'mutineers' were doing. When Goering replied that most were without jobs, Hitler ordered him to give Galland the chance to prove that the Me-262 was a superior fighter by letting him form and lead a squadron of the jets. Galland, in turn, offered Steinhoff a job with the new unit.

This is the story of a great escape. It happened on 25 July 1944 in the skies over southern Germany. A Royal Air Force Flight Lieutenant named A.E. Wall was at the controls of a sleek , unarmed de Havilland Mosquito twin-engined reconnaissance aircraft. At his 30,000-foot altitude, Wall noted the heavy cumulus cloud build-up to the south over the Bavarian Alps near Salzburg. How odd it seemed to him, to be over the heart of the Third Reich and virtually unopposed. Where was the *Luftwaffe*? Since the Allied landings on the Normandy beaches in early June, there had been little serious opposition in the air over German territory, and there appeared to be none today. Minutes later, in the vicinity of Munich, Wall's navigator spotted an enemy aircraft rapidly approaching behind them. Neither pilot nor navigator could identify the type, but Wall reacted immediately, pushing the Mosquito over into shallow diving turn.

This particular Mossie was a fighter-bomber that had been stripped of all its guns to reduce weight and enable greater speed. It was descending at more than 400 mph, and increasing, but, incredibly, the enemy plane was even faster. It tore past the Mosquito – the fastest aircraft Wall and his navigator had ever seen. The stripped-down Mosquito was agile and manoeuvrable and Wall threw it around in a series of frantic moves to elude the enemy machine which kept returning to line up on him. For some reason, it seemed unable to align on its target. Cannon shells came lobbing past without scoring a hit. The strange aircraft kept reappearing, always from behind, but with each successive pass the enemy shells missed. At times, the cannon fire would commence from a considerable distance – 800 to 1,000 yards – effectively out of range. The exhausting tailchase continued for nearly 15 minutes and, at one point, Wall had manoeuvred the Mosquito into a position where, had he been armed, he might have scored some hits on his adversary.

The struggle had taken both aircraft very close to the Alps and provided Wall with the chance of ducking into the cumulus cloud cover. He hid in its shelter for a few minutes before emerging to find that the other plane had disappeared. He learned later that he had encountered, and nearly become a victim of, Willy Messerschmitt's elegant little twin-jet Me-262 *Schwalbe* (Swallow). It was the first documented air combat involving the plane.

Resembling a shark, the swept-wing single-seat fighter was powered by two Junkers Jumo 004 turbojet engines that produced a combined thrust of just under 4,000 lb – not much really, and not enough for the work required of the plane. The production version of the Me-262 *Schwalbe* was capable of 540 mph in level flight and could carry a combined fuel and ammmunition load of nearly 6,000 lb.

Why a jet? The propeller-driven piston-engined fighter planes of the late 1930s and early 1940s had been limited in speed by their propellers. In general, the faster a propeller turns, the faster it propels its aircraft – up to a point. When the speed of the propeller tips approaches the speed of sound, the ability of the propeller to pull the aircraft forward reaches its limit. A simple jet engine like the Jumo 004 turbojet generates a lot of power for its size and weight. The turbine wheels or 'propellers' of the engine spin at thousands of revolutions per minute but have a smaller diameter than that of a propeller and cover a much smaller distance in their spin, thus the tips of the turbine wheels never approach the speed of sound as they spin. One negative characteristic of the Jumo 004 engine was its relatively high fuel consumption rate which, at low altitudes, was more than twice that of a piston engine of similar power output.

In the mid-1930s conceptual and developmental work began on early jet propulsion engines, in Britain by Frank Whittle and in Germany by Hans-Joachim Pabst von Ohain. Von Ohain was still a student at the University of Gottingen when he started working on a gas turbine to power an aeroplane and found that such a powerplant was too heavy for such a use. He continued to work on the principle, collaborating with a mechanic named Max Hahn on the construction of a turbojet demonstration model. The work sufficiently impressed von Ohain's professor that he recommended the young man to the aircraft manufacturer, Ernst Heinkel. Heinkel gave him the opportunity of forming a design team to develop a practical turbojet engine.

In 1937, within months of each other, both von Ohain and Whittle had achieved workable bench-test prototype engines. Initially, von Ohain's engine ran on hydrogen, but with the continuing assistance of Max Hahn, a kerosene-burning engine resulted. Heinkel then approved development of a flight-test engine which was attached to an He-118 dive-bomber and air tests began in May 1939. So confident was the plane maker in the turbojet engine design that the testing led to his development of a pure jet-powered experimental aircraft, the Heinkel He-178. The first engine used produced just 835 lb thrust, but an improved version was soon developed that gave 1,300 lb thrust. The He-178 was a simple high-wing of conventional design. It had a tail-wheel undercarriage configuration and was capable of 435 mph. Its maiden flight took place on 27 August 1939, just before the outbreak of the Second World War. The test pilot commented after the flight that the craft was free of both vibration and torque . . . a smooth and wonderful performer. Von Ohain's progress now leapt ahead of Frank Whittle's. The war climate and a lack of enthusiasm by the British government for the project delayed the first flight of the experimental Gloster-Whittle G-40 until May 1941. Across the North Sea, neither the German Air Ministry nor the *Luftwaffe* were excited by the prospects of the He-178 when they witnessed it demonstrated in November 1939. The little plane had a top speed that was slower than that of their fastest propeller-driven fighter and they told Heinkel that his turbojet was not needed – they would win the war with piston-engined planes. The one and only He-178 completed its testing phase and was turned over to the German National Air Museum in Berlin where it was destroyed in a 1943 Allied bombing raid.

Despite the apparent indifference of the German Air Ministry to Heinkel's experimental jet, it nonetheless pursued turbojet development for aircraft use, encouraging German plane makers to experiment with advanced air weaponry for the Reich. In mid-1938, the German Air Ministry had, in fact, already established a high-priority programme for jet engine, turbojet and turboprop development.

A German engine maker called Bramo was urged by the Air Ministry to develop an axial flow engine, which utilized rings of blades to drive air directly into the engine combustion chambers, as opposed to the centrifugal flow approach of both Whittle and von Ohain in which a compressor pump impellor forced the air into the combustion chambers ringing the engine. Bramo's factory works at Spandau was acquired by BMW in 1939, which then shelved its own turbojet development project to focus on developing the Bramo designs. Their first successfully-tested engine, the BMW-003, was run in 1940. The firm of Junkers, meanwhile, had been working on its own axial flow turbojet engine prototype since 1936 and had been contracted by the Air Ministry for development of the Jumo-004, which was being bench-tested in November 1940.

After flight testing the He-178, Heinkel was hard at work on the He-280 project, a twin-engined fighter to be powered by Heinkel engines. And in 1938, the Messerschmitt firm entered the turbojet race with its own design for a twin-turbojet interceptor fighter. It called for a streamlined fuselage with a triangular cross-section, swept wings with a thin chord for high-speed performance, a BMW-003 turbojet engine centre-mounted under each wing and leading-edge 'slats' on the outer wings, which extended automatically at lower speeds for improved lift and handling. Three prototypes of the plane were ordered in July 1940 by the Air Ministry.

The first experimental prototype airframe, Me-262-V-1, was fitted and flown with a single Jumo 210G piston engine and a two-bladed propeller for preliminary testing which began on 18 April, 1941. The promising results led to the Air Ministry ordering an additional five prototype aircraft. The airframe was then fitted with its two BMW-003 turbojet engines of 1,200 lb thrust each, with the Jumo 210G piston unit retained on the airframe as a safety measure, a wise precaution. Messerschmitt chief test pilot Fritz Wendel flew the aircraft off the Leipheim runway on 25 March, 1942, with the power of both turbojets and the back-up piston engine. As soon as he was airborne, the port turbojet failed and then the starboard engine flamed out. Wendel was able to coax the overlaoded plane around for a landing using only the piston engine. The plane was damaged but Wendel was uninjured. The BMW-003 engine was still unreliable, but the Jumo-004 showed more promise and was fitted to the third prototype aircraft, each engine producing 1,850 lb thrust. To accommodate the larger and heavier Jumo engines, adjustments had to be made to the airframe design. One such change involved angling the wings back to find a balance for the additional engine weight. The change brought an important performance boost for the plane, helping to counter the slowing effects of compressibility – the phenomenon that dramatically increases air resistance as the aircraft nears the speed of sound.

Fritz Wendel guided the Me-262 down the short 3,600-foot Leipheim runway on 18 July 1942, and, when his instrument indicated that he had reached the 112 mph take-off speed, he pushed forward on the stick to raise the tail wheel. There was no response. The plane stayed firmly on the runway, rushing headlong towards the end. Its tail-wheel configuration had caused the 262 fuselage to tilt upward. The engine exhaust was directed at a partially downward angle and bounced off the runway surface as the aircraft accelerated, creating a turbulence that disrupted the air flow across the tail. This eliminated the effect of the elevator control surfaces that raised and lowered the tail. Wendel pulled the throttles back and was able to bring the aeroplane to a stop at the end of the runway. He then met with Messerschmitt engineers who suggested a solution to the problem of how to become airborne in the jet. He climbed back into the cockpit for another take-off attempt. This time, when he reached 112 mph, he tapped the brakes in a single, short movement, causing the aircraft to buck slightly, forcing the tail up from the ground. Wendel climbed and circled the airfield in careful arcs for the next 12 minutes before bringing the plane in for a smooth and uneventful landing. He had been impressed by the performance of the craft. Three weeks later Willy Messerschmitt decided that it was time for a *Luftwaffe* pilot to fly the new jet. Heinrich Beauvais, a civilian engineer and *Luftwaffe* test pilot, came to Leipheim and was greeted by Wendel who briefed him on the known characteristics of the 262, explaining how to advance the throttles gently in order to keep the engines from bursting into flame through a sudden excess of fuel. He told Beauvais about his improvised method of getting the jet into the air and stationed himself along the runway, at the point where he thought Beauvais should jab the brakes. The *Luftwaffe* pilot then began his take-off roll. He was moving too slowly when he reached Wendel and the tail lifted briefly before settling back onto the runway surface. He taxied back to the take-off end of the runway to try again. The same thing happened. At a third attempt the jet became airborne for a few seconds but lacked the necessary speed to continue flying. It touched down again and roared off through a field where the right wing clipped a manure pile. The plane whipped around before coming to a halt. Beauvais was unhurt, but the jet was badly damaged. Eventually, it was rebuilt and flew again.

Other *Luftwaffe* pilots arrived at the Messerschmitt field to fly the jet and managed to learn the tricky techniques involved in the procedure. Within months they were taking the plane to speeds near 600 mph but did not try to go beyond that figure. In that range, approaching the speed of sound, the aircraft began to pitch and shudder and became virtually un-controllable.

Flight testing progressed slowly but steadily and, by October, the German Air Ministry was sufficiently impressed to have ordered forty-five pre-production aircraft. An internal debate was going on at the Air Ministry about whether to order the Me-262 into full production or the new Me-209, the improved version of the piston-engined Bf-109 fighter. After General of the Fighter Arm Galland had flown the Me-262-V-4 prototype, and been favourably impressed by it, he suggested cancellation of the Me-209 and full production of the jet fighter. Within a few days the Air Ministry ordered its first 100 production Me-262s. Professor Willy Messerschmitt, however, continued to lobby for production of the Me-209 as well as the 262 until November 1943 when the Me-209 project was finally abandoned.

Technical development of the jet then began to be overshadowed by politics. Adolf Hitler's concern over the Allied successes in North Africa and Italy fired his desire to create a high-speed Jagdbomber/Jabo or fighter-bomber to deal with the threatened Allied invasion of the European Continent. He needed a specialized air weapon capable of driving the Americans and British back into the sea. In early November 1943 *Reichsmarshall* Goering and *Luftwaffe* Field Marshal Erhard Milch went to the Augsburg plant of Willy Messerschmitt to ask the professor if the Me-262 could be made to carry bombs. Messerschmitt replied that it could deliver at least 1,100 lb of bombs and possibly as much as twice that load in an easily adapted Jabo version of the plane. There followed the famous demonstration and inspection at Insterburg when Hitler asked Goering the same question about bomb-carrying capability for the 262 and received the same answer given to Goering earlier. The Führer ordered that the Me-262 be built as a fighter-bomber, an order largely ignored by Messerschmitt who immediately began production of the aeroplane as a fighter. Aware of the developing American B-29 bomber threat, Milch continued to support producing the 262 as a fighter.

By the early spring of 1944, several Me-262s were being evaluated for combat by the Luftwaffe in a special unit. This activity coincided with the large-scale introduction of the North American P-51 Mustang long-range escort fighter by the U.S. Eighth Air Force in England. The Mustangs were the first and only Allied fighter capable of shepherding the American heavy bombers all the way to the most distant targets in Germany and back to England and making the air defence of the Reich more difficult than ever. To General Galland and the fighter pilots of the *Luftwaffe*, the Me-262 seemed the last and only remaining hope for Germany in the war. Willy Messerschmitt, meanwhile, had severe problems of his own. His vital assembly plant at Regensburg had been almost completely destroyed in an Allied bombing raid on 17 August 1943, forcing him to relocate the plant's production to Bavaria near the Alps. The situation was made worse by the slow-paced delivery of the Jumo-004 turbojet engines. The politcal situation surrounding the Me-262 came to a head on 23 May 1944, when Goering, Galland, Milch, and Armaments Minister Albert Speer met with Hitler at Berchtesgaden to talk about the aircraft production programme. When the discussion turned to the 262 fighter Hitler said that he thought the 262 was being built as a high-speed bomber. He asked Milch how many of the planes had been manufactured to carry bombs. Milch replied "None, mein Führer. The Me-262 is being manufactured exclusively as a fighter aircraft." He went on to state that the plane could not be adapted to the bomber role without major design changes and that, even then, it would be limited to a bomb load of only 1,100 lb. Hitler was furious. At Insterburg in November he had been told that the plane could be adapted to the bomber role and had ordered it built as a fighter-bomber. No one had questioned his decision at the time. All his plans for turning back the expected Allied invasion of the Continent had been based on using the Jabo Me-262 against the amphibious landings. There were no Jabo jets and he had not been told so until this moment. He raged: "Who pays the slightest attention to the orders I give? I gave an unqualified order, and left nobody in any doubt that the aircraft was to be equipped as a fighter-bomber!" Milch would bear the brunt of blame in the matter and was summarily removed from office. Goering's waning popularity with the Führer continued to slide. The meeting ended with Hitler commanding that the work on the jet be concentrated on delivery of the bomber version. He agreed, however, to continued testing of the fighter version, provided it did not slow the production and deliveries of the Jabo. Messerschmitt went to work on the Jabo variant which, at best, would only serve as interim equipment until the purpose-built Ar-234 jet bomber being developed by the Arado company was ready.

A small unit of nine Me-262 Jabos was formed under command of Major Wolfgang Schenk to operate from northern France in opposition to the Allied landing forces in June. The Germans were expecting the Allies to come ashore in the Pas de Calais and positioned the jets accordingly. Nothing was achieved and they were pulled back to a field in Belgium when the Allies accomplished their breakout from Normandy. After this operation, Hitler's order to build the 262 in the Jabo variant was rescinded; once again, the aircraft was being produced primarily in the fighter version.

There is some historical evidence that a man called Hero of Alexandria designed what he referred to as an aeolipile – a crude turbine driven by jet propulsion. John Barber of Nuneaton, England, advanced the science in 1794 with his invention of a type of gas turbine apparatus. And in the 1930s the young Cambridge honours graduate in engineering, Frank Whittle, began work on his contribution to the field. Whittle had been a flight cadet at the RAF College, Cranwell, in 1926 and had completed the flying instructor course at RAF Wittering by 1930 when he married Dorothy Mary Lee. By 1932 he was officer-in-charge of the Engine Test Section at RAF Henlow and had patented his own design of an aircraft engine in which a gas turbine provided a powerful propulsive jet. Forty-seven years later, he was to fly as a passenger at 1,340 mph in an aeroplane called Concorde, crossing the Atlantic from London to Washington DC in 3 hours and 37 minutes – a journey largely made possible by Whittle himself.

Whittle was born on 1 June 1907 in Lancashire, the son of a foreman in a machine tools factory. From his earliest memories as a four-year-old, he had loved aeroplanes and everything about flying. It seemed inevitable that he would grow up to join the Royal Air Force where he learned to fly and in which he began his work on the idea that would change the world. From a concept he had developed in a thesis written at RAF Cranwell in 1929, entitled *Future Developments in Aircraft Design*, Whittle proposed a new type of gas turbine engine that would produce a propelling jet instead of driving a propeller.

Pilot Officer Whittle explained his idea to the commandant at Cranwell who was sufficiently impressed to bring the matter to the attention of the British Air Ministry. The AM soon invited Whittle to come to London with his sketches and calculations where he met scientists at the Air Ministry's South Kensington Laboratory, including Dr A.A. Griffith, whose special interest was gas turbines for driving propellers. Griffith listened to Whittle's presentation and asserted that the assumptions of the young officer were over-optimistic and his calculations flawed. Following the meeting, Whittle received a letter from the Air Ministry stating that the idea he had proposed was impractical. Materials did not yet exist that were capable of withstanding the high temperatures and the stresses for the gas turbine to operate efficiently.

In January 1936 Frank Whittle entered into a four-party agreement with the Air Council (the Secretary of State for Air) to form a company for the purpose of developing a turbojet engine. The company was called Power Jets Limited. In Germany, at about the same time, the separate airframe and aero engine companies of the Heinkel organization were merged and a secret department was established for the development and construction of a turbojet. The Air Ministry in Britain was unaware of this.

The aero engine manufacturers of both Britain and Germany were traditionalists – conservative in their approach to the business and science of their work. Their vested interests lay in piston engines for the fighters, bombers, transports and reconnaissance aircraft of their nations and they were not motivated to learn new technologies or throw out their bread-and-butter production in favour of some unproven turbojet concept. Experience had shown that gas turbines didn't work. In Germany, however, the *Reichsluftministerium* (Air Ministry) exerted pressure on the leading German aero engine makers to devote substantial effort to gas turbine jet technology for aircraft. No such intensity of effort existed in England.

12 April 1937. With the assistance of three fitters, Frank Whittle prepared to start his WU (Whittle Unit) turbojet. The engine was mounted on a test rig at the Power Jets facility, with its jet exhaust pipe protruding from a window. Three sheets of inch-thick steel plating had been positioned vertically as a safety barrier around the engine. Should the engine over-speed, bits might fly off with a force and speed greater than bullets. The instrument panel and controls stood to one side, mounted at the forward end of the truck rig on which the engine was fixed. When he was ready, Whittle ordered the separate fuel pump to be activated and signalled for the starter motor to be turned on. He watched his dials and, as the starter motor reached 1,000 rpm, opened the valve sending fuel to a pilot burner in the combustion chamber. At the same time, he turned the handle of the magneto to ignite the finely atomized spray of fuel emitted by the burner. The pilot light was lit.

When the speed of the starter motor reached 2,000 rpm Whittle opened the main fuel valve. There was a rising shriek as the speed of the engine rapidly increased and the casing of the combustion chamber began to glow in reddish-orange patches. The machine was out of control. Assistants scrambled to get out of the area but Whittle, frightened as he was, stayed put to screw down the control valve. The screaming acceleration continued to climb and reached 8,000 rpm before the revs began to drop. He admitted later that he had never been so frightened in his life. An inauspicious entry into the jet age.

A prolonged period of trial and error, technological and financial turmoil followed. Whittle was weakened by ill health and overwork in his determination to solve the troubles with the engine. Scores of design and material changes, many of them minor but some fundamental, were made before the problems were finally resolved. In the late summer of 1939, as it became clear that war was unavoidable, the British Air Ministry shifted from being uninterested in Whittle's turbojet, to being enthusiastic. Whittle was told that work on the jet engine was to go on even if war broke out. The developmental work had gone well in recent weeks and though combustion problems plagued Whittle, they had successfully attained an engine speed of 16,650 rpm or 94 per cent of full design speed.

June 1940. Frank had been promoted to the temporary rank of Wing Commander. France had fallen and it was clear that Britain was Hitler's next target. Invasion was probable. In the battle for France, the Germans had lost more than 1,000 aircraft and the British nearly that many. The RAF was gravely in need of both fighter aircraft and pilots. Whittle was asked to meet with Lord Beaverbrook, Churchill's Minister for Aircraft Production, whose most immediate task was the urgent manufacture and delivery of Hurricanes and Spitfires for the Few who would have to fly them in the defence of Britain. It is to the credit of the Canadian-born newspaper publisher turned aeroplane supremo that by the early summer of 1940 British aircraft makers were producing 500 fighters a month for the Royal Air Force and the Fleet Air Arm. It is also to his credit that when priority had to be given to aircraft already in production and most new projects were being cancelled, Beaverbrook supported Whittle's priority for his turbojet and the construction of the Gloster/Whittle E.28 – the little plane that would be Britain's first jet aircraft.

April 1941. With completion of the Gloster/Whittle E.28/39 airframe at the beginning of the month, Frank Whittle arranged for his W.1X (proto-type) turbojet engine to be installed in the first of the two E.28 prototypes for the purpose of taxi testing only. The first actual W.1 engine was assembled but not yet bench-tested and he did not want to risk it until he was sure that all significant bugs had been traced and fixed on the W.1X. The W.1, meanwhile, was taken to Brockworth (Gloster) for mock-up fitting in the other E.28 prototype airframe. With the completion of this work, the engined prototype of the plane was moved in secrecy to the safety of a large garage in Cheltenham (a site now occupied by an arcade shopping mall), away from the renewed threat of bombing by the Germans. A small group of skilled craftsmen laboured over the new plane. On 7 April the unairworthy prototype E.28 fitted with the W.1X engine was readied for taxi testing by Gloster chief test pilot Gerry Sayer, but by the time all was set for the trial the daylight was nearly gone and the airfield soggy from a rainshower. The next morning, Whittle elected to run some taxi trials and got the E.28 rolling to a speed of 60 mph, commenting later on the lack of vibration and reduced noise factors compared with conventional aircraft, the simplicity of the controls and the excellent visibility from the cockpit. He was not as positive in his opinion of the engine instrumentation, but, in general, he felt good about the aircraft. After lunch, Sayer continued the taxi testing with a reminder from Whittle that the engine in this prototype was unairworthy. In his next taxi run Sayer ran the power up, released the brakes and began to roll. Well down the Brockworth runway, the E.28 appeared to pitch up slightly and became airborne for a few seconds, covering about 200 yards. Sayer repeated the 'flight' twice more that day, both times covering between 200 and 300 yards. He later commented that the engine was very smooth with no vibration felt in the cockpit but that the throttle control was too coarse, allowing too large an increase in engine revolutions with very little forward movement of the throttle lever. He thought that the engine ran very well in the taxiing trials.

Three days after the taxiing trials, the W.1 engine was test-run for the first time. Prior to the test the modification identified in the debugging of the W.1X engine was incorporated into the W.1, which easily passed its acceptance test. In early May the W.1 engine was installed in the Gloster/Whittle E.28/39. The aircraft and engine were then cleared by the Ministry of Aircraft Production for 10 hours of flight testing. The short runway at Brockworth was considered unsuitable for the maiden flight of the E.28, so the plane was again moved in secrecy, this time to RAF Cranwell, Lincolnshire. It was appropriate that Whittle and his creation would come to fruition where, as a cadet, he had written the thesis which led to the start of his work on the jet propulsion. He was already deeply immersed in planning for the twin-engined Gloster Meteor fighter which was to be powered by the Whittle W.2B turbojet. The first flight of the E.28 seemed almost unimportant to him when, on 15 May, Gerry Sayer taxied the plane out to the end of the long Cranwell runway. Sayer went through his final cockpit checks and made sure the cockpit hood was fully open. It was bitterly cold and windy as he advanced the throttle and the plane began to roll. He kept it straight down the centreline of the runway and after 600 yards the plane left the ground. As it climbed through 1,000 feet Sayer retracted the undercarriage and in seconds the E.28 disappeared into a cloud bank, trailing a faint wisp of smoke. The sound of the jet engine was still audible and soon the plane emerged from the clouds to make a wide circuit of the field. Sayer brought her in for a perfect landing after 17 minutes of maiden flight. Frank Whittle commented: "I was very tense. . ."

When he flew the Me-262 for the first time, Adolf Galland liked it very much, but had some criticism of the design. He recommended that the tail-wheel-configured undercarriage be replaced with a tricycle-gear undercarriage to alleviate the poor visibility afforded on the ground. The V-6 prototype produced in October 1943 had a fully-retractable tricycle landing gear system. During the course of prototype flight testing, some experimentation and modification was carried out to create an ultra high-speed version of the plane, including a special small canopy. The V-12 prototype was used for the modification and it resulted in a top speed of 624 mph being achieved, or 84 mph faster than the standard Me-262.

The Me-262A-1A *Schwalbe* went into production equipped with two Jumo-004 turbojets of 1,980 lb thrust each. The aircraft had an unusual starting system comprised of a little, two-stroke gasoline engine positioned behind the engine nozzle housing. An electric starter was used to crank the gasoline engine and a back-up pull-cord starter handle was also provided. The pilot was protected by armoured front glass and an armoured seat back. There was no ejection seat like those fitted in all modern jet fighters. The aeroplane was armed with four short-barrelled MK-108 30mm cannon mounted in the nose. These were low-velocity cannon of short range but considerable power. They were sighted initially through a Revi 16B reflector gunsight, but this was later replaced by an Askania EX42 gyro-scopic gunsight.

The fighter-bomber Jabo variant was known as the *Sturmvogel* (Storm Bird or Storm Eagle) and its design adaptation consisted mainly of two bomb pylons fitted beneath the forward fuselage for the attachment of two 550-lb general purpose bombs, and the removal of the upper pair of cannon. With its extremely clean shape, the *Sturmvogel* proved a poor dive-bomber, building up far too much speed and often becoming uncontrollable in the dive. It was also unsuited for horizontal bombing, lacking a bombsight device. Armed with a type of cluster bomb weapon, however, it was reasonably practical for low level attacks. The adaptation also required the elimination of most cockpit armour and the addition of an extra fuel tank in the rear of the fuselage for increased range. In practice, the fuel in this extra tank had to used up first to prevent a dangerous tail-heavy condition after the bombs were dropped.

In general it is known that the Me-262A-1A was somewhat underpowered for its weight and mission requirements and required a rather long take-off run. It was quite fast compared to everything else in the air in 1944–45, and relatively good in its handling, although in the higher speed ranges it tended to slither a bit which reduced its stability as a gun platform. The throttles had to be handled with great care as engine fires were a real and constant danger. Reliability was not a feature of the engines which suffered a great many flameouts and burnouts. The Jumo-004 engines, which had been designed with the minimal use of high-strength metals, were really unsatisfactory for operational use as the blades tended to fail frequently and the engines often had to be junked after a mere 10 hours of flight time. Losing the power of one engine in flight was an extreme problem as the aircraft was only barely able to sustain flight on one engine. If the engine loss occurred at an air speed of less than 180 mph, the aircraft would almost certainly be lost as well. The high rate of fuel consumption severely limited the aeroplane's time in the air and its maximum range was 650 miles in optimal conditions. The craft weighed 8,340 empty and 14,080 pounds fully loaded. It was 34 feet 9 inches long, 12 feet 7 inches high and had a wingspan of 40 feet 7 inches.

Operational evaluation of this new and radically unconventional aircraft proved a slow and arduous process, particularly in light of the incessant enemy air attacks on the fields in Germany where the 262 was based late in the war. Operation was further complicated by a limitation which arose when it was found that the fiery jet blast of the early tail-wheeled 262s could actually set fire to asphalt runways, restricting them to concrete runways.

Operating against the American daylight heavy bomber formations, meant a high attrition rate of the jets and pilots. The units flying the 262 in combat consisted of many rather inexperienced fighter pilots (as well as a number of the most experienced surviving elite). The youngsters, while eager and spirited, were having to fly ultra-high-performance aircraft that were a challenge even to the best of the veteran GAF fighter pilots. No solid tactics had been devised for use against B-17 and B-24 formations and controlling the jets as they flashed through and around the enemy bombers made shooting accurately from them very difficult. If a 262 pilot approached the bombers at a slower speed in order to improve his chances of scoring hits, he was an easier target for the gunners in the bombers. Nevertheless, a number of Me-262 pilots of Galland's elite JV-44 unit managed to score several kills before the war in Europe ended on 8 May 1945. The rocket-carrying Me-262A-1Bs had proved especially effective in their attacks. The problem of training and transitioning the inexperienced GAF pilots onto the Me-262 had necessitated development of a two-seat trainer variant, the Me-262B-1A, which had been brought on line in summer 1944. Only 15 of the aircraft were produced. A tandem version of the 262, the aeroplane was fitted with dual controls and the rear seat replaced one of the fuel tanks. The originally specified range was retained by the fitting of two external fuel tanks of 80 U.S. gallon capacity each beneath the forward fuselage. A night fighter variant was also built and, in the final months of the war, the Messerschmitt works was developing a prototype of an improved night fighter, the Me-262B-2A, with a greater fuel capacity and the intended installation of a much-improved radar. Also under consideration for the variant was the installation of an upward-firing cannon in the rear of the fuselage for attacking RAF bombers from the blind spot below their fuselages.

One of the hazards frequently faced by the 262 pilots was ground attack by enemy fighters – P-51 Mustangs in particular – on the airfields of the jets. The Germans tried to defend the Me-262s during their take-off and landing by providing airfield cover with patrolling Focke-Wulf Fw-190 fighters. But shortages of aircraft and fuel limited this to a minimum. These airfields were also ringed with anti-aircraft (flak) batteries, but they were often manned by inefficient crews who sometimes fired on their own aircraft by mistake.

In the last months of the war, only a small number of the Me-262s produced got into action against the enemy. It is unlikely that the German Air Force had more than 200 of the craft operational at any time. Combat records indicate that pilots of the Me-262 shot down approximately 150 Allied planes for the loss of 100 Me-262s. After the war, several of the German jets were collected at the Lechfeld airstrip in Bavaria by the U.S. Army Air Force for evaluation by the U.S.A.A.F. Air Technical Intelligence Group. German test pilots and Me-262 ground crew personnel assisted the Americans in the testing them in Germany. The planes were shipped by aircraft carrier to the U.S. where they went to the air force test facility at Wright Field, Ohio for additional evaluation, including a fly-off against the Lockheed P-80 Shooting Star fighter. The Me-262 was judged superior to the P-80.

In addition to the standard Me-262 fighter and Jabo fighter-bombers, a number of other versions had been produced in small quantities by the end of the war. They included a variant armed with two Mk-108 low-velocity 30mm cannon as well as two high-velocity 30mm cannon and two 20mm cannon; an all-weather version; a ground-attack variant of the *Schwalbe* with extra armour and armament (designed but not built); a *Sturmvogel* bomber with an experimental bombsight system; a few examples of a *Sturmvogel* with a transparent nose and provision for a prone bombardier; a version of the *Schwalbe* armed with a *Rheinmetall* 50mm tank gun to be used against the Allied bombers (in experimental combat trials the gun repeatedly jammed and the bright muzzle flash tended to temporarily blind the pilot); unarmed reconnaissance versions as well as one with two 30mm cannon and either one or two nose-mounted cameras; an interceptor variant with a Walther rocket booster in the tail for improved rate of climb; and finally a *Schwalbe* with BMW-003R turbojet engines and rocket boosters in a version said by its test pilots to be tricky and frightening to fly.

In the 1990s, a private American aviation group organized a project to build five authentic Me-262 flying replica aircraft, authentic in all respects other than the use of modern General Electric J85 non-afterburning turbojet engines instead of the dangerously unreliable old Jumo-004 powerplants. Though smaller than the Jumo engines, the J85s were fitted in the correct Me-262 nacelles without changing the external appearance of the aircraft. The maiden flight of the first 262 replica took place on 20 December 2003. The craft suffered a collapsed landing gear on its second flight and was under repair for the next 6 months. The test pilot was unhurt in the incident. In 2005, two more of the replica aircraft, a single-seater and a tandem trainer version, were nearing completion.

Two other notable high-speed German aircraft had appeared late in the war. Well before the Messerschmitt Me-262 turbojet took off on its first flight in July 1942, designers at the German aircraft firm Arado were at work on Germany's, and the world's, first true jet bomber, the Ar-234, a larger and more sophisticated jet than the 262. They had been working on construction of more than 30 prototypes of the plane to showcase a range of fascinating variants they had planned for the bomber. By the summer of 1944, the new bomber, the Ar-234B, called the Blitz, was in full produc-tion. In trials is delivered a top speed of 461 mph at 33,000 feet and was developmentally much advanced over any Allied bomber. Operationally, the 234B could carry 3,300 lb of bombs and was powered by a pair of Jumo turbojets generating just under 2,000 lb thrust each. Another variant of the plane was a four-engined version, the Ar-234C. The prototypes were used to test a range of advanced concepts including rocket-assisted take-off from short runways, a skid-equipped version which took off after jettisoning a three-wheeled trolley to eliminate the weight and drag of a conventional undercarriage, a pressurized cabin, and even one of the first ejection seats.

*   *   *

Even faster than the Me-262, the Messerschmitt Me-163 Komet was a diminutive, revolutionary rocket-propelled fighter with a stubby fuselage and swept wings made of wood. The Komet was fitted with a 3,750-lb thrust rocket motor that gave it a top speed of 600 mph. Billed as a 'wonder weapon' by the Nazis near the end of the war, the Komet was first encountered by bomber crews of the American Eighth Air Force in the summer of 1944. Its 437-gallon fuel capacity allowed it just four to six minutes of flight after take-off. With a climb-rate of nearly 12,000 feet a minute, it could climb almost vertically and in less than two minutes top out above the Allied formations where it would roll over and dive in an attack bringing into play the devastating firepower of its twin 30mm cannon. In just a few more minutes, with its fuel exhausted the Me-163 engine would quit and the pilot would glide the craft back to his nearby base. The main drawback of the rocket plane was the extreme volatility of the fuel mixture used by it, a blend of methyl alcohol and concentrated hydrogen peroxide, a frequently explosive mixture that caused many Komets of blow up while still on the runway. The terrible, extreme acidity of the fuel mix even melted flesh on one unfortunate *Luftwaffe* pilot of the Komet when a fuel line ruptured, dousing his cockpit with the fumes. One of its pilots called the Komet the most dangerous aircraft ever built. Production of the rocket plane peaked at 279 units, of which only a few entered combat. They accounted for the demise of nine American bombers.

At last the agony of his dreadful burns was partially relieved in the hospital by powerful pain-killing injections. His head and much of the rest of him was wrapped in thick layers of white gauze. For the next several weeks he saw nothing and, in his perpetually drugged state, heard little.

Long, dreary days followed, one after the other. Nurses came to take his temperature or to place a straw in the slit of his mouth so he could suck at liquid nourishment. And more pain-killers. Always pain-killers.

The air raids seemed to be happening more and more frequently and each time they wheeled him down the corridors to the air-raid shelter.

When he was well enough to receive visitors, Galland came to tell him about the squadron and that he thought that the war was nearly over. The Allies had taken the Po Valley and were advancing towards the Brenner Pass. Steinhoff could not talk or respond and after a little while Galland whispered, "See you, Macky", and left the room.

He was getting weaker, the pain overwhelming. And the itching . . . under the bandages it felt as though ants were swarming over his face. His batman, Rieber, arrived to say "We're moving you, sir. You can't stay here. The Americans will be in Munich soon, and anyway the staff here are all cracking up. We're taking you up to Bad Wiessee. There's a smashing hospital there."

After the ambulance trip to Bad Wiessee they gave him injections to make him sleep.

His new doctor came in and told him not to worry, that they would patch him up all right. A kind nurse was there and Rieber returned to look after him. The batman described the hospital to Steinhoff as an old villa not far from the lake. The doctors, he said, were excellent and the food was good too. Sometimes the terrible moments on the airfield came back – the failed take-off, the stench of kerosene, the flames. Galland returned. "Macky, I was admitted here yesterday. I stopped a bit of shrapnel attacking viermots. In the knee – it's not too bad. I hear you're doing well – mending nicely. Don't worry about a thing. Listen, Macky, Lützow didn't get back from a mission against the Viermots over the Swabian Jura. I'm sorry . . ."

CHAPTER SIX

Hans-Joachim Marseille

Hans-Joachim Marseille was one of the most colourful and charismatic fighter pilots of the *Luftwaffe*. General of the Fighter Arm Adolf Galland said of him: "He was the unrivalled virtuoso among the fighter pilots of World War Two. His achievements were previously considered impossible." Like some of the most successful fighter pilots of all air forces in that conflict, Marseille was an individualist, a non-conformist, a brilliant innovator and a free spirit. Eduard Neumann, *Kommodore* of JG 27, Marseille's unit, remembered him as: ". . . a mixture of the fresh air of Berlin and French champagne, a gentleman." He enlisted in the *Luftwaffe* when he was eighteen. By twenty-two he was dead.

Born on 13 December 1919, Hans-Joachim Marseille, like Galland, was a German of French Huguenot ancestry. His father was an army officer, but from childhood Hans had a profound aversion to military ideals. This attitude carried over into his own military career, adding to his reputation as the most 'unmilitary' of all Germany's top aces. After his parents divorced, his mother doted on him and rarely punished his frequently mischievous behaviour.

As a teenager, Marseille joined one of the *Deutsche Lufthansa* flying schools and entered the *Luftwaffe* in November 1939 where he went through the fighter pilot school, benefitting from a complete and unhurried peacetime training regimen. As a Master Sergeant in the Battle of Britain, Marseille shot down seven aircraft and was himself shot down four times. With great personal charm and a devotion to a flamboyant night life, Marseille was often in trouble with his superior officers. His love of American swing and jazz music, and his popularity with young women wherever he happened to be, ultimately led to his being transferred out of IV/JG 52, for 'insubordination'. The commander of that unit, Johannes Steinhoff, recalled:

Marseille was remarkably handsome. He was a gifted pilot and fighter, but he was unreliable. He had girlfriends everywhere, who took up so much of his time that he was often too tired to be allowed to fly. His often irresponsible understanding of duty was the primary reason I sent him packing. But he had irresistible charm.

His personnel file on leaving IV/JG 52 was virtually a catalogue of entries detailing his disciplinary infractions, his recalitrance, and his unmilitary ways.

Marseille, whose friends called him 'Jochen', was posted to I/JG 27 at Döberitz near Berlin, under the command of Edu Neumann. The unit was relocated to the desert of North Africa in April 1941 to provide air support for Field Marshal Erwin Rommel's Afrika Korps. In the desert, Marseille's irrepressible character was tolerated by Neumann who appreciated him for what he was and recognized his considerable potential, his exceptional flying skills, superior eyesight and brilliant sense of tactics. Neumann patiently endured Jochen's frequently sophomoric behaviour on the ground, tolerating his long, non-regulation hair, and his 'playboy' reputation. He worked with Jochen to overcome the aspects of the young man's personality that were interfering with his performance as a fighter pilot, and over time, Marseille evolved into a much more serious and professional airman. He became a better fighter pilot, devising a highly analytical and intensive training programme in order to be the most refined professional possible. His programme consisted of several aspects.

To improve his flying skill, he took advantage of every opportunity to practice extreme aerobatics, which greatly improved his confidence and control in handling the Messerschmitt Bf-109 fighter. He concentrated on sharpening his marksmanship by strafing various ground objects and perfected his ability in the difficult science of deflection shooting. He worked to strengthen his legs and his abdominal muscles to help him tolerate the excessive G forces experienced in dogfighting. His intention was to increase his ability to cope with these stresses for longer periods of aerial combat, to help him wear down and outlast his opponents. He sought to enhance his exceptional eyesight by deliberately shunning sunglasses in the hot, dry desert environment. He found, too, that drinking more milk and less alcohol tended to improve his vision.

Jochen pursued his interest in the enemy by reading voraciously. He focused on the development and refinement of innovative air tactics. He based much of his approach on operating as a small, highly efficient leader/wingman unit which he believed to be the safest and most effective way of air fighting in the high-visibility desert conditions. He preferred to work alone, with his wingman flying at a safe distance away, but close enough to provide warning and cover. He believed that his 'lone wolf' approach greatly reduced the risk of accidentally hitting his wingman when firing at an enemy aircraft, and of colliding with him. He even devised his own unorthodox method of shooting at an enemy plane in a close-range dogfight. With very little time and often minimal opportunity to line up a shot, he worked on perfecting high-angle deflection shots in which he fired a very short burst in the split second when the leading edge (the propeller) of his target aircraft passed the nose of his 109. Forsaking the use of his gunsight, he poured a single snap shot of rounds into the opponent with the intention of scoring hits on the engine and cockpit. He practiced this tactic (without actually firing) and subsequently relied on it successfully in combat. He was a devotee of extreme and intense manoeuvring over high speed in aerial combat, and contrary to the standard group procedure of using full throttle throughout air combat, he would often throttle back and even lower his flaps to reduce speed and shorten the radius of his turns in a dogfight.

In his early days with I/JG 27, Jochen was nothing like the fighter pilot he would become. He had not yet adapted to the stark difference between flying in Europe and in North Africa, and was almost immediately shot down by a Free-French Hurricane pilot. When Jochen had completed his personal retraining programme, he had become a brilliant, supremely confident and capable fighter pilot. His endurance in combat was remarkable, as was his ability to see the enemy before his fellow pilots, and from far greater distances. His flying and his mastery of his Bf-109 fighter were unparalleled in the group. No one in North Africa could match his lethal marksmanship or his high-angle deflection shooting technique in which he averaged a mere 15 gun rounds per kill. He was universally admired for his ability to 'disappear' when manoeuvring around enemy aircraft, only to reappear in a perfect firing position behind, above or below his victim.

Back in Germany, Dr Josef Goebbels, Hitler's propaganda minister, made sure that Marseille's accomplishments were receiving plenty of publicity in the German press. Goebbels used the many and frequent victories of the ace partially to offset the erratic results of Rommel in that theatre of the war. Jochen was becoming a star and a heart throb for breathless young German girls who bombarded him with bundles of fan letters, causing much ribbing from his fellow pilots. The German papers referred to him as the 'African Eagle' and the 'Star of the Desert'. In Italy, Mussolini conferred the Gold Medal for Bravery on Marseille, only the second such award made to a German in World War Two.

After Jochen emerged from his self-imposed retraining, he started a success pattern that provided exactly the sort of story Goebbels craved. The 'new' Jochen first showed what he could do in a fighter sweep on 24 September 1941. He quickly downed a British bomber and rejoined his six-plane formation of Bf-109s. They soon encountered 16 Hawker Hurricanes. Jochen and his wingman were ordered to give cover to four other 109s that were attacking the Hurricanes. On seeing three of the Hurricanes shot down, Jochen ordered his wingman to cover him as he dived on a four-plane formation of the Allied fighters. He pulled up level at the altitude of the enemy planes and managed to dispose of two with a single burst while arcing through a tight turn. He dived again to build up speed and rolled into a steep, climbing turn, firing at and destroying a third Hurricane. The main air battle was over; the two formations having disengaged, but Jochen was not finished. He caught up with the retreating Hurricanes and shot down one more, his fifth victory of the day.

There is common agreement among the fighter aces of the world that their real success started at the moment (readily recalled by most of them) when they achieved a sudden and dramatic breakthrough in their air marksmanship – the moment when their 'shooting eye came in'. When this happened for Jochen, everything changed for him and his opponents. It seemed to occur in conjunction with perfecting his ability to see, evaluate and react instantly, while moving in the three dimensions of an air combat situation – to execute his attack with computer-like precision. He combined that precision with aggressiveness, amazing eyesight, fearlessness, and an efficiency in battle that astonished the other pilots, and his armourers who noted how frequently Jochen returned from a mission with less than half his ammunition expended, having accounted for as many as six enemy aircraft.

The world's third-ranking fighter ace of all time, Major General Gunther Rall, was for a time a member of Adolf Galland's staff, with a responsibility for evaluating German pilot combat reports:

> The wartime combat reports of the *Luftwaffe* fighter pilots were very detailed. [They included] witness, air witness, ground witness, your account of the combat, the type of enemy aircraft involved, the type of ammunition you fired, the armament of your aircraft, and how many rounds of ammunition were used. These reports were a nuisance to us, but when I was on Galland's staff I saw how valuable they were.
>
> We found that Marseille needed an average of only 15 bullets per kill – which is tremendous. No other fighter [pilot] remotely approached him in this respect. Marseille was the real type – an excellent pilot and a brilliant marksman. I think he was the best shot in the *Luftwaffe*.

Jochen's favourite method of attack when he encountered a formation of British aircraft in the desert skies was to hurtle into the midst of the enemy planes at great speed, causing surprise, confusion and uncertainty among the enemy pilots, who would invariably break their formation. This would present Marseille with at least one obviously rattled victim and he would immediately pounce on the hapless man, shoot him down, and come back to the fray to repeat the procedure.

One example of his awesome prowess was the bomber escort mission he flew on 6 June 1942. The German pilots sighted a formation of 16 Curtiss P-40 Tomahawk fighters and ground attack aircraft. Jochen remained with the German bombers for 10 minutes and then left his formation accompanied by his wingman. They dived on the Tomahawks and Jochen closed to within 150 feet of one before getting off a snap shot which sent the Allied fighter into the ground. Pulling up and around quickly, he found a reasonable deflection angle on a second enemy plane and dispatched it as easily as the first and went back for more. At 3,500 feet he caught up with his third victim of the engagement, tried and succeeded with another deflection shot, downing the third enemy plane. He went after his fourth kill of the day, destroying it as easily as he had the others. The P-40 exploded, leaving a long black smoke plume. Passing through the smoke and debris of number four, Jochen dived again to catch the remaining enemy fighters which had descended to a low altitude. He arrived at their level and overshot them slightly, finding that he was alongside one of the Tomahawks. He turned in a partial arc and fired, hitting the aircraft in the engine and the cockpit. The rest of the Tomahawks continued to descend and Jochen chased them again for several minutes before dispatching his sixth and final kill of the day down at near ground level. The entire air battle had lasted 11 minutes and five of Jochen's six victories had been achieved in the first 5 minutes of the action.

Jochen's greatest day of his air combat career is recalled in an extract from the book, *Die Wehrmacht* (The Armed Forces), published by the German High Command in 1942.

The accomplishments of the *Luftwaffe* in the North African campaign will require a special page of glory when the history of this war is written some day. They are equal in greatness to the deeds of the men fighting on the ground. But without the *Luftwaffe* – the fighter pilots, bomber pilots, local and long-range reconnaissance pilots, the transport flyers – much if not all that was achieved by Rommel's men and the soldiers of Italy would have been unthinkable.

We must consider that they found themselves in a very different land and in an unaccustomed climate. One must add the indirect support for the Axis soldiers fighting in the desert sand and rocks of Libya – that is, the fight against the Meditteranean convoys which were to supply the enemy with ammunition, material, and provisions; or the neutralization of Malta, the island aircraft base from which tactical aircraft threatened to disrupt the German and Italian supply system.

Below, the war correspondent First Lieutenant Fritz Dettman tells us about one of them, the most successful one, Captain Hans-Joachim Marseille, squadron commander in the fighter wing. He gave his life for Germany after 158 aerial victories. Only a single day in the life of this flyer will be described: 1 September 1942, the day on which Marseille succeeded in shooting down 17 enemy aircraft by himself, an achievement unparalleled in the short history of aerial war, and one that probably will not be equalled for some time . . . it should be said that even though no one else has equalled this achievement, it is typical of the spirit prevailing in the *Luftwaffe*. The *Luftwaffe* has to fight under conditions which, like those in North Africa, make great demands on each individual.

Before us lies an official document. It provides a silent testimony of the greatest fighter pilot feat of this war to date. The documentation tells in dispassionate terms of the action of a squadron on 1 September 1942, when twenty-two-year-old Hans-Joachim Marseille took off three times and destroyed 17 British and American enemies, all of them fighter aircraft. Here is the case of one man alone fighting a battle, a soldier in the sky above El Alamein who flew into the swarms of his enemies like a winged Mars.

When Captain Marseille, at the time still a First Lieutenant, drove out to the parked aircraft at 0730 on 1 September, there was nothing to indicate that this would be a special day. Marseille had been full of energy for days; the weather was as clear as ever this North African summer. By early morning, the sun shone with almost uncomfortable warmth, and only a light breeze blew in from the sea.

The squadron had orders to provide escort for a Stuka mission headed for a target south of Imayid. At 0750 the squadron had joined the Stuka unit not far from the field. The planes flew away eastward into the clear blue sky of the combat area.

Near the target, they climbed to 3,500 metres when the Chief reported the approach of enemy fighters on the radio. He counted ten planes, tiny dots which were approaching rapidly. When they were close to the target the Stukas prepared to attack.

Marseille pulled up in a short right-hand curve. Then the others heard him say: 'I'm attacking!' Three seconds later his wingman watched the squadron commander swing out of a left turn to get behind the tail-end Curtiss fighter of the formation that was now veering away. He fired from a distance of 100 metres.

As if a fist had grabbed it and torn it from its rapid flight, the enemy plane tipped over on its left wing and plunged to the ground almost vertically, like a rock. It burst into flame on impact. The pilot had not been able to save himself. Marseille's wingman looked at the clock when the smoke mushroom rose from below. It was 0820. Then he checked the map section: 18 km SSE of El Imayid.

The wingman didn't have to look long for his Chief. Right after the first attack, Marseille had changed from the left turn from the Curtiss he shot down to the next one. Two kilometres farther east, a plane was plunging, leaving a black trail. It was 0830. The flames of the second crash fire flared up only a few hundred metres from the plane destroyed 2 minutes earlier. This time, too, the bullets scored a direct hit in the cockpit.

By now, the Stukas have dropped their bombs. The comrades have already turned away for home and are flying back at an altitude of about 100 metres. The squadron, which had assembled in the meantime, plunged down in a steep dive. An unnoticed Curtiss had turned north, and, flying low, was trying to get near the German dive bombers.

At 0833, as the enemy machine was getting ready to attack, it was the Captain's chance. Out of a sharp left turn, his burst of fire hit the target with millimetre precision. Only 100 metres down, the earth's surface was suddenly illuminated by a giant flash and the fire consumed man and plane. This was 1 km SE of Imayid.

Just as the squadron was about to turn away westward, the cry of 'Spitfire!' blared over the radio. The other crews were already in front with the Stukas. Alone with his wingman, Marseille seemed vulnerable as the six enemy planes, close as a phalanx, came at him from six o'clock high. But Marseille knew the right moment to break. He held for that perfect moment. Head cocked backward to the left, he watched the leading enemy plane, which had separated from the rest, approach almost within firing range.

He could clearly see the muzzles of the cannon and machine-guns. But as he said: "As long as I look right into the muzzles, nothing can happen to me. Only if he pulls lead am I in danger". Flames spurt from the muzzles and the fine, silky smoke trails lance downward, then float in the air. The Englishman, firing constantly, had approached to within 150 metres of the young Captain. At that moment, Marseille suddenly made a sharp left turn. The Spitfires soared away under Marseille and his wingman at tremendous speed. This was their chance.

The Germans could now turn the tables – taking advantage of the big radius of turn the British had to fly in order to get into attacking position again. Marseille figured correctly. He pulled to the right and within seconds was 80 metres behind the last Englishman, fired and hit him. This time too the defeated pilot did not have time to remove his canopy and bale out.

It was 0839 and the wreckage of a crashed Spitfire was burning itself out 20 km ESE of El Imayid.

At 0914 Marseille's squadron landed. The flight mechanics and armourer approached and congratulated the Chief. Without any excitement though, because it was nothing unusual for Marseille to shoot down four adversaries on a mission. The armourer replaced the ammunition belts. The flight mechanics were already busy with the engine. Electricians and radio mechanics checked circuits. When the armourer refilled the belt, he found that the Chief had consumed 20 rounds of cannon shells and 60 rounds of machine-gun ammunition. That too was nothing special. It was normal ammunition consumption for Marseille.

Alam El Halfa is neither a city nor a settlement. A dot in the desert 30 or 40 kilometres south-east of the coast, it has a well and a few native huts battered by the winds. Here, hardly 2 hours later, Marseille was to experience his greatest triumph.

His squadron was again ordered to escort a Stuka strike in this area. At 1020 hours the Chief had taken off with only one flight. Just before the Stukas' objective, only 8 to 10 kilometres south of his position, Marseille suddenly caught sight of two British bomber formations – 15 to 18 aircraft in each – and two formations of escorting fighters each with twenty-five to thirty aircraft.

Numerical superiority of his foes never impressed Marseille. He had been familiar with British numerical superiority ever since he came to Africa. Marseille knew that it is not the number of aircraft that decides the outcome, but the better man. He waited now for a few moments, until he saw what he was anticipating.

A squadron of the British escort fighters with eight Curtiss P-36s peeled off from their escort duties and went after the Stukas. Marseille and his wingman met them halfway. The British saw what was coming. They turned and formed a defensive circle. This tactical measure would normally suffice, but not against Marseille.

Adjusting his speed, he was suddenly sitting in the middle of the enemy merry-go-round and shot down a Curtiss from 50 metres, out of a sharp left turn. Half a minute later the second enemy dropped from almost the same manoeuvre. Abruptly the aircraft that had held together the defensive circle were dispersed. Their leader had lost his nerve.

The remaining British fighters split into two-ship elements and flew off to the north-west. Two minutes later, Marseille had again approached to within 100 metres. A third plane plunged down. The other five Curtiss fighters turned east and drew close together again. Marseille raced after his foes.

When they took a north-westerly course toward the Meditteranean in a shallow dive from 3,500 metres, there were only four left. Two minutes later at 1101, the fifth P-36 went down. Direct hits by Marseille's guns exploded the British machine in mid-air. The sixth fighter went down at 1102 when the tenacious Marseille from a left-hand climbing turn shot down the remaining aircraft.

The combatants had meanwhile worked their way eastward. Marseille's two-ship formation was close together and climbing when more Curtiss fighters appeared below, flying east. They had not seen the Germans. Flying straight, Marseille plunged toward them like an arrow, taking them from the right rear. Under the impact of Marseille's guns, the fuselage of a Curtiss exploded.

Now the young Captain led his two-plane element north, to return to the field. Again, a Curtiss appeared a few hundred metres below them, flying eastward with a white trail of smoke. Marseille attacked immediately, firing from a distance of 80 metres, and saw the fuselage and tail assembly disintegrate. The fuselage spun downward and when he flew past, the victor could see the pilot dead in his seat.

Eight enemy aircraft had been downed by his fire. Marseille had been victorious over a whole squadron in an aerial battle of 10 minutes. Not till we place the downing times next to each other do we get a real picture of this amazing achievement: 10:55, 10:56, 10:58, 10:59, 11:01, 11:02, 11:03, 11:05.

Half an hour later Marseille appeared in the squadron's operational JQ. Field Marshal Kesselring had come. Marseille reported the return of his squadron from its mission with 12 victories.

'And how many of these 12 did you get?' asked the Field Marshal.

'Twelve, sir!'

The Field Marshal shook hands with the young officer, took a chair and sat down without saying a word.

The day had now become hot and oppressive. Anyone else would have called it a day. Marseille too, perhaps, on some other day. But this day he felt full of energy – strong enough to go up again. He waited for the next mission in the bunker of his squadron. But at the 1358 take-off he had to stay behind. His plane had a flat tyre.

It was almost 1700 when he took off again with his squadron on his third mission. Once more the fighters would escort bombers, Ju-88s this time, to Imayid. What now happened was similar to the morning action.

A formation of 15 Curtiss P-40s tried to attack the Ju-88s while the big bombers were diving on their target. Marseille cut into the British fighters with his squadron and dispersed the enemy formation. The aerial combat that followed lasted 6 minutes. In this time, at altitudes between 1,500 and 100 metres Marseille shot down five British aircraft.

The first four went down at precise 1 minute intervals between 1745 and 1750 hours. The fifth one was shot down at 1753. The victory sites were 7 km south-southwest of Imayid.

With a total of 17 victories in one day (16 were reported in the Wehrmacht report, because one downing was not confirmed until 12 hours later, through the statement of a witness) Captain Marseille had established something that is without comparison. A performance of singular greatness, a magnificent victory, it was enhanced by the squadron's lack of losses. In a day filled with fighting, they lost no men or aircraft.

During September 1942, Hans-Joachim Marseille shot down an astonishing total of 61 enemy aircraft. His final total of victories: 158. On the occasion of his 125th kill, he was awarded the Diamonds decoration to his Knight's Cross with Oak Leaves and Swords. It was to have been presented to him by Hitler later in the year. By 30 September, Rommel's elite Afrika Korps was all but defeated as the Allies threatened an assault before El Alamein. The pilots of JG 27 fought on. At 10.47 that morning, Jochen took off on yet another mission escorting obsolete Ju-87 Stuka dive bombers on a raid against targets in Egypt. After the Stukas had delivered their bombs, Jochen and his squadron were returning to their base when they were directed to intercept a flight of enemy aircraft south of Imayid. They failed to find the enemy planes and continued back towards their airfield. At 11.35 a few of the other pilots noticed a thin wisp of black smoke trailing from Jochen's new, specially-modified Bf-109. At that moment, they heard him call on the radio, "There's smoke in my cockpit", followed by a cough. The smoke trail became heavier, venting out in thick, black billows. He was seen to be writhing in the cockpit, apparently losing control. "I can't see. I can't see." His fellow pilots tried to help him by calling out directions and urging him to stay with the plane for a few more moments, until they had crossed back into German-held territory. Seconds dragged by and he began to suffocate. He rolled the fighter onto its back, releasing the cockpit canopy. He had undone his restraining straps but, instead of sucking him out, the slipstream pinned him in the smoky cockpit. The weakened pilot forced his way out of the trap. The other pilots were relieved to see him clear the cockpit and then shocked as his body struck and careered off the fighter's tailplane. Unconscious, the body of Marseille tumbled to the desert floor, his parachute unopened.

They buried the Star of Africa where he fell. A small monument marks the gravesite 7 kilometres south of Sidi Barani. His epitaph: Undefeated.

Of Jochen, his commanding officer, Colonel Eduard Neumann said later:

> When Marseille came to JG 27 he brought a very bad military reputation with him, and he was not at all a sympathetic fellow. He tried to show off, and considered his acquaintance with a lot of movie stars to be of great importance. In Africa, he became ambitious in a good way, and completely changed his character. After some time there, it became a matter of some importance to movie stars to know HIM. He was too fast and too mercurial to be a good leader and teacher, but his pilots adored him. He thanked them by protecting them and bringing them home safely.

CHAPTER SEVEN

Other *Luftwaffe* Pilots

In the Second World War the German *Luftwaffe* produced hundreds of well-trained, high-achieving fighter pilots who, in many cases, flew and fought from the first days of the war until the last. They participated in the early Blitzkrieg attacks, in the Battles of France and Britain, in North Africa, the Mediterranean, the Soviet Union, and in the final defence of Germany. They flew and fought until they were killed, or injured too seriously to fly again, or until the war ended. Like their more celebrated comrades whose wartime careers form the major portion of this book, they were unfairly blamed and unjustly ridiculed by *Reichsmarshall* Hermann Goering for every failed campaign in which the *Luftwaffe* took part.

Their American and British adversaries, on the other hand, freely acknowledged that the courage and skill of the German fighter pilots was beyond question. As one American bomber pilot put it, "They had unlimited guts, and they were good!"

Feldwebel Horst Walter Petzschler, was born in Berlin on 1 September 1921. He worked as an apprentice aircraft builder after high school and volunteered in April 1941 to serve in the *Luftwaffe*. He received his pilot training at Grottkau in Upper Silesia at *Flugzeugführerschule* A/B-9 and narrowly avoided becoming a Heinkel He-111 bomber pilot, transferring from that assignment late in 1942 to a fighter pilot school at Prenzlau, near Berlin. His first operational fighter wing was JG 105 Fighter School's 1st Staffel based at Villacoublay, near Paris, in March 1943. In April, Horst took part in an encounter with more than 200 B-17s of the American Eighth Air Force over Paris. It was his first air combat mission.

By late August, his training on the Focke-Wulf Fw 190A-2 had been completed in southern France at the Toulouse-Blagnac base of the Fighter Pilot Training Group East. Fw. Petzschler was assigned to JG 51 'Mölders' on 23 August 1943, which was operating on the Russian Front under the command of *Oberst* (Colonel) Karlfried Nordmann. From then until April 1944, Horst flew the Fw 190A-4 on 126 fighter-bomber sorties against tanks, ammunition dumps and bridges in the Smolensk-Terespol region.

While flying through heavy Russian flak during his first such mission, he was shot down, but eluded capture and was rescued by a German tank crew of the 3rd SS Panzer Division.

On 5 November Horst achieved his first aerial victory shooting down a Yak-7 and, 5 days later, added two more kills, downing a pair of IL-2s. In March 1944 he received the awards of the Iron Cross 2nd Class and days later, the Iron Cross 1st Class.

With the growing size and scope of the American daylight heavy bomber attacks on German targets, the defence of the Reich received high priority. Horst Petzschler was one of many *Luftwaffe* fighter pilots transferred in the spring of 1944 to help meet this need. His new unit was JG 3 'Udet' , the 4th Staffel of the 2nd Gruppe, which was commanded by *Oberleutnant* Walter Bohatsch. Horst's fourth and fifth victories came on 12 May when he attacked and downed a B-17 Flying Fortress and a P-51 Mustang, both in the Frankfurt-am-Main area. Flying a Messerschmitt Bf-109, he engaged in a frontal attack on the bomber, watching his bullets and cannon shells strike the wing fuel tanks of the big plane. An inboard engine of the B-17 exploded and Horst's gun camera recorded the scene as a wing of the bomber began to break off and a small group of parachutes trailed from the stricken American aircraft. As a flight of top-cover Mustangs fell on him, he reacted by pulling up and around to face the enemy fighters head-on. He began firing immediately and saw strikes appear on the lead Mustang, which exploded in a massive fireball.

28 May 1944. In their largest assault to date, 1,282 American heavy bombers arrived to strike at the German oil industry. Their equally massive escort was a force of more than 1,200 P-38 Lightning, P-47 Thunderbolt and P-51 Mustang fighters. Opposing the Americans were a combined fighter force of 300 Bf-109s, Fw 190s and Me 410s which were assembled in the Magdeburg area awaiting the American bomber stream.

Horst in Black 14, and his wingman, were flying at 32,000 feet as a great flock of Mustangs dived on the German fighters. The two Germans climbed towards the Mustangs at full power and, as the distance rapidly shortened, the lead Mustang pilot begain shooting. His bullets struck and shot down the Messerschmitt of Horst's wingman. Horst was able to get in a few snap shots from his cannon as the same Mustang passed over him and saw the P-51 sag briefly as it began trailing coolant. The Mustang pilot jettisoned his canopy and rolled the fighter inverted twice in an effort to leave the cockpit. He succeeded on his thrid attempt. Horst noted that the time was 2.20 p.m. The parachuting American pilot landed a few moments later near Eichenbarleben, south of Magdeburg. He then became a prisoner of war.

The action was not over for Fw. Petzschler. The wingman of the downed Mustang pilot fired at Horst's 109, scoring several hits. The German baled out and landed near a group of American airmen who had baled out of their crippled bomber. The gun camera of Horst's destroyed 109 was retrieved from the wreck and the film from it confirmed his Mustang victory. On that day, 32 American heavy bombers and 14 escort fighters fell to German fighter defenders and German flak.

In late September 1944, Horst was posted to Fighter Pilot Training Group North at Liegnitz, Lower Silesia, as a fighter pilot instructor where he retrained bomber pilots to be fighter pilots. He served at Liegnitz until February 1945 when he asked to be sent back to the Eastern Front. His request was granted and he reported to Oberleutnant Anton Lindner, commander of 10/JG 51, at Danzig on 15 February. Horst was made a flight leader and his unit was flying the latest and best of the Bf-109s, the G-10. With his new unit, he increased his score to a final total of 26, the last being a Russian Pe-2 downed on 27 April , 1945, less than 2 weeks before the end of the war.

In the last days of the war, Horst's group commander ordered 15 of his pilots to fly their aircraft to Copenhagen and surrender them to the British forces. After take-off Horst discovered that his outer wing fuel-tank was leaking. Unable to make it to Copenhagen, he was forced to make a dead-stick landing at Bulltofta in Sweden. At Bulltofta he was told that he and his aircraft would be interned for the duration of the war and was assured that he would be treated according to the dictates of the Geneva Conventions. He was asked to relinquish his 7.65mm Belgian Browning pistol and not to sabotage his aircraft by setting off the explosive charge placed between the control column and the fuel tank. He was then escorted to the officers' mess and treated to an excellent dinner.

The war in Europe ended formally on 8 May 1945 but Horst remained in Swedish custody until January 1946. To his horror, he and the other German internees at Bulltofta were then turned over to the Russians. They first took him to Latvia and then on to Russia where he was imprisoned until 22 September 1949, when they finally released him.

In the course of his 297 World War Two missions, Horst Petzschler scored 26 aerial victories and was shot down 13 times, 12 of them by flak and the other by an enemy fighter.

Horst's post-war career has included a stay in Canada where he was an auto mechanic. He later relocated to the United States where he worked in the aircraft industry for Boeing, Lear, Northrop, and Beechcraft.

20 July 1940. In the night sky over the Ruhr a twin-engined Messerschmitt Me-110, the aircraft that had proved such a dismal failure as a long-range escort fighter, was about to establish its capability as a night defensive fighter. *Oberleutnant* Werner Strieb was at the controls. In the next 5 years of war Strieb would account for 66 Allied aircraft destroyed in the night-fighting campaign, believed by many historians to be the most successful aspect of German air power in that conflict. During the Royal Air Force bombing raid on Nuremberg in the night of 30/31 March 1944, the night-fighters of the *Luftwaffe* shot down 107 British bombers, the largest fighter victory of the war at night.

None of the air forces of the main combatants in the Second World War had much interest in aerial night fighting in the years leading up to the war. The apathy of Britain and Germany in the subject severely handicapped them later when they were forced to defend themselves against aerial bombing at night. This attitude related directly to the common view that bombardment was of far greater importance than pursuit, with fighters being regarded as of secondary importance to the design, development and manufacture of bombers. So extreme was this negligence on the part of the U.S. Army Air Force that it entered the war without a single fighter aircraft type of equivalent capability to the main fighter weapons of Germany and Japan at the time, the Messerschmitt Bf-109 and the A6M Zero, respectively.

Werner Strieb tried to ignore the blinding searchlights that illuminated the patch of sky through which the R.A.F. Whitley bombers were flying en route to the Ruhr valley, the industrial heart of Germany. He had the advantages of height and speed over the Whitleys and he concentrated on one of the enemy aircraft as he dived through the intense bright light of the beams. German flak was bursting around his Me-110, as well as around the Whitley. His superior speed soon brought him into position for a shot at the British plane, droning slowly on towards its target. When he fired his 20mm cannons he was annoyed to see the shells go wide of the bomber. The Whitley continued on course. Coming around in a hard bank, Strieb passed through the searchlight beams again as he tried to line up on the bomber. On the second try, he put several deadly shells into the fuselage and bomb bay of the Whitley, which poured burning aviation spirit before exploding violently. The action was the first kill by a night fighter over Germany.

By early in 1943, morale in the *Luftwaffe* was wilting as many of its officers saw the futility of Hitler's and Goering's determination that the air force would remain strictly an offensive weapon. Bomber manufacture and production flourished with fighter production receiving a much lower priority. It would result in a desperate need for pilots and aircraft in the defence of Germany as the Allied strategic bombing capability grew. At the beginning of the year, the German daytime fighter defence force numbered only 200 single-seat aircraft. While their fighters were good – the Focke-Wulf Fw 190 and the Messerschmitt Bf-109 – it was a ridiculously outnumbered force to cope with the large and burgeoning American bomber raiders. The highly manoeuvrable Fw 190A-3, recently added to the GAF inventory, was powered by a BMW 1,700-horsepower radial engine which gave it a top speed of 418 mph. Unfortunately for the Germans, they didn't have nearly enough of them. The nightfighter force of the *Luftwaffe* was somewhat better prepared, with about 390 aircraft, largely Messerschmitt Me-110 twin-engined fighters.

By spring, Major General Josef Kammhuber, chief of the *Luftwaffe*'s night defence fighters, had persuaded *Reichsmarshall* Hermann Goering of the need to expand the German night defence force to at least 2,100 aircraft. When Kammhuber's plan was submitted to Hitler for approval, the Führer refused to listen to the general's view that the Reich would shortly be suffering the effects of the Allied air forces' rapidly increasing bombing capability. Kammhuber was proven correct in the next few months.

As General of the Fighter Arm Adolf Galland recalled:

> For 2 years we had been on the wrong track. After the Battle of Britain we should have switched over to defence in the west. We should have given the fighter priority over the bomber, as the British had done when they were threatened by the German raids, before they took the offensive again. Only the re-establishment of air superiority over our own territory would put us into the position that one day would allow us to resume the offensive.

Known as 'the Falcon', Wolfgang Falck accounted for only seven victories in his career as a Me-110 nightfighter pilot, but he was far more important to the *Luftwaffe* than that total would seem to indicate. He would become the 'Father of the German Night Fighting Force'.

Falck trained at the German Air Transport School at Schleissheim where he soloed in 1931 at the age of twenty-one. He was then selected for fighter pilot training at Lipetsk in the Soviet Union as part of the German-Russian training agreement. Falck:

> Our staff was German but all the mechanics, hangar workers, and maintenance people were Russians – Russian Soldiers – as it was a Red Army base. We flew the Fokker P-3, a Dutch-designed aircraft with a British Napier Lion engine, flown by German pilots in Russia using technical manuals written in Spanish. We had a hell of a time with those manuals. Germany was not allowed [by the terms of the Versailles Treaty after the First World War] to have aircraft, so the machines had been bought by a South American government, I don't know which one, and then sold and re-shipped to Russia for German use. At least five nations were thus involved in the 'secret' training of German pilots in Russia.

At the age of twenty-four, Falck was promoted to Lieutenant and was immediately ordered to write to the Minister of War and tender his resignation from military service. When the resignation was accepted, he was made an instructor at the Schleissheim fighter pilot school. With the German reoccupation of the Rhineland, Falck and the other fighter instructors at Schleissheim joined a new fighter group being established at Kitzingen, near Frankfurt. Falck:

> We were the only group at that time that had real machine-guns and
> ammunition. The other groups were as harmless as moths. One
> French fighter wing could have obliterated the entire German Air
> Force in those days.

The Falcon was soon transferred to the Richthofen Fighter Wing as
commander of the First Squadron. With establishment of III Gruppe of
the Richthofen Wing, he was given command of a squadron in the new unit
and just before the start of the Second World War, III Gruppe was transferred to a Destroyer Wing, ZG-26 (*Zerstörergeschwader*), which was
equipped with the Me-110.

The twelve 110s of Falck's squadron were the first German aircraft
airborne in the war which began on 1 September 1939. After participating
in the Polish campaign, his unit was moved to the German Bight, where it
took part in the largest air battle since the First World War, between the
Germans and the British, on 18 December. In the encounter, the *Luftwaffe*
fighters intercepted a big force of R.A.F. Wellington bombers raiding
Wilhelmshaven. The attack proved disastrous for the British and resulted
in a major propaganda coup for the Germans. They exploited it heavily as
a *Luftwaffe* victory which, according to German newspaper and magazine
accounts, had produced three new air force heroes: Lieutenant Colonel
Carl Schumacher (the Wing Commander), and Johannes Steinhoff and
Wolfgang Falck – two of Schumacher's finest squadron commanders.
Steinhoff had led the Bf-109 fighters and Falck the Me-110s. The editor of
the British aviation periodical *The Aeroplane* said of Falck, who he had met
before the war:

> He looks like a falcon. He is not big enough to be an eagle. But he has
> the aquiline features which artists and novelists love to ascribe to
> heroic birdmen. He speaks excellent English and is a charming
> companion.

Falck's participation in the Wilhelmshaven air battle made him one of the
most famous squadron commanders in the *Luftwaffe*, and a few months
later General Albert Kesselring ordered him to Düsseldorf to take charge
of I/ZG-1.

Falck's unit was based at Aalborg near the Danish border in 1940 and
was frequently the victim of pre-dawn bombing and strafing attacks by
the RAF, and the Falcon often found himself, with his fellow pilots,
stretched flat and face down in the mud of a slit trench as the enemy
planes arrived.

> There we were, fighter pilots, lying in ditches. How we hated it. We
> had a young radar officer with us, and he would give his predictions.
> 'The British are coming across the bay. They will be here in 10

minutes . . . 8 minutes . . . 3 minutes.' Then all hell broke loose. In this time, radar was very new to us – that is easily forgotten now that it is so commonplace. Then, the proper ways of using this instrument had not yet been devised. But I thought that if we knew where the bombers were, and when they were likely to arrive, there must be a good chance of intercepting them. Anything was better than being in a ditch waiting for a bomb on my head. I thought that there had to be a way to take off before they came, and then after the raid to fly out to sea with them in the darkness and fly with them until daylight. Then we could shoot them down. I worked out a system for this after meetings with the searchlight commander and the radar man. We set up a specially coded map. I first tried it with three crews to see if we could fly at night with the Me-110. In retrospect, this seems incredible, but it shows how little we knew in those days and how ill-prepared we were for what was to come.

During one of the night attacks by the RAF, Falck became so infuriated at being powerless against the enemy force, that he said to his pilots: "Let's take off and go get those Englishmen." They raced to their planes and, without helmets, parachutes or even radios, took off. There could be no communication between the Me-110 pilots. They chased and caught the British bombers and engaged in brief exchanges of gunfire to no apparent result. But the exercise proved to Falck that, with radar and good communications, it would certainly be possible to intercept and shoot down the enemy raiders. He later wrote a report on the experience, giving his conclusions and his theories about night fighting. It went to the German Air Ministry and got immediate action. Falck received visits from Ernst Udet, Colonel General Erhard Milch, and General Albert Kesselring. It began to look as if the time had come for an effective *Luftwaffe* nightfighter force.

With the Battle of France, any such plans were shelved. Wolfgang Falck and ZG-1 fought in the Battle operating from a base at Le Havre and, at its successful conclusion, Kesselring ordered him to bring a squadron back to Düsseldorf where he was to form a new nightfighter wing to defend the area against RAF attack. At Düsseldorf, Falck received the cooperation of the Lieutenant Colonel running the searchlight operation, but ran into trouble when he encountered the commander of a Bf-109 squadron which had been experimenting with nightfighter operations. The commander was an obstructionist and a Major, whereas Falck was a mere Captain. As Falck worked to organize the new Me-110 nightfighter wing, he was ordered to a meeting at The Hague, to discuss his theories of nightfighting with Goering, Kesselring, Udet, Chief of Personnel General Kastener, and General Bruno Loerzer, a friend and mentor of Goering.

In the meeting, Goering made Falck Wing Commander of *Nachtjagdgeschwader* 1 (NJG-1), but did not promote him. He would be the only captain in the history of the *Luftwaffe* to serve as a wing commander. He told Goering of the problem he was having back in Düsseldorf with the uncooperative major, and the *Reichsmarshall* told him to go back to Düsseldorf and fire the major. "Pick out a new officer to command that 109 group. You also need a good radar man and a good flak man. You have your pick of officers in the *Luftwaffe*." On his return to base, Falck sacked the recalcitrant major and promoted Johannes Steinhoff to command II/NJG-1. The next problem for Falck was the commander of the area flak unit, who was also uncooperative, to the point of impugning the courage of the nightfighter pilots. Falck then arranged for the man to fly on a night mission in a Me-110 the next evening: "I want you to see how it is, Colonel, up there in the dark, with your own flak firing at you and British gunners shooting multiple machine-guns at you." The colonel declined the invitation and proved the soul of cooperation thereafter.

Soon Falck's nightfighter wing began to grow far larger than a normal fighter wing. He received two squadrons of Dornier Do-17s to fly as intruders in nightfighter operations over RAF bases in England. As the night fighting activity grew and the unit's successes mounted, Kesselring decided to appoint Colonel Josef Kammhuber of the General Staff, to be Night Fighter Division Commander responsible for the coordination of searchlights, radar and air operations. Falck:

> I did not know Kammhuber very well then. He came to my office and said, "Please can you tell me about these operations from your viewpoint?" He told me to stay seated and was kindness itself. In a few days all that changed, of course, but we were as close as twins for the next three years. Kammhuber was outstanding, capable, and realistic, and I admired him.

With the evolution of the *Luftwaffe* nightfighter organization under Kammhuber and Falck, came many important and innovative developments leading to a highly efficient operation. Instead of running three fighter groups as was standard practice for a wing commander, Falck found himself in charge of eight groups spread geographically from Norway down to the Brest peninsula. He rose to the rank of Colonel, functioning in effect as a division commander and became deputy to Kammhuber, who was promoted to General. Finally, after three years of working successfully together, their differences in approach to the massive problems of the nightfighter operation caused them to part company.

After his departure from Kammhuber's staff, Wolfgang Falck held a responsible role in the day and night fighter defence of the Reich until summer 1944 when he contacted his old friend, Adolf Galland, to ask for a flying job. Galland offered him Fighter Leader in the Balkans, with a headquarters near Belgrade, a job that dissolved a few days later when Rumania and Bulgaria switched sides in the war. In March 1945, Falck was given a fighter command in the Rhineland, but on his arrival in the area he was unable to track down either his staff or his headquarters. He spent the last weeks of the war in southern Germany and became a prisoner of war of the Americans on 3 May 1945.

The British later brought the Falcon to Bielefeld to work with the Royal Engineers overseeing German workers. It ultimately led to him working for North American Aviation, as a consultant in Bonn. Adolf Galland, whose excellent book, *The First and The Last*, told of the rise and fall of the *Luftwaffe*, said of him:

Wolfgang Falck was not only one of 'The First' who flew in 1939, but also one of the greatest in terms of pioneering and innovations to the new art of night fighting. He was one of our best men.

Bibliography

Baumbach, Werner, *The Life and Death of the Luftwaffe*, Coward-McCann, 1960.

Bekker, Cajus*, The Luftwaffe War Diaries*, Doubleday & Co., 1968.

Bergel, Hugh, *Flying Wartime Aircraft*, David and Charles, 1972.

Brown, Eric, *Wings of the Luftwaffe*, Airlife Publishing, 1993.

Bishop, Edward, *The Battle of Britain*, George Allen and Unwin, 1960.

Brickhill, Paul*, Reach for the Sky*, Collins, 1954.

Caldwell, Donald L.*, Top Guns of the Luftwaffe*, Ivy Books, 1991.

Collier, Richard, *Eagle Day*, Pan Books, 1968.

Crook, D.M., *Spitfire Pilot*, Faber & Faber.

Deighton, Len, *Fighter*, Ballantine Books, 1977.

Emde, Heiner, *Conquerers of the Air*, The Viking Press, 1968.

Faber, Harold, *Luftwaffe: A History*, Quadrangle-New York Times Books, 1977.

Forrester, Larry, *Fly for your Life*, Bantam Books, 1973.

Freeman, Roger A., *Mighty Eighth War Diary*, Jane's, 1981.

Galland, Adolf, *The First and the Last*, Ballantine Books, 1954.

Gallico, Paul, *The Hurricane Story*, Four Square Books, 1967.

Gelb, Norman, *Scramble*, Michael Joseph, 1986.

Gilbert, James, *The Great Planes*, Ridge Press, 1970.

Golley, John, *Whittle*, Airlife, 1987.

Gunston, Bill, *Fighter!*, Parragon, 1997.

Gurney, Gene, *Five Down and Glory*, Ballantine Books, 1958.

Hall, Roger, *Clouds of Fear*, Coronet Books, 1975.

Hess, William, and Ivie, Thomas G., *Fighters of the Mighty Eighth*, Motorbooks International, 1990.

Heilmann, Willi, *I Fought You From The Skies*, Award Books, 1966.

Infield, Glenn, *Big Week!,* Pinnacle Books, 1974.

Johnson, J.E., *Wing Leader*, Ballantine Books, 1957.

Kent, J.A., *One of the Few*, Corgi, 1975.

Laming, Tim, *RAF Fighter Pilot*, W.H. Allen, 1991.

Lee, Asher, *Goering-Air Leader*, Hippocrene Books, 1972.

Lyall, Gavin, *The War in the Air*, Ballantine Books, 1968.

Mason, F.K., *Battle Over Britain*, McWhirter Twins, 1969.

Mosley, Leonard, *The Reich Marshal*, Doubleday, 1974.

Nesbitt-Dufort, John, *Scramble: Flying the Aircraft of WW2*, Speed and Sports Publications, 1970.

O'Leary, Michael, *Mustang, A Living Legend*, Osprey, 1987.

Quill, Jeffrey, *Spitfire*, Arrow Books, 1985.

Toliver, Raymond F., and Constable, Trevor J., *Fighter Aces*, Macmillan, 1965.

Toliver, Raymond F., and Constable, Trevor J., *Horrido!*, Macmillan, 1968.

Toliver, Raymond F., and Constable, Trevor J., *The Blond Knight of Germany*, Ballantine Books, 1970.

Steinhoff, Johannes, *The Final Hours*, Nautical and Aviation Publishing, 1977.

Steinhoff, Johannes, *The Last Chance*, Hutchinson & Co., 1977.

Steinhoff, Johannes, *Messerschmitts Over Sicily*, Stackpole Books, 2004.

Time-Life Books, *The Luftwaffe*, 1982.

Townsend, Peter, *Duel of Eagles*, Simon and Schuster, 1970.

Turner, John Frayn, *The Bader Tapes*, The Kensal Press, 1986.

Wagner, Ray, *Mustang Designer*, Orion books, 1990.

Weal, Johm, *Bf 109F/G Aces of the Western Front*, Osprey, 1999.

Index